Y0-CCW-980

CONFLICT, COMPETITION, OR COOPERATION?

SUNY Series in Education and Culture:
Critical Factors in the Formation of Character and
Community in American Life
Eugene F. Provenzo and Paul Farber, Editors

Conflict, Competition, or Cooperation?

Dilemmas of State Education Policymaking

DOUGLAS M. ABRAMS

State University of New York Press

For information, address the State University of New York Press,
State University Plaza, Albany, NY 12246

Production by Bernadine Dawes
Marketing by Fran Keneston

Library of Congress Cataloging-in-Publication Data

Abrams, Douglas M., 1945–
        Conflict, competition, or cooperation? : dilemmas of state
education policymaking / Douglas M. Abrams.
                p. cm. — (SUNY series in education and culture: critical
factors in the formation of character and community in American
life)
        Includes bibliographical references and index.
        ISBN 0-7914-1677-1 (alk. paper) : — ISBN 0-7914-1678-X
(pbk. : alk. paper) :
        1. Education and state—United States. 2. Higher education
and state—United States. 3. Education and state—Utah—Case
studies. 4. Higher education and state—Utah—Case studies.
5. Politics and education—United States. 6. Politics and
education—Utah—Case studies. I. Title. II. Series: SUNY series
in education and culture.
        LC89.A54   1993
        379.73—dc20   92-43401
                                                                                               CIP

1 2 3 4 5 6 7 8 9 10

To the memory of

Scott M. Matheson

leader, citizen-politician, and former governor
of the state of Utah, who believed that education—broadly conceived—is the most chal-
lenging policy area facing his state.

CONTENTS

LIST OF FIGURES

FOREWORD

Douglas Abrams has illuminated an increasingly important yet virtually ignored policy realm in *Conflict, Competition, or Cooperation? Dilemmas of State Education Policymaking*. His case analysis of the political relationships between public schools and higher education over the better part of a decade (1983–89) in the state of Utah provides important insights into how interlevel cooperation and competition play out in the highest echelons of a state's policymaking structure.

A misleading myth has impeded our understanding of the American education system and its operations. This myth has perpetuated the notion that there are two inherently distinct types of education: elementary and secondary and "higher" education. Our uncritical acceptance of this separation of the education levels has exacerbated the fragmentation of the enterprise. The isolation of the levels must be broken down during a period of fiscal constraints and rapidly changing demographics. For example, higher education will be increasingly dependent on the quality of public schools if the pipeline of college students is to be maintained. Colleges and universities obviously must be concerned with the caliber of education provided in public schools to the growing numbers of poor and minority students who are enrolled.

As the nation faces the daunting economic, social, and political challenges of the 1990s and the impending twenty-first century, the sharp division between the educational levels must be bridged. We simply can no longer afford the interlevel schism that so artificially divides the educational enterprise. Any rational planning for the future (not only for higher education but also for the nation's overall well-being) must be predicated upon increasingly serious concerns about the quality of elementary and secondary education and related issues such as inadequate student learning outcomes (which have generated substantial remedial costs for higher education), significant dropout rates, large class sizes, school violence, tracking, and inadequate school facilities. Indeed, we must explore ways to rationalize and more effectively operationalize the concept of a more coordinated, articulate, and interdependent education system.

Emulation is alleged to be the highest form of flattery and I must confess to some bias as I read this volume. More than twenty years ago (1969), the late David Minar, Emanuel Hurwitz, and I wrote a volume entitled *Education and State Politics: The Developing Relationship Between Elementary–Secondary and Higher Education*, which analyzed on a case basis the relationship of elementary–secondary to higher education in twelve populous states. In all candor, I must admit that the publication was largely a non-event. It received polite but relatively limited attention among policymakers and academics. In some ways, we might have been ahead of our time in identifying an issue whose saliency was not resonated to during an era of escalating educational budgets and unbridled growth.

Times certainly have changed, and Dr. Abrams's more recent and relevant in-depth case study of education policy elites generates important information about the deeply embedded institutionalized separation that continues to exist between the education levels in every state. The author's intensive analysis of interlevel relationships develops important understandings of how the two educational worlds and cultures currently interact or in too many cases do not interact in virtually every jurisdiction. Indeed, this analysis of political relationships has broad and important applicability to the education policy process in each of the states today.

The politics of education and the formulation of policy rapidly is becoming a far more open system. Political and business leaders, for example, are becoming more engaged in raising fundamental questions about the purposes, funding, content, and outputs of the educational enterprise at every level. The citizenry at large has made a massive investment in both public and higher education without raising very legitimate questions as to why these sectors do not relate more closely to each other. The luxury of separation is no longer tenable for both fiscal and substantive reasons. Educators themselves had best anticipate the closer public scrutiny which the current structural arrangements will receive in the immediate future. Financial and political realities will compel the development of closer linkages between the levels despite their different purposes, priorities, histories, constituencies, cultures, funding, and organizational patterns. There are growing numbers of encouraging but still isolated and fragmentary examples of efforts to break down the barriers. Such critically important efforts and the ultimate basic institutional restructuring which will have to take place will be facilitated by the insights and understandings to be derived from this important analysis. Indeed, Douglas Abrams's *Conflict, Competition, or Cooperation? Dilemmas of State Education Policymaking* is an important and timely contribution with valuable messages for educators, public policymakers, and the citizenry at large.

MICHAEL D. USDAN
President

The Institute for Educational Leadership
Washington, D.C.

PREFACE

The education policy area is massive, both in terms of the dollars (public and private) that it commands and its organizational complexity. In organizational terms there has been a systematic evolutionary (some would say revolutionary) change in the organizational context of education policy-making. Two groups of scholars (those primarily interested in elementary-secondary education, and those focusing on higher education) have worked separately to describe parallel developments within the governance of the public schools and public colleges and universities. Collectively, their works document an increasingly influential and responsible role for state governments with regard to both the public education and higher education sectors. Interestingly, neither group has fully explored the political implications for its own area of primary interest of what the other group has to say.

Recognizing and understanding the implications of these institutional changes for the political dynamics between the public and higher education sectors and the state-level policy elites who guide them is essential, for there is little question but that the future will bring added financial stringency to the public sector, and inevitably an increasing competition for limited resources. This study brings an unconventional perspective to education policy in the states in that it focuses the spotlight of description and analysis directly on the organizational interface between education sectors where many issues of importance to the public interest will be addressed and resolved. If we can better understand the differences between education sectors, we will better understand how they can cooperate, and why they must compete.

The analysis presented here seeks to establish the reality of an important aspect of the education policy process within the states by minutely analyzing certain relationships that have been instinctively understood and acted upon by education policy leaders for some time. In the same way that political scientists and sociologists have sought greater understandings of, for example, the exercise of political power, or the evolution of cultural conflicts within the local community by studying intensively a New Haven, Connecticut, or a Muncie, Indiana,[1] I have sought to understand more fully the political dynamics of organizational competition and cooperation between public and higher education policy elites within state government by focusing on a single state jurisdiction, the state of Utah.

It may appropriately be asked whether the Utah education community, or the state of Utah generally, is a typical case. There are reasons for characterizing Utah as an extreme—if not a deviant—case, for cultural values and demographic patterns have created extreme circumstances in funding education. Robert and Helen Lynd and Robert Dahl, whose studies I have just cited, claimed a degree of representativeness for the political jurisdictions that they analyzed in depth. For the purposes of this study, I make no claim that Utah is representative of other states except in the sense that the development of the state's education governance structures and general funding relationships with regard to both education sectors over the last quarter century is typical of such developments nationwide during this period. The burden of chapter 2 is to describe the broad commonalities of institutional development in education governance within the American federal system, and to describe and delineate the reflection of these general patterns within the state of Utah. While specific circumstances and policy structures within the various states are diverse, the political dynamics of organizational competition and cooperation are universal.

The study partakes of all of the strengths and weaknesses of the case study method: it trades broad, objective knowledge for in-depth, subjective understanding. It seeks to reveal the general through the specific; there is nothing in the case that does not illuminate general principles and relationships by exemplifying them in concrete circumstances. Utah education policy elites and the specific governance structures within which they interact are not the focus of this study; Utah is merely the setting of the action. The study focuses on the dynamic political relationships between public and higher education policy elites within the organizational structures of state government as they seek, through the use of strategies of political competition and cooperation, to optimize the benefits to the organizational interests they represent. A central purpose of the study is to present an approach to viewing and understanding the politics surrounding the education policy process in each of the states today. I intend the book to serve both as an invitation and as an incitement to others to look more carefully at the political relationships between public and higher education policy leaders within the policy arenas of their own state governments.

The setting of the study within a single state jurisdiction was dictated not only by the practical constraints facing a single researcher but also by the nature of the political phenomena being studied. Only through an intensive analysis of a relatively small number of education policy leaders —education administrators and governing board members from both sectors, legislators, state executives, and teachers' union officials—interacting together over an extended period of time within several different issue contexts could I gain the understandings of elite behavior that I sought. What emerges from the investigation is a clearer picture of the political culture of upper-echelon education policymaking at the state level.

Protagoras is reputed to have said that "man is the measure of all things." This study analyzes the political actions and interactions of men and women who, working within impersonal organizational structures and confronting organizational roles and constraints that they could not ignore, gave these roles substance and changed them with their unique human qualities. The cases present the thoughts and actions of real people, defending real organizational interests according to the roles dictated by their placement within the organizational structure, and within real personal and organizational constraints. The scope of the issues raised and the magnitude of the stakes won or lost are not so important as is understanding the reality of these interactions.

To help describe and explain these political interactions, I have drawn relevant theoretical perspectives from several research traditions including interest group politics, organization theory, and comparative politics. While a consistent and probing use of the newspapers identified and clarified issues and prominent actors at the initial stages of the research, the two primary sources of information and data for the study were the meeting minutes of state education policy bodies and personal interviews with policy leaders.

The formal meeting minutes of the two state-level education boards and their liaison committee were scanned and read selectively in depth for all meetings held during the nearly seven years from the fall of 1982 through the spring of 1989. From these minutes I took extensive notes by date of each organization on all topics that, in my judgment, related to organizational competition or cooperation between the public and higher education sectors. From this review of these sources I identified four issue area cases for intensive study. Using the notes from the minutes, I placed the activity and actions of each of these organizations chronologically on matrices using three columns, side by side—one column for each organization. This created a visual, spatial representation of relationships in time between the actions and reactions of the three organizations, and the decision makers within them, as they worked to deal with the separate issues treated in the issue area cases.[2] This technique was essential in describing and interpreting the policy process.

The study relied heavily on personal interviews using elements of both Lewis Dexter's "elite-specialized," and Robert Merton's "focused" interview techniques.[3] Over the seven-year period that was studied in depth (1983–89), there were multiple occupants of the various organizational positions within the state's education policy community who carried the authority as well as the responsibility to establish and support political strategies for their organizations. Obviously, some were more influential than others. An understanding of events as they were to unfold and the roles that specific individuals reputedly played guided the final selection of individuals to be interviewed. Ultimately, sixty-three interviews were held with fifty-five individuals representing the major organizational actors in the decision process. The majority of the interviews were held between November 1989 and July 1990. This intensive interview process, extending over nine months, was at the same time the most personally demanding, stressful, and personally rewarding aspect of the research. The research design required personal interviews with many responsible individuals whose time was at a premium.[4] Almost all received me graciously and were generous with their time and experience. I thank them sincerely for their generosity. They bear no responsibility for the interpretations I have made of their comments, nor for any misstatements of fact which undoubtedly are to be found within the cases. For these I bear full responsibility. My intent always has been to accurately reflect the circumstances as I understood them.

I acknowledge an intellectual debt to the following friends and professors who broadened and tested my perspectives in areas of inquiry of importance to the study: Anthony W. Morgan, Betty Malen, L. Jackson Newell, and Cecil G. Miskel in education administration and policy; James B. Mayfield in organization theory; Robert P. Huefner in state and local government; and Edward C. Epstein in elite/rank-and-file relationships as studied in comparative politics. I feel a particular sense of gratitude to Ronald J. Hrebenar, whose guidance in a seminar on interest group politics in 1983 focused my attention on the dynamics of political competition and cooperation between organization elites and whose mentoring counsel given eight years later helped to make this book possible. Dr. Hrebenar carefully read the original study in the form of a doctoral dissertation and made numerous valuable suggestions. I benefitted greatly, as well, from the sympathetic guidance of Paul Farber (who provided several well-turned phrases that I have used) and Eugene F. Provenzo, Jr., each of whom read an early version of the manuscript and offered encouragement as well as wise counsel in making it a worthy book. My father, Milton C. Abrams, has been a consistently encouraging friend in this and other endeavors, and facilitated several key interviews for this study at a time when my spirits were lagging. I express my admiration for the vision and principled commitment of the SUNY Press, its editorial board, and its editor, Lois Patton, who persevered in developing a manuscript of some promise and potential public importance that several individuals found to be of questionable marketability. I consider their decision to publish this work to be in the best tradition of the university press. I am grateful to the publishers of the *Journal of Education Finance* for their generous permission to use revised segments from an article that I previously had published in the journal. While each of these individuals or groups may rightfully claim a share of any value that the book may have, its shortcomings are exclusively my own. Finally, I thank Kathleen, and our teenagers, Karen and Bradley; my association with them serves to make my life endlessly interesting and rewarding regardless of my personal successes or failures in the world.

1. Prologue

Much of the thinking and writing that addresses competition and cooperation presents these complementary social phenomena in terms of individual
personal actors or in terms of internally undifferentiated organizational
entities implicitly represented as acting as individuals.[1] Such assumptions
may allow the observer to operationalize complex social phenomena, but
they obliterate fundamental characteristics of organizational competition
and cooperation. The very fact of organization conditions and constrains
the commitments, decisions, and actions of individuals according to their
placement within the structure of the organization. Consequently, the social
phenomena of competition and cooperation between individuals are
different from competition and cooperation between organizations. At the
heart of an adequate understanding of these phenomena lie the horizontal
relationship between organization elites in different organizations and the
vertical relationship differentiating organization elites and their rank and
file, both in function and perspective.

ORGANIZATION ELITES AND THE RANK AND FILE

Formal organization, Max Weber's ideal type "bureaucracy," is the basic
element of social control in the modern, industrialized state. Because
"bureaucracy is *the* means of carrying 'community action' over into
rationally ordered 'societal action' . . . it is a power instrument of the first
order—for the one who controls the bureaucratic apparatus."[2] The "bureaucratic apparatus" is controlled only by those at the very top, the organization elites who exclusively make the decisions that determine the
organization's actions. According to Weber, action from within the rank
and file is unimportant in the face of the irresistible power of bureaucratic
discipline, which requires the suspension of criticism, and the exact
execution of orders received from those above.[3] Weber's description of

1

authority relationships within bureaucratic structures has been shown to be an incomplete explanation of the interaction of people within organizations.

The Three-Tiered Organization

More recent students of organization observe important political interrelationships among the organization's functionally differentiated levels, which differ markedly from Weber's concept of organizational discipline. Talcott Parsons identifies three levels (systems) in the hierarchical structure of organization and describes the vertical relationships among them and the discontinuities within the organization at the "point of articulation" between each level.[4] The technical system is responsible for actually performing the primary functions for which the organization has been established, for example, the teaching of elementary school children or university graduate students in the classroom. The managerial system administers the organization's internal affairs, procures and manages the resources needed to perform the technical function, and mediates between the organization and the external situation. Decisions made within the managerial system necessarily take precedence over those made at the technical level. Finally, the institutional system mediates between the particular managerial organization and the general community interests that it is intended to serve. Boards of trustees (or directors) and school boards, for example, control the managerial organization by applying generalized norms, through control mechanisms that are between the management system and the general public interest, and in some cases by bringing the managerial organization directly into a structure of "public authority," that is, through an organ of government. This is the case, for example, with state-level executive agencies that, along with their boards, govern and coordinate public and higher education.

Parsons notes that there is a qualitative break in the continuity of "line" authority at the two points of articulation between the three systems or organizational levels at which there is a two-way interchange of essential inputs and outputs. Because the input from each level is qualitatively different, by withholding its necessary contribution each system is able to interfere seriously with the functioning of the other systems and the larger organization as a whole. All participants thereby exercise some power within the system; while the central authority remains in control, it is subject to, and constrained by, the interests and demands of others.

The differentiation of essential functions within the organization focuses our attention on the possibility (and actuality) of political relationships between organizational levels and groups within the organization that are not envisioned in Weber's description of bureaucratic discipline. Coalitions of individuals within the organization bargain with the central authority or among themselves in defining the goals of the organization, as well as organizational outcomes. Because both individuals and groups within the organization hold goals that are distinct from those of the organization as a whole, the larger organization is a "politically negotiated order," in which power is distributed more broadly than is assumed within a rationalist definition of the organization.[5]

Boundary Personnel

The concept of boundary personnel, those within the organization who interact directly with the organization's environment, adds an important perspective to this conceptualization of the organizational hierarchy.[6] At the technical system level there may be many boundary personnel performing the primary operations of the organization who collectively (but not individually) have a significant impact on the relations of their organization within the larger environment. Public school teachers and university professors are prime examples of such boundary personnel. At the managerial system level, managers (fewer in number) are involved with tactical decision making and goal formation, and their impact on interorganizational relations is probably greater than that of the technical staff. However, the institutional system level, which consists of organization policy elites (top executives as well as members of boards of trustees), focuses on strategic decision making and goal formation for the organization as a whole. The number of boundary personnel at this level is substantially fewer, and the decision-making power of these people in interorganizational matters is much greater, for it is at the institutional system level that decisions on the adoption and use of political strategies intended to integrate the organization with its environment are made and implemented.

Because all organizations inhabit a larger, more comprehensive world of organizations, each must interact with others in the larger universe so as to obtain the resources that it needs to accomplish its goals. In Richard Scott's homey terms, "Some sort of working accommodation with the neighbors must be achieved."[7] Working out an accommodation with the closest neighbors often seems most pressing. It is to organization elites that this responsibility is given; that is, they must interact with their peers in these other organizations in such a way as to secure the interests of the organization of which they are a part and for which they exercise responsibility. It is organization elites who play the key role in setting the tone and substance of their organization's relationships with other organizations. These relationships can vary from conflict and competition, to noninvolvement, to cooperation.[8] Organization elites must choose what political stance to take with regard to other neighboring organizations. Will the interests they serve benefit more by competing with a given organizational neighbor at a given time on a given issue, or by cooperating with it? Or should the strategy be one of noninvolvement? Is such a course possible given other contextual variables?

Interaction of Organization Elites

The vertical relationships within a given decision unit between the organization's elite and its rank and file establish important constraints on the horizontal interactions between policy elites in separate organizations, who have the greatest and most direct impact on decisions governing the political stance of their organizations within the broader environment.[9] In effect, these relationships are two sides of the same coin. Organization leaders who exercise boundary-spanning responsibilities "become vulnerable to pressures from outside as well as inside [the organization]."[10] This is most clearly the case when such interactions involve the exchange of resources or joint decision making to provide the necessary resources for the organization. In these political relationships, leaders often come to identify with their peers, analogous elites in otherwise competing organizations with whom they interact on an ongoing basis, and with whom they may develop a sense of community based on their common responsibilities of leadership and their personal interaction in meeting these responsibilities.[11] This interaction is sometimes facilitated through temporary, or even permanent, organizational structures that provide a forum in which leaders can meet to discuss their needs and reach mutual accommodation. Such mediating organizational structures can support cooperative decision making by insulating organization elites from the pressures and demands of their rank and file.[12]

CONFIGURATIONS OF ORGANIZATIONAL POWER

Henry Mintzberg's analysis of the dynamic ebb and flow of power in and around the organization enhances and adds explanatory power to the theory of the three-tiered organization. According to his elaborate model, the political behavior of organizations derives from a power game in which influencers try to control the decisions and actions of the organization through energetic and skillful use of the systems of influence available to them.[13] Influencers, who may be either internal or external to the organization, form coalitions of people and groups who bargain among themselves to establish a distribution of organizational power favorable to their own interests.

The Internal Coalition

Internal influencers (analogous to Parsons's technical and managerial systems) are those full-time employees charged with deciding and acting for the organization on a permanent basis. Their decisions and actions actually run the organization. At the apex of Mintzberg's Internal Coalition is the chief executive officer. This individual—typically the most powerful person in the system—receives often contradictory demands from external influencers and must reconcile them in order for the Internal Coalition to deal with them. Other influencers within the Internal Coalition include the top general management of the organization; the operators, those who produce the products and services for which the organization was created; line managers; organizational analysts; and organizational support staff.

We can define two different Internal Coalitions within the two organizational complexes comprising the public and higher education sectors in each of the states. Actors in the public education Internal Coalition include the state superintendent of public education, associate state superintendents, superintendents of local school districts, public school teachers, and a wide variety of support staff as diverse as school librarians, guidance counselors, and physical plant maintenance staff. Actors in the higher education Internal Coalition include the state commissioner (or chancellor) of higher education, associate commissioners, college and university presidents, the professoriate, and a similar variety of support staff including legal counsel, librarians, student services providers, and food services personnel.

The organization defines and establishes different roles for different people depending upon their position within it. The requirements and constraints that accompany and are imposed by individuals' organizationally defined roles are of considerable importance in explaining their needs, their preferred goals for the organization, and their behavior. The needs and interests of the various influencers within the Internal Coalition are reflected in the goals that they favor. The chief executive officer seeks organizational survival and growth. Line managers seek growth of the units they supervise, often favoring a balkanization of the organization that would enhance their autonomy. Analysts and support staff seek organizational efficiency, well-planned change, and excellence in performance. Operators seek autonomy, the enhancement of their specialty within the organization, and protection of the social group. In each case, the needs and interests of the members of the Internal Coalition, both individually and collectively, fall short of a perspective that can successfully integrate the organization with its external environment.

There are several types of Internal Coalitions, each defined according to the predominant system of influence within it. That configuration that concentrates power to the greatest extent within the Internal Coalition is based on the personal control by the chief executive officer. This Personalized Internal Coalition, as Mintzberg calls it, dominates the organization through the chief executive officer by precluding or discouraging the internal systems of politics, expertise, and bureaucratic control.

The External Coalition

The prime component of Mintzberg's External Coalition, which consists of part-time influencers, is the board of directors.[14] Other components are the owners, those who hold title to the organization; the associates, those who trade and even compete with the organization; the organization's publics, which include groups as diverse as families, public opinion leaders, and special interest groups; and, very significantly, employee organizations. Regarding employee organizations, Mintzberg notes that it is the impotence of the operators (employees) within the Internal Coalition that drives them to act collectively in the External Coalition.[15] Again, we can define two different External Coalitions associated with the public and higher education sectors within each of the states. Actors in the public education External Coalition include the state board of education, the state legislature and the governor, the policy elites of higher education (the complementary education sector—the "associates"), the teachers' union, and a wide variety of education interest groups. Actors in the higher education External Coalition include the state board of higher education (the regents), the state legislature and the governor, the policy elites of public education, and other opinion leaders and interest groups.

The External Coalition potentially wields considerable power with respect to the Internal Coalition. It uses social norms, pressure campaigns, formal constraints, and various controls to work through internal influencers to affect organizational decisions and actions. The most influential configuration of power in the External Coalition occurs "to the extent that the organization experiences some form of dependency on its environment as well as the concentration of its external power either in the hands of a single group . . . or else in an active consensus among its external influencers."[16] This configuration is called a Dominated External Coalition. In spite of its power and legitimacy, it is highly fragile, for the dominant consensus upon which it is built can easily break up over differences of opinion within the coalition, or simply evaporate as central actors leave the stage.

Political Behavior of the Organization

The power relationships between the External and the Internal Coalitions are reciprocal. For example, the Dominated External Coalition reduces the power of the Internal Coalition. Should the Dominated External Coalition be divided, the Internal Coalition is encouraged to become politicized; should it become passive,[17] power shifts to the Internal Coalition where it is most often exercised by the chief executive officer, who establishes a Personalized Internal Coalition that dominates the organization. These various configurations of power have important implications for the political strategies used by organizations in the larger environment. It is the External Coalition (a prime component being Parsons's institutional system) that performs strategic decision making and goal formation for the organization as a whole. If the External Coalition becomes divided or passive, power will revert to the Internal Coalition, and interorganizational political strategies will change accordingly. Because the organizationally defined needs, interests, and goals of influencers within the Internal Coalition are parochial, political strategies of cooperation with other organizations are not only improbable, but impractical, for the Internal Coalition lacks both the motivation and the political and organizational resources required to negotiate and implement cooperative strategies. This is not to say that cooperative strategies will always result from a Dominated External Coalition. Rather, a Dominated External Coalition is a necessary—though not sufficient—condition for cooperative strategies to emerge.

SUMMARY

Implicit in this brief discussion of formal organization has been the open systems perspective, by which the organization has been defined as "[a coalition] of shifting interest groups that develop goals by negotiation; the structure of the coalition, its activities, and its outcomes are strongly influenced by environmental factors."[18] In the organization conceived as an open system that must interact with the larger environment to survive, it is organization elites who play the key role of establishing the relations of the organization with the larger environment through which it exchanges goods and services with other organizations. It is a primary function of organization leaders to see that their organization's exchange relationships with the larger environment are favorable in the sense of assuring that resources of dollars, people, work to do, and the authority to do it are always available. Thus, organization elites will seek to maintain and increase, if possible, the resources made available to the organization—resources that will allow it to meet its currently defined purposes, as well as future purposes planned by organization leaders. They must also defend organizational interests against attacks from the outside that might jeopardize established sources and levels of support.

Organization elites pursue these various activities in support of their primary goal of maintaining favorable exchange relationships with the larger environment usually by cooperatively joining with—or competing against—other relevant organizations. The subtle and complex activity making up these political relationships between organization elites is highly ambiguous and subjective, and is conditioned by the hopes, desires, intentions, past experiences, and personalities of individual actors. Most significantly, organizational roles and structures and the configuration of organizational power in and around the organization heavily condition the decisions and actions of individual leaders. In these political relationships between the decision elites of different organizations, the organization rank and file often play an important constraining role.

A final word on the study of organizations and organizational decision making is needed. Organizations exist within organizations much like Chinese boxes, nestled one within another. A complex formal organization is comprised of "a comprehensive network of subordinate formal organizations."[19] Thus, an organizational configuration that is identified for study can be easily modified conceptually by simply changing the level of aggregation and analysis. Regarding the interorganizational decision-making process, Matthew Tuite has written,

The phenomenon of interorganizational decision making can be found at any systems level . . . [T]here are fundamental similarities in the phenomenon [of interorganizational or intersystem decision making] whether the interacting systems are semiautonomous departments and divisions within an organization, or organizations, or multi-organization confederations, or various system combinations.[20]

In the spirit of these observations on organizations and their implications for organization theory, the diverse concepts presented here and in subsequent chapters will be freely used and applied to the action of the cases to suggest understandings and relationships useful in describing and explaining the tension, interplay, and balance between organization actors working within formal organizational structures according to the roles established for them. Collectively, these organizational concepts are of central importance in understanding the political interactions of public and higher education policy elites in state government.

2. Education
   Policy
   Structures

National Patterns and Their Reflection in Utah

Organization is the universally accepted mechanism for achieving collective purposes. Within a society, government itself is the most comprehensive organization of all. It aggregates interests and establishes administrative structures to control them.[1] The administrative structure of government, particularly the executive, represents an attempt to simplify, rationalize, and mirror broader, more complex interests within the society as a whole, over which government is required or seeks to exert control. The agencies of government establish organizational connections to and control over activities of importance to the state. In total, they are a microcosm of those broader, more complex, and competing interests found within the state as a whole. One such complex activity of central interest to the state is education.

Every society must educate its people. Formal education is the central formative cultural influence in a nation's public life. In modern societies, government has undertaken this enormous task. In the United States, the education enterprise, broadly conceived, consumes more public tax dollars (local, state, and federal) than any other governmental activity, with the significant exception of national defense.[2] Historically, education has been the basis of the American dream, supporting the liberty and opportunity of the individual, and assuring both individuals and groups of economic security, and social integration and mobility. More recently, as modern technology has increasingly required a technically trained, rather than a mass, labor force, formal education has been viewed as the means of assuring national economic well-being in a highly competitive global marketplace.

Given the central position of education in our common public life, it is a striking fact that in the United States the education enterprise is carried on by two organizational complexes, each a world unto itself. One education world is centered around children and youth in elementary and secondary schools, the other around adults in a diverse array of institutions

11

ranging from the community and technical college to the research university. State governments have always played an important—if not the central—role in the funding and governance of each education sector. Both constitutionally and by statute the administrative structures and procedures of state governments divide education along these lines in tacit recognition of a separateness based on fundamentally differing lines of historical development, of organization, constituencies, funding sources, priorities, and purposes.

Since the Second World War, state governments have established new, and strengthened existing, organizational connections to and administrative controls over both the public schools and public institutions of higher education. Governmental actions in response to economic and demographic circumstances have propelled a dynamic evolution of intergovernmental relations that represent pragmatic readjustments in the relative authority and influence on education policy of the various levels of government in the American federal system. These changes have had major implications for the ways in which government deals with education and for the political processes surrounding the education policy area, shifting the arena as well as the prime actors involved in framing education policy issues and in achieving the authoritative allocation of public resources to education. State governments have moved to center stage.[3] A brief survey of the evolving governance and funding relationships supporting the public schools and public higher education reveals the chief historical reasons—quite different in each education sector[4]—for this ascendancy in the education policy role of the states.

NATIONAL PATTERNS IN PUBLIC EDUCATION

Public education funding policy has passed through several characteristic intergovernmental patterns beginning with local government predominance, and moving to local-state partnership, which has evolved now, with the support of the federal government, to state-level predominance.

Local Government Predominance

While local control and funding of schools had been an established practice in the colonies before the writing and ratification of the Constitution, the constitutional basis of the conventional understanding that public education is a "state function administered at the local level" lies in the reserved powers doctrine of the Tenth Amendment.[5] The states, in turn, delegated their power and authority over the schools to local governmental entities, the local school districts. It is this local control of public education that historically has been a hallmark of American education, in sharp contrast to other Western countries.

In terms of the layer-cake metaphor used to describe intergovernmental relations under dual federalism, these local school districts, creatures of state power established and maintained through constitutional and statutory provisions of the various states, make up the bottom layer of the cake. There was a time when this layer of the cake was very broad indeed. In 1931, as the Depression deepened, there were nearly 130,000 local school districts.[6] These governmental entities were responsible to the citizens within their jurisdictions, had corporate status, and were empowered to tax, spend, and incur debt to provide for public education. Assuming an average school board size of five persons, plus one superintendent per school district, in 1930 there were well over three-quarters of a million people at the local level intimately involved in making primary decisions on public education operational policy and funding.[7]

Popularly elected local boards established tax rates on real property located within the boundaries of the district for the support of education. Property tax monies were administered at the local level by the school superintendent according to needs and priorities established at the local level through administrative and political processes in which he himself was usually the single most influential figure, to be followed by members of the school board and other elected officials. There was little interaction, or need for such, between governmental levels.

This conventional layer-cake view (popularly held into the 1960s), in which the separate layers of government have little or no involvement with each other in their exclusive areas of responsibility, was inadequate and even simplistic, even as a representation of the reality of education funding and governance three decades earlier.[8] Nevertheless, if one looks at the numbers of people involved at the local level in public education policy and funding decisions, as well as the percentage distribution of total dollars spent on public education by level of government, there is a clear justification for asserting the predominance of local government in influencing public education policy through the first half of this century. In 1920, for example, local government supplied more than 83 percent of the funds spent on public education; twenty years later, in 1940, that figure was still by far the greater part at 68 percent.[9]

Local Government/State Government Partnership

If a theoretical justification for an areal division of power is that of keeping government close to the people, thus protecting liberty, there is an equally inevitable and practical implication of such a division, that being the strong likelihood of the unequal areal distribution of real property across political jurisdictions. The smaller the jurisdiction, the greater is the likelihood for such inequality. Reliance upon the local property tax to fund public education created inevitable, and often glaring, inequalities in school systems attributable to the unequal distribution of wealth across school district boundaries.[10] Opportunities for education were much greater (or less) for one student than for another, simply because of where that student lived. These built-in problems of inequality were exacerbated by the Depression, which limited the ability of local governments to fund services through the property tax.

In response, state governments adopted equalizing "foundation formula" strategies to deal with the problem, in addition to making state funds available to local school districts for assistance in building capital facilities. The purpose of the foundation formula approach was to assure a minimum level of financial support to all school districts within the state regardless of the local property tax base by requiring every district to establish a minimum mill levy, with the state government making up the difference to the established minimum standard of support with state monies.[11]

Decisions in both state and federal courts served as a basis for what has come to be known as the school finance reform movement.[12] The primary objective of the reform movement was to equalize the differences in per capita expenditures for education that are the result of differences in taxable wealth per student among the states' school districts. During the 1970s, thirty states reformed their school finance systems or were in the process of doing so by court order.[13]

For the immediate purposes of this study, the importance of state foundation formula strategies to equalize the funding available for public education does not lie with the formulas themselves or their technical application, but rather in the impact that these state-level actions have had on intergovernmental relations, and the relative influence and power of state governments vis-à-vis local governments with regard to education funding policy. The funding formulas and capital facilities dollars institutionalized the necessity for ongoing interactions between local and state-level administrators. Local autonomy on funding matters was reduced as states mandated minimum mill levies and established operational procedures for the ongoing administration of equalization programs. The clear-cut assignment of responsibilities that previously had separated state and local government—at least in theory—came to be blurred as administrative and fiscal interaction between state and local levels of government increased. The layer cake had become a marble cake in which interaction between governmental levels was routine and pervasive.

The local-state partnership in education that progressively evolved during the five decades from 1930 to 1980, is most graphically reflected in two primary indicators. The first of these is the changing funding pattern for public education; the second is the transformation of local-level governmental and administrative structure supporting public education. The two factors are closely related.

Relative percentages of total dollars spent on public education by local, state, and federal governments in 1920, 1940, and 1960 indicate a progressive decrease in the percentage spent by local government (83.2 percent, 68.0 percent, and 56.5 percent for these years respectively), and a progressive increase in state-level spending for the same years (16.5 percent, 30.3 percent, and 39.1 percent). The relative percentage of local and state funds spent for public education was very nearly equal in 1980, with local governments accounting for 43.4 percent, and states contributing 46.8 percent. Across the same time span, 1940 to 1980, the federal share moved from less than 2 percent prior to World War II, to 9.8 percent two years into the Carter administration. This high-water mark in the federal percentage of education funding achieved under a strongly pro-education president fell to 6.5 percent by 1985 under the education policies of the Reagan administration (see figure 1).[14]

Given this significant shift in the distribution of costs for public elementary and secondary education from local governments to the states, it is instructive to review as well the growth of total costs of public education. Total revenue receipts of public elementary and secondary schools in 1940 were $2.3 billion; in 1985, they were $137.4 billion, an increase of nearly sixty-fold (see figure 2).[15]

In gross figures, total state aid dollars increased from $684.4 million in 1940 to approximately $66.9 billion in 1984–85, an increase of nearly ninety-eight-fold.[16] The relative percentage increase in state-level funding is in large part attributable to the equalization programs of the states.

Of equal significance to the transformation of intergovernmental relations in education policy has been the dramatic consolidation of local school districts nationwide since 1930. From the school year 1932 to 1977, the total number of local school districts declined by 112,360 districts, a reduction of 88 percent (see figure 3).[17]

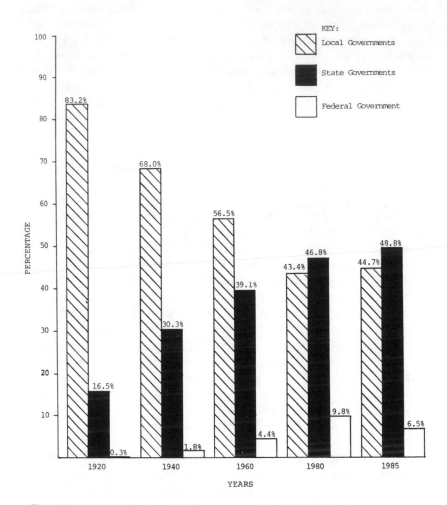

Fig. 1. Percentage distribution of total revenue receipts of public elementary and secondary schools from local, state, and federal governments, 1920–85. (Source: see note 14.)

This consolidation of school districts, which rapidly accelerated in the late 1950s and early 1960s, is an important evidence of the growing influence of state education agencies, for in most cases the consolidation was actively led by state departments of education.[18] Often, rather than using a piecemeal approach, state legislatures passed statewide reorganization plans with state education agency functions also specified in the law.

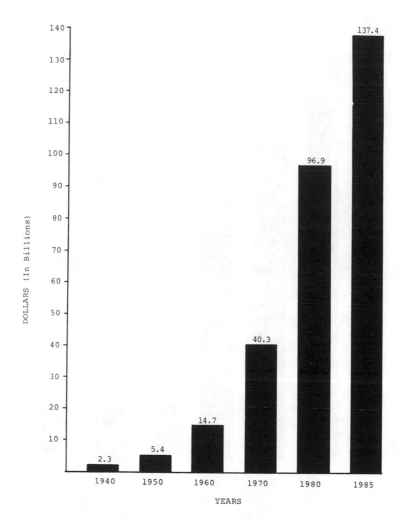

Fig. 2. Total revenue receipts of public elementary and secondary schools (in billions of dollars), 1940–85. (Source: see note 15.)

Historically, a prime justification of school district consolidation was the equalization of wealth and educational opportunity through the creation of larger jurisdictions; school district consolidation was a logical policy complement to state foundation formula equalization programs.[19] The impact of the two reform policies in conjunction with one another on the

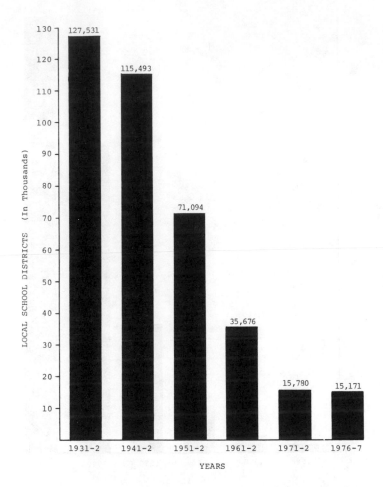

Fig. 3. Total number of basic local administrative units (independent school districts in the United States and the District of Columbia), 1932–77. (Source: see note 17.)

balance between state and local influence was major. By the early 1960s, state education agencies and their administrators were playing a more visible and influential role in their interactions with local school districts. The local superintendent and school board remained the senior partner in this intergovernmental partnership, but a strong foundation had been established through state equalization programs and school district consolidation to support a progressively growing and influential state presence.

The Federal Government as Kingmaker:
State Government Predominance

The importance of the federal government in the funding of public education was minimal through the early post–World War II period.[20] The turnabout in the federal government's involvement in public education came in 1965 with the passage of the Elementary and Secondary Education Act (ESEA), legislation intended primarily to channel funds to meeting the educational needs of children disadvantaged through poverty.[21] Yet, more important than the monetary contribution of the federal government has been the impact of ESEA on the structure and intergovernmental relations of public school funding. ESEA has been characterized as being an example of "policymaking with finances at the fulcrum for influencing outcomes in IGR (intergovernmental relations)."[22] Previous to ESEA the state education agencies were involved most typically in collecting data and in dispensing money. The norm was noninterference. Sparsely staffed state agencies deferred to local control. ESEA brought an end to this relationship.

During the late 1960s state education agencies nearly tripled the size of their professional staffs. By 1972 thirty-five states had more than one hundred full-time professionals and only four had fewer than fifty.[23] More than this, state agencies were required through laws and regulations to provide leadership and to monitor programs. An additional evidence of the sustained and growing power of state education agencies is the fact that between 1961 and 1977 there was a further 57 percent reduction in the number of local school districts nationwide, decreasing the total from 35,676 to 15,171.

All of these factors entailed a fundamental change in the local-state partnership in public education. The power and influence of the states in public education funding issues was greatly augmented, while the relative authority of local districts was diminished through state and federal laws and regulations. Specifically, there has been a dramatic increase in state influence in public education since 1960 in major education policy areas and initiatives including education finance, the administration of federal categorical grants, state requirements for educational accountability, state specifications and programs for children with special needs, and state education agency efforts to stimulate innovation and experimentation.[24] The augmented role of the state in the governance of education is reflected in greatly increased involvement of both governors[25] and legislators as education policymakers. Legislatures have moved actively to exercise legislative oversight of public education, a trend supported by constitutional and statutory language, as well as recent court interpretations.[26]

Current observers see an unclear pattern in the relative influence in public education policy among state-level actors, including state education agencies, legislatures and their committees, governors, and legislative and executive budget staffs. What seems not to be in question is that "the states will continue to be the pivotal actors in school finance."[27] The implications of this fact for the practical political processes surrounding public education are considerable. Because of the currently established locus of public education funding decision making, today's and tomorrow's policy actors in the area of public education "are more apt to focus their lobbying efforts and attention on the governor, state legislature, and state board of education than on the local school district."[28]

NATIONAL PATTERNS IN HIGHER EDUCATION

In contrast to the shifting intergovernmental funding patterns found in public education in the United States, from colonial beginnings, through the emergence over the last century of large state systems of higher education, to the present, the states have always been the primary source of funding for public higher education. Throughout most of this history the states have operated within a tradition of recognizing the autonomy of institutions of higher education based on what has been characterized as the "self-denying ordinance," by which states paid the bill but did not dictate policy.[29] The evolution of state policy from granting institutional autonomy under the self-denying ordinance to the centralized state-level coordination and governance of higher education, which characterizes the fifty states in the 1990s, is of central importance to the political processes surrounding the policy area of education.

Individual Institutional Autonomy

Higher education began in the American colonies as an arm of the church with the establishment of Harvard College in 1636. A century later, in 1740, nonsectarian colleges (beginning with what has come to be known as the University of Pennsylvania) began to be established, though the vast majority of colleges founded between the American Revolution and the Civil War were established and supported by religious interests.[30] Following the Revolution, state governments sought for a time to absorb these colleges into their administrative structures. The Supreme Court put an end to this endeavor of the states by establishing the legal inviolability of state charters to private colleges; thereafter state governments began to establish colleges of their own.[31] The state university movement, which began soon after the Revolution, accelerated by the 1850s, strongly supported by the federal government, which provided important incentives in the form of land grants for the establishment of state colleges and universities.[32] While federal law and policy supported the initial establishment of colleges and universities, the role of the federal government in higher education through World War II was minor. The states, by tradition, and the Constitution played—and have continued to play—the primary role in establishing, maintaining, operating, and controlling public institutions of higher education.

During this formative period, as states established institutions of postsecondary education, they turned for their models of public account-ability to the private sector in which state legislatures had granted charters to legally established entities called boards of trustees (or directors) who thereby governed the institutions with very few controls by the state. Normally, agencies of state government were required to operate within both fiscal and administrative structures and procedures that would ensure strict conformity to the budgetary and fiscal procedures outlined for state government as a whole. It was this self-restraint of state government with regard to institutions of higher education that constituted the "self-denying ordinance" alluded to above.[33]

By 1940, many state governments had established an array of individual institutions of higher education falling into a four-tiered pattern. In an ascending order of progressively broader and more comprehensive curriculum offerings and institutional missions were the vocational and junior college, the teacher's college, the land-grant college of agriculture and mechanical arts, and finally the state university that offered programs from the bachelor's degree to the doctorate in the arts, sciences, and professions. While the precise institutional configuration within each state differed according to local history and circumstances, there were common-alities. Rural locations for colleges and universities were the rule, and higher education was commonly of modest cost, both to students and state governments.

Characteristically, these diverse institutions of higher education, both public and private, were regarded as being completely independent entities, each established separately and governed by an autonomous board of trustees. The presidents and boards of public institutions petitioned state legislatures directly for funds and authorizations to develop their own programs, functions, and educational philosophies. In such efforts, little concern or thought, in the sense of coordination, was given to other colleges and universities. There were few exceptions to this condition by 1900.

Centralized State-Level Coordination and Governance

In 1905, Florida established a single board to govern its institutions of higher education, to be followed by Iowa the next year. Eleven states had established single governing boards for higher education by 1932.[34] By 1972, forty-seven of fifty states had established either consolidated state-level governing boards or coordinating boards responsible for state-wide planning and coordination of two or more governing boards.[35] Thus, by the mid-1970s the overwhelming majority of the states had at least supplemented, and in most instances supplanted, the original governing relationship in which institutions interacted directly and freely with the state government. In place of this bilateral relationship, legislatively established governing or coordinating boards were interposed between the institution, on the one side, and the governor and legislature, on the other. These boards would deal with separate institutions on a multilateral basis and inevitably narrow their freedom. In 1958, Lyman Glenny characterized these emerging centralized governance relationships with higher education as "a spectacular departure" from traditional modes of institutional control;[36] a quarter of a century later, in 1985, he pronounced the new forms to be "'institutionalized' as a part of state government."[37] To what factors can this dramatic institutional evolution toward centralized state-level governance and coordination of higher education be attributed?

In the broad perspective, demographic and economic factors came together after World War II in such a way as not simply to prompt, but to require, increased and systematic attention to higher education by state governments. Three variables (the total number of students enrolled in institutions of higher education, the total number of higher education institutions, and the total dollars expended in support of higher education) graphically document the explosion of higher education services in the United States since 1940 and the role of state governments in supporting this striking growth.

Between 1940 and 1980, higher education in the United States moved from an elite to a mass base. While the general population was increasing less than twofold, there was nearly an eightfold increase in the number of students enrolled in institutions of higher education. The number moved from 1.5 million students just before World War II to 11.6 million students four decades later in 1980 (see figure 4).[38]

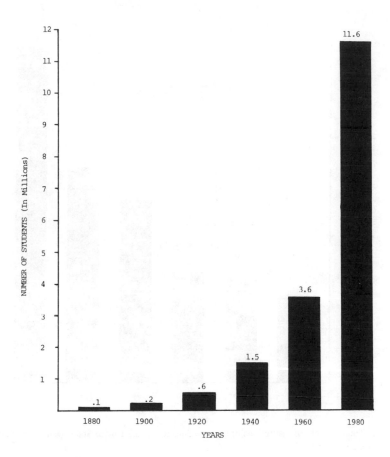

Fig. 4. Total number of students enrolled in institutions of higher education (in millions), 1880–1980. (Source: see note 38.)

Veterans returning from World War II, aided by the GI Bill, provided the initial surge in enrollments. However, the educational patterns of young people changed substantially to sustain the initial postwar growth. Since 1945, increasing proportions of the younger generation have been motivated, financially able, and academically qualified to enroll in higher education programs. Before World War II, 47 percent of the nation's high school students graduated, and about 13 percent went on to some form of higher education. In 1980, 75 percent graduated from high school and 40 percent enrolled in college.[39] By 1985, total enrollments in institutions of

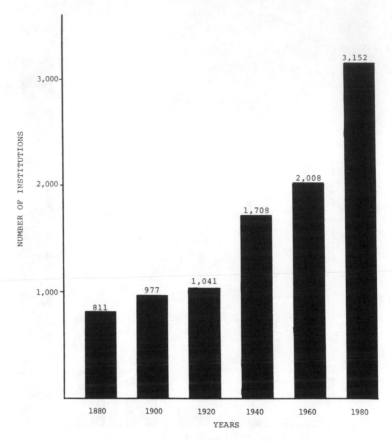

Fig. 5. Total number of institutions of higher education in the United States (both public and private), 1880–1980. (Source: see note 41.)

higher education equalled 12.2 million; 77 percent of the total, or 9.5 million, were in public institutions.[40] The postwar surge in college and university enrollments was met in the major part by the states through their support of public institutions of higher education.

With the dramatic increase in students there was a corresponding increase in the number of higher education institutions. From 1,708 colleges and universities in 1940, the number grew to 3,152 in 1980, an increase of 85 percent. Nearly half of these were publicly funded (see figure 5).[41]

In addition to the proliferation of institutions, there was an evolution in institutional mission as well in which the number of doctorate-granting institutions nearly doubled between 1948 and 1976, increasing from 64 to

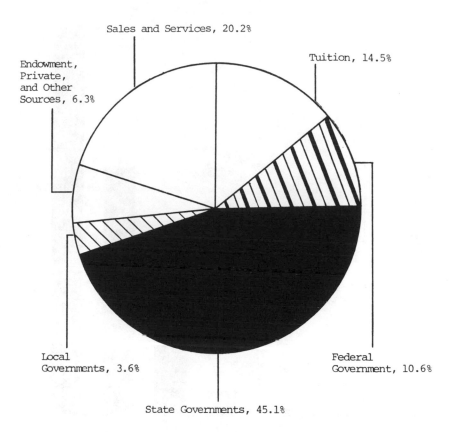

Fig. 7. Percentage distribution of sources of revenue for public institutions of higher education, 1984–85. (Sources: see note 44.)

119. (Many teachers' colleges had been "graduated" to a more expensive doctoral degree granting status.) While there were 162 teachers' colleges and 22 complex liberal arts colleges in 1948, by 1976 there were 354 comprehensive public institutions. Public two-year colleges increased from 250 in 1948 to more than 900 in 1976.[42]

Most striking, perhaps, has been the increase in the current fund revenues of higher education institutions (see figure 6). The remarkable growth in the total number of students and of institutions was necessarily paralleled by a corresponding increase in the allocation of financial

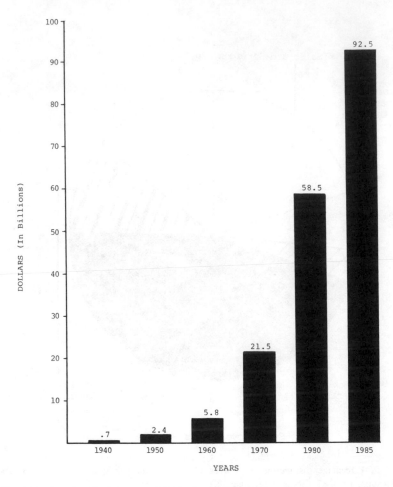

Fig. 6. Total current fund revenue of institutions of higher education (in billions of dollars), 1940–85. (Sources: see note 43.)

resources to higher education. In 1940, these revenues were just over $715 million. By 1985, current fund revenues had increased to nearly $92.5 billion, an increase over four decades of nearly 130-fold.[43]

In 1985, the states were the largest single source of revenue to public institutions of higher education, providing 45.1 percent of their fund revenues, while the federal government supplied 10.6 percent, and local governments provided 3.6 percent (see figure 7).[44]

The current distribution of the costs of public higher education among local, state, and federal governments does not represent a change from the past, in that state governments have always borne the primary responsibility for organizing, staffing, funding, and maintaining the nation's public colleges and universities. There has, however, been a remarkable change in the magnitude of financial resources channelled to higher education by the states. The vastly increased size, complexity, and cost of higher education created financial and programming problems that could not be solved within the traditional framework of institutional autonomy. These pressures have forced the states to modify the self-denying ordinance by moving to centralized governing relationships in which "in numerous matters, decisions once made by the university are now the province of a variety of state government agencies."[45] Knowledgeable observers predict an increasing trend to the centralization of higher education governance at the state level. The dominant role of state governments in the governance of higher education—clearly evident in the 1980s—is reflected in John Millett's graphic assertion with reference to centralized state governance of higher education, that higher education in America does not have three thousand different futures, roughly corresponding to the number of individual colleges and universities in the country, as was suggested by a Carnegie Foundation report; rather, higher education has fifty different futures corresponding to the fifty state governments within the United States.[46]

EDUCATION INTERESTS IN STATE GOVERNMENT: THE IMPLICATIONS OF THEORY[47]

The details of the evolutionary changes in education policy structures described in general terms above are as varied as the states themselves, yet the institutional relationships associated with them are uniformly characterized by the gravitation of power from local school districts and individual institutions of higher education to the states, largely through separate, state-level agencies for each education sector. This fact has fundamental implications for the political dynamics surrounding the education policy area at the state level.

James Q. Wilson proposes an axiom that organizations that oppose one another do not typically compete.[48] For example, a League to Abolish Capital Punishment does not compete for resources of time, money, or prestigious members with a League to Bring Back Hanging. This is because each organization appeals to individuals who are very different on at least one point: their attitude toward capital punishment. The resources lost by one organization would not likely be gained by the other. Rather, competition exists where two organizations do not oppose one another with respect to their objectives and must, therefore, appeal to similar or identical contributors. To extend Wilson's playful example, the League to Bring Back Hanging will likely compete with the League to Bring Back Execution by Firing Squad, in that they both seek limited resources from a segment of the population which, while disagreeing on the means to an end, agree on the end itself.

Viewing the agencies of state government as a microcosm of competing interests within the state, each of which petitions the same source—the legislature—for limited resources, places them theoretically in a highly competitive situation in the budget process, which Aaron Wildavsky sees as "recording the momentary outcome of the political struggle over who gets what from government."[49] Within the narrowly restricted field of legislative budget politics, potentially every department competes with every other department for limited resources. However, the competition between agencies is tempered by budgetary practice in which separate function areas, each of which is granted legitimacy, are allocated a budget base that is subsequently modified incrementally.

Within these restrictions, and on the basis of Wilson's axiom on group competition, by analogy we hypothesize that two departments of state government, each of which is charged with the responsibility of education (albeit a relatively clearly differentiated segment of education), are in a more competitive situation *in relation to each other* than either one of them would be individually in relation to a department of health, transportation, industrial development, or agriculture, for example.

In support of the hypothesis, Robert Berdahl observes generally that fiscal problems within the states "have exacerbated tensions associated with a zero-sum game approach to state funding of various educational levels [i.e., public and higher education]."[50] Susan Fuhrman has predicted further that "there will probably be increased contention between elementary and secondary education and higher education as the latter sector experiences severe enrollment declines."[51] Fuhrman's statement, based on the empirical observation of declining enrollments in higher education nationwide, could be generalized to theoretical advantage by saying that either increasing or declining enrollments within either education sector will increase contention between the two. The sector experiencing increases in enrollment will push for increased allocations to match enrollment, while the sector experiencing decreases will fight to hold on to the established resource allocation. Thus, the existence of close and potentially conflictual relationships between public and higher education interests within the structure of state government is acknowledged by informed students of education politics.

Organizations, including the institutions of government, are really structured patterns of behavior, both of groups and of individuals within them. It is within the stable relationships established by organization that political dynamics are played out. Structure is not an independent determinant of policy outcomes, but a conditioner of the political process by which those policy outcomes are achieved. It contributes to the ways in which issues are formulated, and the shape and quality of the political dynamics surrounding them.[52] Because of the increased influence of state-level policy actors (most particularly in education funding decisions) public and higher education interests must now, more than ever in the past, compete in the same policy arena of state government for limited resources.[53] There are growing pressures for interrelationships between public and higher education leaders at the state level that hold potential for conflictual, as well as cooperative, relationships in areas as varied as funding, curriculum development, program evaluation, teacher education, and vocational education.[54] The current structure of state-level education governance and politics creates pressures for both competition and cooperation which confront a relatively small number of centralized leaders with the recurring dilemma of choosing between the two in their search for political strategies intended to optimize the resources made available to them.

While we hypothesize particular political relationships between state education policy leaders, we lack in-depth empirical studies of these relationships upon which to base subjective understanding. An essential purpose of this investigation is to explore with care and in detail the political interrelationships of state education policy elites within just one of the fifty states: the state of Utah. Utah reflects fully the broad national patterns of evolution and development in education governance structures sketched in the historical perspective above, while at the same time being small enough to allow a degree of comprehensiveness and unity of analysis.

The discussion below orients the reader to the public and higher education governance structures in Utah and describes contextual political relationships that permeate and constrain the education policy process within the state. Recognizing that education governance structures, as well as the subjective relationships constraining policy leaders who must act within these organizational structures, vary from state to state, the discussion is broadly relevant to the organizational and political relationships in each of the other states.

EDUCATION POLICY STRUCTURES AND CONTEXTUAL
POLITICAL RELATIONSHIPS IN UTAH

To speak of "education" or the "education lobby" in Utah—or any other
state—as being monolithic is highly misleading. The education community
in Utah is divided characteristically into two organizational complexes, one
centered around the public schools (kindergarten through high school) and
the other centered around the state's colleges and universities. The state's
constitution, statutes, and administrative structures and procedures divide
education along these lines in recognition of a separateness based on
differing priorities and purposes, constituencies, lines of historical
development, and organizational and funding patterns.

Public Education Policy Structures in Utah

The complex of organizations charged with governing and administering
public education in Utah includes structures at both the state and local
levels. The state-level governance structure charged with coordinating the
state's public schools is established by the Utah constitution. It consists of
the State Board of Education, made up of nine members popularly elected
from the nine school board election districts into which the state is divided;
the board's chief executive officer which it appoints, the state superintendent for public instruction; and the Utah State Office of Education.
The State Board of Education is viewed by some—most notably selected
members of the State Board of Education—as the fourth coordinate branch
of government, equal in constitutional status and authority with the
executive branch, the legislature, or the supreme court. This view was
strongly expressed by a former chair and current member of the State
Board of Education, who asserted in an interview that public education is
independent and that the legislature and governor exceed their constitutional charge when they intrude into education policy matters. Members of the
board have been defensive of their (the board's) prerogatives, and this view
has lead the State Board of Education to actions that have been, in the
judgment of some observers, politically ill-advised.

The State Board of Education is designated by statute as the State
Board for Vocational Education in order to meet requirements for receiving
federal dollars in support of vocational education. At times over the last
decade, this board has established a formal meeting schedule in which it
alternates meeting dates, meeting first as the State Board of Education,
then as the State Board for Vocational Education. On vocational education
issues, higher education institution presidents periodically approach the

State Board for Vocational Education with hat in hand as their vocational education programs are reviewed by the board.

While the constitutionally established responsibility for public education in Utah lies with the state, the state in turn has delegated operational responsibility for the public schools to forty legislatively created school districts, each of which has a popularly elected board.[55] There are more than two hundred persons statewide who serve on local school boards, having been elected by their fellow citizens to exercise this public responsibility defined by statute. Each local district has a superintendent named by the board and responsible to it. One urban school superintendent recalled an instance when the governor of the state, a personal friend, had called and asked him to do something that potentially violated the established protocols in his relationship with his board. He politely reaffirmed to the governor, "I work for the board, not the governor." Another district superintendent asserted that "local boards are powerful in determining the actions of local superintendents." Thus, it can be said that public education in Utah is operationally decentralized. Local property taxes levied by each school district and supplemented by monies from the state's Uniform School Fund are administered through a foundation formula program to provide financial support for the public schools.

Numerous state-level associations represent various components of the public education community statewide. The Utah School Boards Association, the Utah Association of Elementary School Principals, the Utah Association of Secondary School Principals, and the Utah School Employees Association all provide continuing organizational opportunities for people at the local level to meet with their peers across the state, and to unite with others in making their voices heard in education policy-making. The local school district superintendents have organized into the Utah Society of School Superintendents, an organization that fosters communication among the state's top local school district administrators on matters of mutual concern and seeks to play an advisory role to the state superintendent and the State Office of Education. Roald Campbell found the Utah School Boards Association and the Utah Society of School Superintendents to have as much, or more, credibility and influence with the legislature as the powerful Utah Education Association.[56] A former chair of the State Board of Education viewed the small local districts as the "natural constituency" of the State Board of Education. Yet, in his view, the board had "frittered away" its political capital with the local districts to the point that by 1990 the Utah School Boards Association was generally antagonistic to it. The Parent-Teacher Association has cultivated and maintains a reputation for organizational strength, objectivity, and consistent commitment to children and solid educational programs, giving it much influence both in the legislature and with the population at large.

Public school teachers are highly organized into a three-tier organizational structure consisting of the local district education association, the Utah Education Association (UEA), and the National Education Association (NEA). Membership in all three levels—local, state, and national—is high throughout the state, in part because membership in simply the local or state-level organization is not allowed. Statewide membership in the UEA in 1990 was approximately seventeen thousand persons. A competing organization, the American Federation of Teachers/Utah Teachers United (AFT/UTU) claims a membership of somewhat over one thousand persons. The AFT/UTU has a reputation both nationally and within the state of being more aggressive than the mainstream UEA/NEA. However, in terms of political clout within Utah state politics, the UEA wields by far the greater influence. The UEA is taken more seriously outside the State Office of Education than within it. A former education advisor to the governor reflected that the State Office of Education has "tunnel vision on UEA. They sell the organization short." Her assessment was validated indirectly by an associate superintendent at the State Office of Education who indicated that the teachers' union has "little impact on education policy." However, his definitions and interpretation are undoubtedly too narrow. In direct contrast, a current regent, formerly a member of the state legislature, sees the UEA, not the State Office of Education, as being the driving force behind public education funding. What adds interest to the education policy process is that many view the UEA as being, in the words of a former education advisor in the governor's office, "a maverick," both unpredictable and hard to control.

The UEA has a professional, full-time staff and is very active, aggressive, and powerful in lobbying for the interests of Utah's public school teachers. The organization seeks to establish an identity in the mind of the public between the interests of school children and those of school teachers. In the interviews, a former executive director of the UEA indicated that while the organization is interested in many different educational outcomes, "they all come a distant second to maintaining and increasing teacher salaries." In relative terms, the UEA has been effective in a difficult economic and political environment in protecting and augmenting teacher salaries. In 1987, while expenditures per pupil in Utah ranked fiftieth (lowest) in the nation, teachers' salaries ranked thirty-fifth.[57] The economics of the seniority system currently prevail in determining teachers' salaries. The UEA has taken a characteristic union stance with regard to salaries, consistently and strenuously opposing the merit principle

in teacher compensation. The relationships between individual superintendents and the respective district education associations have come to be
analogous to labor/management relationships in private business, particularly in the negotiation of annual contracts, in which considerable conflict and
confrontation are not uncommon. The professional staff of the UEA
believe that if they do not look out for the interests of school teachers, no
one else will. Significantly, when asked about the State Board of
Education, members of the senior staff of the UEA expressed some
distrust, which was either increased or lessened by the stance of the state
superintendent on specific issues. The organization has been very
successful over an extended period in establishing itself as a political
power within the state.[58]

Public education, involving as it does the majority of parents and
children throughout the state, is unquestionably the single most pervasive
activity of government. The general purposes of public education enjoy a
high level of acceptance and the active support of the state's population.

Higher Education Policy Structures in Utah

There are nine publicly supported institutions of higher education in Utah.
Each college or university has a president, as well as an institutional
council that advises the state's higher education governing body, the State
Board of Regents. Regents, sixteen in number, are appointed by the
governor with the consent of the state senate and often are politically
powerful individuals in their own right. Lawyers and businessmen have
played particularly important roles on the Board of Regents during its
relatively short history. It is expected that appointments to the board reflect
an appropriate geographic distribution. Additionally, one place on the board
traditionally goes to a general authority of the Church of Jesus Christ of
Latter-day Saints. In an interview, a former governor indicated that he
considered appointments to the State Board of Regents to be the most
prestigious and important appointments that he could make. The commissioner of higher education, appointed by the Board of Regents, is the chief
executive officer of the board. The commissioner does not supervise the
presidents of the institutions. The individual institutional presidents, each
of whom is named by and directly responsible to the regents, are organized
into a council of presidents. While the council has no formal authority, it
is thought to serve usefully as a forum for the discussion of common
interests and concerns, and it seeks to play an advisory role to the State
Board of Regents.

The voluntary organization in higher education in Utah that is organizationally analogous to the Utah Education Association is the Utah Association for Academic Professionals. It is a polite and well-behaved organization that in the tenor, substance, and impact of its activities is in no way comparable to the UEA, even though it is the only political organization that represents the professoriate in bread-and-butter matters. The organization's political weakness is largely attributable to the fact that the economics of the market govern faculty salaries in higher education rather than the seniority system, as in public education. The best-known organization in higher education in Utah is the American Association of University Professors (AAUP), but the AAUP is primarily known for fighting battles on tenure and academic freedom, not salaries.

The state's publicly supported institutions of higher education are typically in a state of tension with the communities in which they are located. The traditional love/hate relationship prevails in which the community takes pride in the athletic prowess of university teams and the practical research capacity of departments of applied science, yet distrusts and feels threatened by many of the university's values and ideas that are out of harmony with those of the population as a whole. The fact that education beyond high school is not mandatory places a different, lower priority on higher education than on public education in the minds of the general public.

Such, in outline, are the formal organizational structures and internal contextual political relationships defining each of the two education sectors in Utah. How do leaders in both sectors view the interests they represent within the larger policy community? More particularly, what is their perception of the political relationship between education sectors? With regard to the institutionalized separation between education sectors, in 1981 Roald Campbell cited one important legislator as saying, "We can hardly get the two groups to speak to each other."[59] What was the perception of education leaders in 1990? Almost all of the interviews with policy-level decision makers in the public education and higher education sectors (board members, state agency administrators, local/institutional administrators, and Utah Education Association staff) were initiated with an open-ended question asking for the subject's perceptions about the closest organizational competitors for limited funds within state government. The question was posed as follows:

> Theoretically, each organization that is funded substantially by state government is in competition with all other state-funded organizations for limited funds. Are there other organizations or activities funded substantially by the state whose budgets and programs are of greater

and more consistent interest or concern to (higher education/public education) decision makers than others? If so, what are they?[60]

The responses to this open-ended question were instructive. Various agencies of state government having the largest budgets were named by subjects in both education sectors. Predictably, among these were the departments of social services, corrections, transportation, and health. Invariably, the complementary education sector was named (public education for higher education subjects, and higher education for public education subjects); most often it was the first named agency; in many instances it was the only agency named. The language of some of the responses indicates the tenor and quality of the relationship as perceived by policy-level decision makers. Responses from decision makers in higher education included the comments given below.

> "There is a fierce battle [between public and higher education] for education funding."

> "Public education is the primary competitor—there is inherent conflict between the two."

> "Public education is the major competitor."

> "There is a functional interdependence between [public education and higher education], as well as competition for dollars."

Responses from public education decision makers included the comments given below.

> "We are concerned with the education pie and want to keep an appropriate balance [between public and higher education]. We don't have high concern with other agencies beyond fair shares."

> "Higher education is the only [agency] observed by public education. And public education is the heaviest hitter."

> "There is competition with higher education. It is rare that concern is given to other agencies. UEA looks to UPEA [Utah Public Employees Association] salaries, but not superintendents and boards."

> "Higher education is the major funding competitor."

There were several recurring themes found in the responses from leaders in both sectors. There was an often expressed concern with maintaining a percentage share of the state's budget dollars, as well as the historically established proportional distribution between public education and higher education, in which a percentage point translates into millions of dollars. Leaders in both sectors recognize the importance of enrollment trends in heightening the competitive dynamics between the two. A former associate state superintendent expressed the matter in this way: "The growth rate of public education enrollments has peaked, but the growth rate in higher education enrollments is still increasing. Higher education wants additional dollars to match the increase in students, but public education cannot let funds go because it is already funded at the lowest level per student in the nation." The size of the budget allocated to an agency was repeatedly cited as the basis for interest and concern. As a university president explained, "The magnitude of the public education budget has serious implications for higher education."

These were the perceptions of Utah education administrators and board members in 1990. Some elements of the competitive relationship appear to have declined in recent years. A former regent noted that "in the early days [the 1970s] the competition was greater." A former state superintendent substantiated this assertion, recalling that in the 1970s it had been a common practice, based on distrust, for public education and higher education state agency staff to sit in on each other's legislative budget hearings to make sure that nothing was being done behind their backs that would disadvantage the interests they represented. Since 1983, a liaison committee between the two boards has served as a forum in which leaders from both agencies have openly shared their budget plans and strategies prior to the legislative session. This committee will be discussed in more detail later in this chapter.

A recurrent theme, arising spontaneously in numerous interviews except those with persons in public education at the state level, was the relationship between an elective or an appointive state board and the policy process. The most repeated objection to the election of the State Board of Education was that, in the words of a former chair of the Board of Regents, "regional election brings with it biases and hidden agendas." The factionalism attributed to the election process was seen by many as a source of political weakness with the legislature. Another regent observed that "election creates a false sense of autonomy," which leads the board, on occasion, to pursue politically unsound courses. Few members of the State Board of Education raised the issue of the composition of the board, or its elective status. One member of the State Board of Education who did raise the issue of the composition of the board saw the various "groupings" on the board as representing "a useful mix of experience and perspectives."

A former gubernatorial advisor observed, in comparing the State Board of Regents and the State Board of Education, that "the power brokers won't run for the State Board of Education." The objection of a former governor to the election of the State Board of Education is a more principled restatement of this view. He argued that the public's supreme interest in public education requires that the most able and competent people available serve, and this cannot be the result of a process in which only a very small minority of the state's voters cast ballots for people they don't know. His personal commitment to establishing a strong State Board of Education within the existing framework played a central role in the cases analyzed later in this study.

A former chair of the regents argued that elections yield both "good and bad" people, but that the rigorous scrutiny preceding an appointment leads more consistently to qualified people who are "well rounded and less provincial." In the orientation lecture that he traditionally delivered to new appointees on their system-wide responsibilities, another former chair of the regents presented an idealized view of the operation of the appointed State Board of Regents. He concluded that "the regents have geographic, occupational, and political diversity, but unity in policy." Ideally, each regent, qua regent, looks objectively at the needs of the system as a whole and does not yield to the particular interests of a locality or region. An influential state senator, however, sees a reassertion of regional factions within the regents, supported by the legislature, while a small college president sees an imbalance in the Board of Regents predisposing that body in favor of urban institutions.

The political strength of the two state education boards relative to one another has waxed and waned over the years. Political strength or weakness in this context is a function of the relationship the board has with the legislature. In 1981, Roald Campbell described a politically healthy State Board of Education, but a State Board of Regents that, by comparison, was politically unresponsive, arrogant, and even less than fully competent. Campbell writes that "legislators have . . . been known to indicate that the regents do not properly do their job," and quotes one legislator as saying, "They [the regents] don't know we exist."[61] Six years later, in May of 1986, a prominent legislator, then majority leader of the Utah House of Representatives, was quoted in the minutes of a meeting of the State Board of Education as saying that "the regents are more politically powerful than the State Board of Education." He went on to exhort the board to develop closer relations with the legislature.

In 1990, interview subjects reaffirmed this theme. One regent, a former legislator with a background in public education, indicated that the regents' credibility has improved, perhaps because of a unified policy stance that comes from an appointed board. From his perspective, the State Board of Education has relatively less credibility and political clout with the legislature because of the hidden agendas and resultant divisiveness associated with an elected board. Several interview subjects representing both public education and higher education sectors attributed much of the decline in the prestige and influence of the State Board of Education to the board's extended difficulties in dealing with the state superintendent of public instruction, whom the board appoints. Through the 1980s four state superintendents had come and gone, with a fifth appointed in 1990 and a sixth in 1992. In the strongest judgment voiced by interview subjects, a local district superintendent with substantial experience at the state level in both public and higher education reported a conversation with an influential legislator who saw the State Board of Education—as now constituted—in very serious trouble with the legislature and not likely to survive in its present form.[62] The very fact that public education had serious problems in 1990 was given more than once by respondents as a reason for higher education to steer clear of direct involvement or identification with it.

All of this should not be interpreted as giving a clean bill of political health to the Board of Regents. In an interview in early 1990, a former governor voiced his opinion that a recent decision to change the name of two component institutions within the Utah System of Higher Education from college to university reflected "a deterioration of the power of the Board of Regents," which, in effect, had capitulated to regional interests within the board and the legislature. An influential senator, chair of the Higher Education Joint Appropriations Subcommittee, likewise saw this decision as a resurgence of regionalism within the Board of Regents.

Education and Utah State Government:
The Executive and the Legislature

The organizational structure of Utah state government formally recognizes the basic separation between the public and higher education sectors, having established two coequal department-level agencies within the executive branch, each with separate governing boards, to oversee and coordinate policy in each area. Over the last decade, two different governors have each had on their staff prominent education advisors whose primary assignment has been public education. The governor's connections with higher education through his personal appointments to the Board of

Regents and the governor's education specialists in the Office of Planning and Budget seem to have made unnecessary a special advisor for higher education.

The executive, and very specifically the governor, is a central education policy actor. A local district superintendent expressed the opinion that "the executive plays a more important role in education policy than is generally recognized." Over the years covered by the study, two governors brought strikingly different personal, political, and administrative styles to their office. These differences had important concrete implications for other actors within the education policy process, and for the process itself. What follows is a composite of the views expressed by some of the interview subjects on the contrasting personal and political styles of these two central actors. The first governor was at ease in the role of governor, exerting what one associate state superintendent called "power leadership." He was impatient with the legislative process. He was well briefed and formulated his own conclusions from the advice of experts. He had a personal agenda for education that was manifest through a proactive personal stance in building the stature of boards and pushing education reform. He had much formal education and was at ease in higher education circles, though frustrated by many in public education. The second governor came up through the ranks of legislative leadership and was more comfortable as a manager of the legislative process than as the chief executive of the state. He lacked background in formal education and relied instead upon "native intelligence." He had no personal agenda for education (beyond reducing the administrative costs of public education), but was rather staff-driven, relying upon his staff advisors to establish the education agenda of his administration.

A former education advisor to the governor indicated that the UEA plays a significant role in gubernatorial decisions. Because of its strong power base, the UEA is able to run and elect candidates to local school boards, the State Board of Education, and the legislature. Consequently, the governor must pay attention to the UEA. Over the last decade, personal styles and philosophy determined how the governor paid attention. One fought the UEA publicly and deliberately excluded it from decision making on the grounds that it is a special interest group. The other sought to avoid public fights with the UEA, and to this end met personally and directly with its leaders to resolve conflicts. One local superintendent observed that "the governor's discussions with UEA have immobilized local super-intendents. It will be difficult to rein them back in."

The state legislature mirrors the administrative pattern described above, with the exception of some modifications to the committee structure implemented during the late 1980s. The full membership of the legislature constitutes the appropriations committee of the legislature. In 1990, there were joint appropriation subcommittees for both public education and higher education. Both the Senate and the House of Representatives had a single standing committee on education, the policy purview of which extended to public and higher education. Additionally, there was a Joint Interim Study Committee on Education. Earlier, in the late 1970s, as reported by Campbell, both legislative houses had standing committees for both public education and higher education, and there was an interim study committee covering each education sector as well. The current legislative committee structure is an appropriate response to 1980s education policy approaches, in which the two sectors were considered more explicitly to be complementary rather than simply separate and unrelated activities of state government.

Campbell, in 1981, described a State Board of Education that, because of a long tradition of autonomy, in his view was more independent of the legislature and the recognized constituency of local boards and superintendents than the Board of Regents.[63] A decade later, in 1990, some in public education felt there was too little autonomy. An associate superintendent at the State Office of Education saw conflict with the legislature arising from the legislature's proclivity to enter the arena of education programming, rather than limiting itself to broad policy decisions. The legislative perspective on this relationship was different. An influential "education" legislator observed that as public education seeks to develop an advocacy relationship with the Public Education Appropriations Subcommittee, the legislature unavoidably is drawn into the role of a "super school board."

A local superintendent described the legislative budget process in the Public Education Joint Appropriations Subcommittee as competitive. "The governor, the State Office of Education, the Utah Education Association, and others compete for a role, and all ask to be heard." Competition in this context relates to a lack of unity within the public education community, a recurrent observation of respondents in public education. In comparing the contrasting approaches in each of the education appropriation subcommittees, one local district superintendent saw the differences as rooted in the relative degree of organizational complexity, and the ambiguity of governance relationships within each education sector. "In public education there is more complexity and ambiguity in governance than with higher education." Within the Public Education Joint Appropriations Subcommittee, courses of action are contested in the committee and the proceedings can be abrasive. The former superintendent of a large urban district indicated that "legislators have, on occasion, been aggressive, negative—even insulting—in demanding budget reductions."

Budgets for the state's nine institutions of higher education have been consolidated under the Board of Regents. Presidents submit institutional priorities to the regents, who then prepare a single budget request for higher education to the legislature. As one member of the legislature's Executive Appropriations Committee put it, "The institutions have little say; the regents define the budget." As of 1990, the leadership of the Higher Education Joint Appropriations Subcommittee had been in place for years, had acquired considerable expertise in the higher education budget, and had exercised tight control over the process. As a local school district superintendent phrased it in comparing the process to that followed in public education, "The decisions are made almost before the hearings begin." A senior institutional staff member, commenting on the consolidated higher education budget under the regents, saw the lack of institutional competition within the legislative budget process as a detriment to higher education overall. Because of the cut-and-dried, highly controlled nature of the process, the subcommittee's agenda and procedures are less interesting, even disappointing, to the members. Powerful people choose to go where big decisions are made. When given a choice between the public education and higher education appropriations subcommittees, they choose the public education subcommittee. He cited as a case in point a rising young senate leader from a university town who chose to go to the public education subcommittee rather than the higher education subcommittee. If it is true, as asserted by a local superintendent, that the two education appropriation subcommittees are "plum" legislative assignments, the concern of some in higher education is that one plum has become sweeter to rising legislative stars than the other. They see a possible diminution over time of higher education influence in the legislative budget process.

The Executive Committee of the Joint Appropriations Committee serves as the gatekeeper on all appropriations for all state programs. The co-chairs of this centrally powerful committee have traditionally been "education" legislators, serving either on the Public Education or Higher Education Joint Appropriations Subcommittee. An individual who had served formerly as both the state superintendent of public instruction and the commissioner of higher education explained the competition between public education and higher education: the fact that both boards "are hustling for the same dollars." He reaffirmed a point made by numerous other interview subjects that this competition is manifested most clearly in the "hatchet committee," the popular and functionally descriptive name of the Executive Appropriations Committee of the legislature.

The Evolution of Governance and Liaison Structures

The establishment of the State Board of Education and the State Office of Education, as central—if not preeminent—policy actors in public education is attributable to the gradual effect over time of factors discussed earlier in this chapter, and not to the specific creation at a single point in time of new education governance structures within the state. The current governance structure in higher education, however, reflects a very pronounced shift of authority and power from the individual institutions to the state level through the creation of new structures and relationships. What happened in Utah is characteristic of a national trend that peaked in the early 1970s, whereby numerous state governments across the country adopted centralized state-level governance structures over publicly funded institutions of higher education.[64]

In 1959, the Utah legislature authorized the creation of a Coordinating Council for Higher Education, which would do just that: coordinate the services and programs of all publicly supported colleges and universities, each of which was relatively autonomous, having its own board of trustees. Ten years later, with the Utah Higher Education Act of 1969, the legislature abolished the coordinating council, establishing in its place the State Board of Higher Education, the name of which was later changed to State Board of Regents to avoid casting the "other" State Board of Education in an unfavorable light. (This semantic oversight had angered some persons in public education.) The State Board of Regents was given direct authority over all publicly supported colleges and universities, thus consolidating the state's control over higher education. The separate institutional boards of trustees were abolished and advisory institutional councils established in their place, subject to the overall authority of the regents. (In 1991, more than two decades after they were created, the legislature changed the name *institutional council* back to the more prestigious *board of trustees*. However, the powers of the new boards of trustees remained the same as those of the institutional councils. The change in name was intended to enhance the status of institutional boards without diluting the central authority of the State Board of Regents.)

The consolidation in 1970 of state-level governing relationships over higher education set the stage for a classic battle over turf between public and higher education leaders. One point of controversy during the legislative debates on the Higher Education Act had been the status of the state's two technical colleges. One influential state senator had sought specifically to exclude the two technical colleges from the governance charge given the new board, on the grounds that they would become "stepchildren."[65] With its creation, the fledgling State Board of Regents initiated strong action to integrate the technical colleges into the new Utah System of Higher Education, and thereby precipitated a head-on collision with the State Board of Education that escalated to all-out warfare between the two education agencies.

The State Board of Education determined to challenge the act itself in the courts. Suit was brought in the Third District Court, claiming that the Utah constitution vested exclusive responsibility for all education in the State Board of Education, and that the statutory establishment of a separate board for higher education was, therefore, unconstitutional.[66] The district court, emphasizing the language of the constitution, sustained the claims of the State Board of Education. The State Board of Regents appealed the decision to the Utah State Supreme Court, where it was reversed in a split decision.[67] The supreme court interpreted the language of the constitution in the context of established practice in which "the state and its officials have acquiesced for years in the fact that the State Board of Education has exercised no direct controls over post-high school education."[68] Accordingly, it affirmed that the legislation correctly assumed the legitimacy of these traditional relationships.

The litigation on the Higher Education Act extended over eighteen months and lay open to public view the political conflict created by the establishment of new governance structures, not simply the discord between the public and higher education agencies, but also within the system of higher education itself. Previously autonomous institutions of higher education had enjoyed the "benign neglect" of the State Board of Education and now chafed under the newly established centralized governance structure established by the act. As the suit was filed initially with the district court, the state attorney general in a letter to the Utah Board of Examiners asked support for a request by the Utah State Board of Higher Education to hire outside counsel. He extended the request to include individual colleges as well, "inasmuch as [the colleges'] interests may not be identical in all particulars with those of the Board of Higher Education."[69] There were, in fact, differences of organizational interest, for in arguments fourteen months later before the Utah Supreme Court, an attorney representing the University of Utah argued with the State Board of Education against the regents.[70]

In 1990, there was a clear recognition among higher education leaders of the competitive dynamics between institutions within the Utah System of Higher Education. A former chair of the regents noted "the continuing interplay of institutional interests within the system." A university president expressed concern with "the system tendency to leveling, which disadvantages larger institutions." A small college president voiced dissatisfaction with what he characterized as the unbalanced composition of the Board of Regents, which favors institutions in urban areas (the larger institutions), and disadvantages the smaller institutions located in rural areas of the state. He further noted that institutional self-interest surfaces in the activities of the council of presidents, in which the larger universities play a disproportionately large role. Another university president acknowledged the tendency of officials of institutions to seek advantages for their own college or university through the political process and found such incipient competition within the system to be tolerable, provided it does not directly conflict with the interests of other institutions or the system as a whole. Such a relationship, he admitted, requires institutional administrators to watch each other as well as public education and the legislature, for "there will always be some end-runs."

The 1971 court case and its aftermath created, in the words of an associate commissioner of the Utah System of Higher Education, "an environment of isolation, mistrust, and suspicion between public education and higher education agencies," which characterized the 1970s. The supreme court's decision in 1973 clarified the relationships between the two education boards and established a framework within which proper—if not cordial—working relationships between the two boards could be built, but the language of the constitution upon which the conflict had been based remained unchanged. The statutory status of the State Board of Regents, relative to the constitutional status of the State Board of Education, continued to trouble higher education leaders. They viewed the language of Article Ten as a loaded gun potentially threatening their existence at a future date, for a subsequent challenge to the split decision of the court might break the other way. In the very conflictual and contentious relationship that had existed between the highest governing and administrative levels of the two education sectors, those in higher education felt an implicit threat from public education, specifically in the person of the state superintendent of public instruction who had pushed the constitutional issue into the courts in the first place. With the filing of the initial suit in 1971, the chairman of the State Board of Regents, a prestigious Salt Lake City attorney, roundly criticized the state attorney general for submitting the controversy between the two education boards to litigation rather than seeking other remedies—most appropriately, in his view, a constitutional amendment that would establish beyond question the legitimate intentions of the legislation.[71] For more than a dozen years thereafter such an amendment was a high priority for the most influential members of the Board of Regents.

During the period of this study, two concerns dominated the legislative agendas of the two boards on governance issues. The issues were different, yet inextricably intertwined. First, higher education decision makers—the State Board of Regents, specifically—sought a constitutional amendment clarifying and affirming their status. This effort was at least passively resisted by many in the public education sector and their proponents. Yet, under the compelling leadership of a newly elected member and chair—an outsider to the public education community—the State Board of Education in May 1983 voted to recommend an amendment deleting from the constitution all language suggesting that the State Board of Education had responsibility for higher education governance. In the context of a meeting of a newly energized joint liaison committee, the State Board of Education chairman "requested the support" of the regents for the amendment. In his words, "[The State Board of Education and I] are determined that the education family be united in facing the difficult education issues ahead, and that our joint efforts not be diluted by prolonged and unproductive debate over governance issues."[72] This overture was received by the regents as a "statesmanlike approach" from public education. The 1984 legislature debated the proposal for two days, amended it nineteen times, and failed to pass it, whereupon the chairman of the State Board of Education recommended that the two boards "leave it alone for a while," which they did. The minutes of the meetings of the Board of Regents and the liaison committee reflect a continuing interest in the problem over the next two years by those in higher education.

The 1986 legislature failed once again to pass a resolution calling for a constitutional amendment that would put the regents on an equal constitutional footing with the State Board of Education. A referendum submitted to the electorate in November of that year did the next best thing by deleting all references to higher education from the constitutional charge to the State Board of Education, just as had been proposed in 1983. Yet, the State Board of Regents still remains a statutory body, which the legislature can modify or abolish as it chooses. This point is of considerable importance to powerful legislative advocates of public education who were willing to amend the constitution to bring it into conformity with long-established and widely accepted practice, but who would have strongly opposed granting the State Board of Regents constitutional status.[73]

The second concern of the two boards focused ultimately on protecting their established authority against legislative action. With the organization in May 1983 of a legislative study committee on education governance, both boards operated under an implicit threat to their power and autonomy. The organization of the committee had been prompted by an extended period of legislative dissatisfaction with the two boards' bickering and fighting, primarily over vocational education issues, which had characterized their relationship during the previous decade. The committee was discussing such rearrangements of governance structures as a separate third board that would govern vocational education completely, or a superboard that would govern both education sectors and all vocational education programs of the state. Both the State Board of Regents and the State Board of Education had a common interest in forestalling legislative incursions into education governance, for both would lose if such arrangements were implemented. Minimally, such changes would be very disruptive of established relationships that were at least familiar, if not entirely comfortable for both parties. The cooperative strategy used by the two education boards to protect the status quo in education governance was the formation of the State Board of Education/State Board of Regents Joint Liaison Committee. The successful establishment and organization of the liaison committee as a viable policy decision structure was the first task of board members and senior administrators. The second was achieving statutory recognition of the committee by the legislature, thus implicitly obviating the need for further legislative action on education governance. Placing the liaison committee in the statute books required a persistent effort, led by the regents, over a period of five years.

Over the last decade there have been several mechanisms, both formal and informal, whereby the higher education and public education communities maintained contact. It was not unusual in the 1980s for board members and senior administrative staff to attend each other's board meetings. In these instances they often appeared listed in the minutes as special, acknowledged visitors. This represents a change from the 1970s when such attendance would have been viewed as threatening. Senior faculty and the deans of colleges of education have long participated in public education commissions and study groups. Several ad hoc committees or commissions involving both public and higher education will be discussed and analyzed later in this study. Clearly, however, the most important effort at establishing a consistent and continuing liaison between the two organizations has been the State Board of Education/State Board of Regents Joint Liaison Committee.

The beginnings of the liaison committee were highly informal and sporadic, consisting first of annual—then biannual—breakfast meetings between the two boards in the late 1970s. Both boards approached the liaison committee with much more consistent and serious intent beginning in 1983. The concerted action and influence of three individuals—the chairmen of the two state education boards, and a second influential regent—provided the initial direction and momentum of the liaison committee. The chair of the State Board of Education immediately established the priority status of the committee by formally requesting that the chair of each state board sit on the committee, each serving as a co-chair. Additional members included the two chief executive officers—the state superintendent of public instruction and the commissioner of higher education—along with additional selected members of each board. The senior staff of the two boards—associate superintendents and associate commissioners—provided administrative support to the liaison committee. This initially established pattern has persisted and appears to be institutionalized, although the committee membership is not specified in law. The operative understanding between the boards was that the proceedings of the liaison committee would "not bind the official actions of either board, but would express the intent to share information and facilitate cooperation between the boards" on vocational and technical education matters.

Over the first few years, concurrent with the legislative study committee on education governance, the minutes of the liaison committee, as well as those of the State Board of Regents, reflected a recurrent focus on the closely related issues of education governance and vocational education. In October 1983 the chair of the Board of Regents reported to the liaison committee (obviously for public consumption) that the liaison committee was functioning well, thus eliminating the need for a third board for vocational education, or a superboard. In October 1984 it was reported to the regents that the vocational education recommendations in a new master plan could be implemented under the current governance structure through the liaison committee. A month later in the liaison committee, the chair of the regents moved the adoption of a resolution opposing a superboard for education. At this point, statutory recognition of the liaison committee was deemed by the regents to be a useful secondary goal should efforts to obtain a constitutional amendment clarifying the status of the regents fail, which they did. After repeated failures over the next several legislative sessions, the 1988 legislature formally recognized the liaison committee in its amendments to the education title of the Utah Code.[74] The State Board of Education at least once during this period (in September 1986) had voted not to take a position on legislation formalizing the liaison committee, which was periodically referred to in its minutes as the "Regents' Committee."

Achieving statutory status for the liaison committee was the centerpiece of a cooperative effort between the higher education and public education agencies (in which the regents were the more energetic) to defuse legislative concern over education governance issues by demonstrating that effective decision making could be accomplished without major changes in the governing relationships of education. In 1990, a highly influential and articulate "education" legislator rendered his judgment that "the jury is still out on the question of the liaison committee." Asked whether the committee had been able to quiet the concerns of the legislature on education governance, he continued, "Most members of the legislature do not even know that there is such a committee."[75]

SUMMARY

Each of the two education sectors in Utah is an organizational complex very much different from the other. Power, as the ability to act significantly within the policy process, is distributed far differently within the public education sector than in the higher education sector. Within public education that distribution is wide, with public decision power established independently through both constitutional and statutory definitions of office. More than two hundred persons sitting on forty-one elected boards of education at the state and local levels have an explicit public charge to decide public education issues. In the words of a local district superintendent, "Public education has populist appeal." The State Board of Education and its administrative arm, the State Office of Education, are central policy actors, but they are not alone. Many different organizations exercise important influence in public education policymaking. There is a lack of unity. Consequently, the public education policy process is unwieldy. A former state superintendent of public instruction—an outsider to the public education community—saw "a deliberately fragmented system" in public education "with decision power dispersed among local elected boards, an elected state board, legislators, the teachers' union, and the business community." Further, in his view, education is staffed by people who set a priority on protecting their own jobs. A former education advisor to the governor put the same idea in somewhat less pejorative terms when she said, "The corporate culture in public education is different. Local superintendents, who are often career types, work under the imperative 'Don't rock the boat, or risk being fired.'" All of these factors constrain and impede individual decision makers at the top of the public education policy pyramid.

The power to decide and act is distributed much more narrowly in higher education. It emanates down from the top, rather than building up from the bottom. The State Board of Regents is the central policy actor, along with the Utah System of Higher Education as its administrative arm. The higher education sector exercises the power of prestige and of political sophistication and experience. In the words of a local district superintendent, higher education "courts the influential well."

Of considerable importance to the political behavior of state-level education policy leaders is the configuration of interest groups surrounding each education sector. There are a dozen or more organizations at the state level within the public education sector representing not only special clientele groups, but almost every organizational component associated with educating children and youth. The teachers' union, the Utah Education Association, is predominant among them. Each of these organizations seeks actively to have an impact on policy. Such organizations in the higher education sector are almost nonexistent. Thus, the political constraints— arising both from legally established structure, and interest group activity— on state-level leaders in public education and higher education are clearly different. While their organizational and political circumstances are different, the interviews established that the leaders in both education sectors are similar in one important characteristic: they both view the complementary education sector as their closest competitor within state government for limited resources. It is within the organizational structures and contextual political relationships elaborated above that state-level education policy elites in Utah must interact in seeking to further the organizational interests that they represent.

3. Education Policy Elites in Action

A Microanalysis of Political Interrelationships

Objective descriptions of current education governance structures in each of the fifty states are readily available for both public and higher education,[1] yet we lack the detailed, subjective understandings of political dynamics between state-level education policy elites in each sector that define political results in specific circumstances. One purpose of this study is to develop an understanding of the education policy process at the state level by carefully analyzing these relationships and interactions within the state of Utah. While the issue area cases that are presented in subsequent chapters have intrinsic interest and instructional value, the fullest benefits of the study (and the intent of the author) will be realized only to the extent that readers apply the theoretical perspectives and conceptual framework developed here to describe, interpret, and better understand the political relationships between state education policy elites in circumstances that are familiar and of personal interest to them. In terms of social science, this is the ultimate purpose of the case study method.[2]

This chapter further describes the political context and the organizational actors (already introduced to the reader in chapter 2) that will play central roles in the issue area cases that follow. Each of the four issue area cases is briefly presented and placed in relationship with the others. Finally, the formal conceptual framework used to describe and analyze the political dynamics of the cases is presented and discussed.

THE ORGANIZATIONAL ACTORS

Education in Utah is, in Roald Campbell's terms, a "high saliency issue."[3] The centrality of the education policy area within the state is reflected in, and largely explained by, several contextual factors. A measure of the traditional commitment within the state to quality in education and to an egalitarian distribution of educational opportunity is the proportion of the

51

state's budget (well exceeding 50 percent in recent years) allocated to
education. In 1986 there were proportionally more school-age persons
within Utah than in any other state (37.2 percent of the population was
under eighteen years of age, compared to the national average of 26.2
percent),[4] yet Utah has nearly the lowest average per capita income in the
country (forty-eighth of fifty states in the nation at $10,981 annually as
compared to the national average of $14,641 annually) with which to
finance the education of its students.[5] These two facts taken together
account for chronic and severe problems in funding education at all levels
and condition in a fundamental way the political relationships among
education policy leaders.

Education interests in Utah are thought to be among the most
politically powerful and influential in the state. In a 1983 study in which
legislators ranked Utah interests according to perceived political influence,
four of the top nine cited were education-related. Specifically, these
interests or groups were the Utah Education Association (UEA); "education," referring to the public education administrative establishment, which
includes the Utah State Board of Education, its administrative arm, the
Utah State Office of Education, and other state-level organizations
representing local school districts; "higher education," referring to the Utah
State Board of Regents, its administrative arm, the Utah System of Higher
Education, and its component institutions, the state's colleges and
universities; and the Parent-Teacher Association (PTA).[6] These politically
powerful organizations, and the policy elites who lead them, had numerous
occasions to interact during the decade of the 1980s. This study analyzes
four salient issue area cases of high theoretical importance to the problem
of organizational competition and cooperation in which both education
sectors were involved. One case comes early in the decade, two come later
in the decade, and a fourth issue area was (and continues to be) a lingering
source of potential friction.

THE CASES

Beginning in 1983, education policy elites in both education sectors
experimented with cooperative budget strategies to optimize legislative
appropriations. The basis for the political dynamics of this case was
established by a report published in the spring of 1983 by a national
commission that focused on public secondary education. The commission
had been organized and was chaired by Utahns, and the report, *A Nation
at Risk*, was a catalyst in forming an unprecedented, publicly acknowl-

edged, cooperative lobbying strategy between public and higher education in Utah. The cooperative strategy was the exclusive creation of an ad hoc committee, organized under the aegis of the governor, which included the state's most powerful policymakers in public and higher education, and the legislature. At issue was a $150 million legislative appropriation above the established budget base for the support of public *and* higher education. The Utah Education Association, representing the public education rank and file, was a central element in structuring the dynamics of this unusual alliance between public and higher education policy elites.

The highly ambiguous area of vocational/technical education is of substantial interest to both public and higher education. A second case analyzes the conflictual relationships between the two sectors associated in competition for domain. As a domain issue, vocational education raises the question of organizational autonomy for each education sector. There may be more interorganizational conflict over domain issues than over the allocation of financial resources. In actuality, the determination or redefinition of a domain in an established service context allocates resources as well. The vocational education issue area provides an ongoing opportunity for competition and even conflict over turf, as well as over the dollars needed to maintain it.

The 1988 Utah general elections culminated a very hard-fought political battle over popular legislative initiatives aimed at limiting state and local taxes. With more than 50 percent of the public monies (both state and local) expended in Utah going to public and higher education, education interests were at the center of the controversy, both as a prime target of tax protesters, and as political participants defending their vital interests. The tax rebellion was the major threat of the decade to education interests in terms of potentially lost budget dollars; passage of the initiatives would have constituted a crisis for both education sectors, as well as other publicly supported organizations. Informal cooperative patterns between the two sectors emerged to fight the passage of the initiatives. Ultimately, however, the defeat of the initiatives at the polls was attributed to the grass-roots political activity of the Parent-Teacher Association in local communities across the state.

A statewide study on libraries (academic, public, and school) funded by the Utah legislature and conducted in 1988 provided an opportunity for political cooperation between the public and higher education sectors. The policy problem prompting the study was a request by the Utah System of Higher Education for $170 million in capital facilities construction for academic libraries. Higher education policy leaders successfully used the organizational symbols and rhetoric of cooperation to achieve their ultimate aims, but their clear attempts to engage the public education sector in a substantively cooperative political effort to obtain from the state legislature the additional resources needed to build academic library buildings simply did not bear the desired fruit. The issue itself of libraries and library service was deemed to be sufficiently useful that public education policy elites adopted it and put together their own legislative funding proposals for elementary and secondary school libraries.

Collectively, the case studies demonstrate not only the characteristic organizational differences between the public education and higher education sectors, but also the impact upon the education policy decision process of individual policy leaders and the organization rank and file acting within impersonal organizational structures. The studies are highly abstracted representations showing the nuances and subtleties that define the complex fabric of interests and contingencies that education policy-makers respond to in specific political circumstances.

THE ANALYSIS

Much detail has been given in each case so that the conclusions drawn about the political relationships in each issue area are, in fact, implied and supported by the description of the political dynamics presented. The analysis of political relationships and dynamics in each case focuses on four factors that have been shown to be useful in describing and analyzing political competition and cooperation between organization elites.[7] The four factors are represented below as a pyramid, with the most fundamental (Factor 1: The Functional Definition of the Organizations) serving as the base, and the most contingent (Factor 4: Mediating Organizational Structures) serving as the apex (see figure 8). The discussion of each factor thereafter develops its substantive content and suggests the interrelationships among factors.

The Functional Definition of the Organizations

The functional definition of an organization includes several different elements based ultimately on a description of the primary work of the organization, or its domain. Is the domain of the organization (its reason for being) defined clearly and distinctly, or vaguely and ambiguously? What are the exchange relationships and interdependencies that it has with other organizations in its environment? From which organizations does it

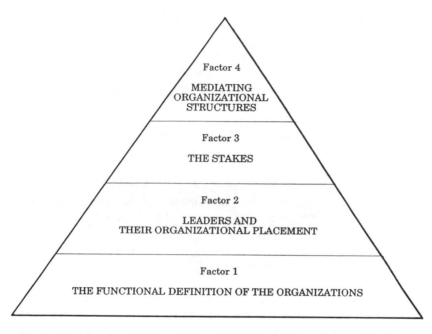

Fig. 8. A four-factor model for analyzing political competition and cooperation between organizations.

obtain the resources needed to meet its purposes? Which organizations consume its products? Very specifically, from what sources does it obtain its funding? Which other organizations draw upon the same pool of resources? What are the governance structures of the organizations? What is the distribution of formal power? Is power broadly or narrowly distributed in the organization? Is it centralized or decentralized? For organizations in the public sphere, what are the constitutional or statutory definitions of the organization's authority and domain? What is the composition of the organizational community of which the single organization is a part? Are membership and placement within the community compulsory and relatively fixed, as in the case of education agencies of state government, or relatively fluid and susceptible to modification? What is the interest group structure surrounding the organization? Answers to these and related questions constitute the functional definition of the organization. Two organizations with closely related functional definitions will be in a more competitive stance toward one another than two whose functional definitions are very different. In summary, elements of central importance to the functional definition of the organization include the following:

- Definition of organizational domain
- Organizational size and complexity
- Organizational exchange relationships/interdependencies
- Funding sources
- Distribution of formal power
  Governance structures (centralized/decentralized)
- Interest group structure surrounding the organizations

The analysis and development of the functional definition of state-level education governance structures for both public and higher education has already been largely completed in chapter 2.

Leaders and their Organizational Placement

Leadership, in the sense of articulating a vision and drawing others to the support of that vision, can be exercised by individuals at all levels of the organization. However, the focus of this factor is upon leaders at the apex of the organization—high-level administrators, executives, and legislators—and upon the interactions between analogous leaders of related organizations. Traditional and intuitive understandings of such relationships focusing on the personal and interpersonal characteristics of participating policy actors are highly relevant. What are the personal circumstances and predispositions of individuals occupying leadership positions? Are they territorial and ideological in their orientation to their roles, or are they pragmatic and instrumental? What are their work experiences and professional associations? How much tenure do they hold in their positions? Have they inherited an institutional memory? What are their personal relationships with their peers in related organizations? Is there "bad blood" between them? Are they easy or difficult to work with? How do leaders view each other?

Organization leaders are not free agents. Persons in policymaking positions speak for, and act as part of, formal organizations. The constraints and requirements imposed by their organizational roles are of great significance in explaining their actions. These constraints are largely derived from the elements in the functional definition of the organization, and include prominently not only the organizational domain, exchange relationships, and distribution of formal and informal power within the organization associated with the rank and file, but also the interest group structure surrounding the organization. The organizational placement of the leader is of great importance. Cooperative interorganizational dynamics require leadership at a particular position in the organization and within a particular configuration of the reciprocal power relationship between coalitions of policy actors both inside and outside the organization. To summarize, core elements in this factor include the following:

- Personal characteristics of leaders
    Ideological-territorial/Pragmatic-instrumental
    Experience (history)/Tenure
- Interpersonal relationships among peer leaders
- Leaders placement in the organization power structure
- Configuration of informal power—Internal/External Coalitions
- Organizational constraints on leaders

The Stakes

The stakes can be defined in terms of "what we can avoid losing," as well as "what we can win." What are the benefits and incentives available to the parties? What are the mechanisms and decision rules (fair shares, the parity principle, winner-take-all) for distributing these benefits? Those benefits that are won or lost can be concrete (such as the allocation of dollars) or abstract (such as the extension or withdrawal of authority). James Wilson asserts that "the behavior of persons occupying organizational roles [of leadership] is principally . . . determined by the requirements of organizational maintenance and enhancement . . . ."[8] In a political vacuum, it may be that organizations would above all seek autonomy, which implies neither competitive nor cooperative relationships with other organizations, but rather self-sufficiency and noninvolvement. In the realities of a political world of limited resources, however, interaction with other organizations is required. It is in pursuit of the twin goals of organizational maintenance and enhancement that organization leaders in the real world adopt strategies of competition or cooperation. The strategy that in the judgment of leaders provides the greatest benefits in support of organizational maintenance and enhancement is the strategy that, presumably, is followed.[9] In fact and application, a political strategy of competition or cooperation is not determined by a simple process of objective measurement and quantification; rather, it is through a very complex, often undefined decision process ultimately based on the subjective judgments of organization leaders that such strategies evolve.[10] This already complex relationship is further complicated by the fact that organizational incentives for cooperation are both objectively and subjectively different for different organizational actors at any given point in time. Moreover, the stakes change over time for the same actor. Presumably, cooperative organizational relationships provide benefits for each party; if there are no perceived benefits for each party, there will be no substantive cooperation. In summary, central elements in this factor include the following:

- Benefits/Liabilities
  Specific/Vague or undefined
  Tangible/Intangible
  "What can we win; what can we avoid losing?"
- Distribution of Benefits
  Decision rules—fair shares/parity principle/winner-take-all

Mediating Organizational Structures

Mediating organizational structures provide circumstances in which representatives from two or more interacting groups are brought together organizationally for joint decision making. This factor is placed last in this discussion because in the logic of the political relationships we are examining it is most contingent. The logical relationship among the factors in most instances appears to be "if Factor 1: if Factor 2: if Factor 3: then Factor 4." In other words, if mediating organizational structures are absent, yet are necessary to achieving a given end, then leaders intent on achieving that end will create them. In this sense, they are instrumental, yet this is not to depreciate their political value. Questions of central importance to this factor include the following: What is the membership of the mediating organization? Where are the representative members placed in the power structure of their own organizations? Does the decision power they exercise derive from within the Internal Coalition of their organizations, or is it grounded in the External Coalition? The composition of the group regarding this single point will have a great impact on the substantive results of the group's actions. If such mediating structures are to function in support of substantive interorganizational cooperation they must contain the true decision elite from each organization.

There is a very close relationship between leaders and mediating organizational structures. Mediating structures, whether ad hoc or permanent, provide the framework and organizational machinery within which small group dynamics can come into play, allowing decision elites to reach an accommodation by reducing the psychological constraints associated with pressure from their rank and file. Two elements central to this factor are

- Membership of the mediating organization
- Placement of representative members in their own organizational power structure—Internal/External Coalitions

The four factors of the model described above are mutually supportive and interactive. In effect, numerous complex contingencies embodied within the core elements listed in the discussion of each factor served cumulatively to define and explain either a competitive or a cooperative interaction between organization policy elites. The model was used to organize ideas, to guide and direct the research, to sort and analyze data, to determine relationships, and to help the author to interpret, understand, and explain the complex organizational and political relationships between the public and higher education policy elites who were the focus of the study.

Each of the four issue area cases consists of three parts. An introductory section reviews relevant theoretical concepts, establishes the policy context for the issue area, and presents the institutional and political relationships that are needed to understand the dynamic political interrelationships of the case. A second section—the body of the case—presents a detailed description of the political dynamics between public education and higher education policy elites. A concluding section discusses and analyzes the dynamics of the case in the light of relevant theoretical perspectives. Each case is separate and distinct, yet there are close interrelationships between them, both in time and substance. The issues in the various cases mix and blend, policy actors appear in one case and reappear in another, and personal and organizational relationships and activities from the past heavily condition both the present and the future. Indeed, one case cannot be fully understood without reference to the others.

The issue area cases are not intended as history or as ends in themselves. Rather, they are presented as opportunities to examine in some depth the political relationships among groups of elite decision makers within specified organizational structures. Taken as a whole, the case studies are a complex, multifaceted description and analysis of the political dynamics found at the organizational interface between the public and higher education sectors in state government. A more thorough understanding of political relationships within this only tacitly acknowledged—and largely unscrutinized—policy space can usefully inform the education policy process in each of the states.

4. Optimizing Legislative Appropriations

Cooperative Budget Strategies[1]

Students of the public sector predict an extended decline at least through the end of the century in the availability of resources to government, coupled with an increase in public demands for services. Such circumstances highlight the difficulty of managing decline and emphasize the need for policy leaders to accommodate conflicting interests.[2] Accommodation implies the use of cooperative approaches. Yet, it is intuitively assumed by many that the level of organizational conflict or cooperation is a direct function of the availability of resources: scarcity of resources promotes competition or conflict; an abundance of resources supports cooperation. If the relationship is as simple and direct as this, how then are we to account for instances of cooperation in times of scarcity?

James Wilson's analysis of competitive and cooperative behavior between groups is particularly relevant.[3] Competition between organizations can be very costly. The costs of competition can be reduced through cooperation. Consequently, two or more competitive groups will often seek to minimize such costs to themselves through cooperative behavior. David Truman labels cooperative behavior between groups that is aimed at "the development of a common strategy . . . that bears some substantive relation to the interests of each" an alliance, which may be continuing and formal, or informal and temporary.[4] Wilson suggests an expanded taxonomy of cooperative organizational behaviors to include the *coalition*, which is an enduring arrangement for the ongoing, explicit coordination of actions of coalition members, and the ad hoc *alliance,* which is a loose, cooperative relationship between organizations with respect to the attainment of a particular end or the performance of a specific task.[5]

Wilson's distinctions between a coalition and an alliance add an important dimension to the theory. While groups seldom form coalitions, in Wilson's meaning, alliances between groups are common. Circumstances in which the autonomy or resources of prospective members are severely threatened (as in a crisis), or in which there is an opportunity to significantly augment the autonomy and resources of prospective members provide strong incentives for cooperation, either in the form of an alliance or a coalition.[6] The coalition, which is intended to endure over time, requires widespread acknowledgment and acceptance within the various levels and general membership of each participating group. The costs of establishing and maintaining such a consensus are often great and explain in large part why coalitions are not often formed.[7] In the ad hoc alliance, the role of leaders is central. The alliance, intended as it is to bring about short-term cooperation that is expedient for each participant in reaching clearly defined, specific, and limited goals, is the result of the interaction and agreement of group leaders—the rank and file play no active role.

The alliance is a common form of cooperation between groups precisely because it furthers the interests of the group without incurring the organizational costs associated with widespread member participation. As Wilson states,

> The reason ad hoc alliances can form at all is that . . . they are purely leadership activities in which the constituent associations are not deeply or formally implicated. Associational leaders and executives respond to a number of partially incompatible incentives: a desire to maintain the organization and one's position in it, as well as a desire to acquire the support and goodwill of other key associational executives and to achieve certain policy ends, even some not much in favor by their rank and file.[8]

In terms of the political interactions between organization elites, actual social situations are seldom purely competitive or cooperative. It is possible for related organizations to be cooperatively interdependent with regard to one goal and competitively interdependent regarding another related goal.[9] For example, public education and higher education policy elites can be *cooperatively interdependent* regarding the issue of additional state funding for education, but *competitively interdependent* with regard to the specific distribution of the added dollars between them.

In their 1969 study of the developing relationship between elementary-secondary and higher education, Michael Usdan and his colleagues identified several issue areas of substantial interest to both that would bring them progressively closer and require potentially conflictual interaction. Public funding headed the list. For a half-dozen years, from 1983 through 1989, Utah education policy elites explored the dynamics and implications of cooperative legislative budget strategies. The interactions between education sectors on funding issues have evolved from a stance of antagonism and distrust in the 1970s, to an unprecedented—and unrepeated—

joint lobbying strategy in 1983–1984, to a more distant, though still open and mutually supportive, approach (within the principle of fair shares) to education funding later in the decade.

POLITICAL DYNAMICS

"Pull together for strength, and share the benefits."

On 12 October 1983, approximately ninety days before the opening of the twenty-day budget session of the Utah State Legislature, an important meeting of the Utah State Board of Regents was reported in the press.[10] The Board of Regents was seeking an increase of $51 million over the current operating budget for higher education from the upcoming legislature. The presidents of the state's nine publicly funded institutions of higher learning had submitted requests to the regents totaling $80.5 million in additional money.

Having approved the motion to request an additional $51 million, the regents then immediately adopted a resolution calling for a joint lobbying campaign with public education "for no less than a $150 million increase." Because the public education budget was 2.5 times greater than that of higher education, higher education would receive 28.3 percent (42.5 million) using the existing ratio, with public education receiving $107.5 million. Regents chairman Kem Gardner indicated that they were trying to be realistic in the supplemental appropriation request, and that key legislators and the governor seemed willing to go only as high as $150 million total for education. Limited radio reportage of the unusual proceedings of the regents' meeting was carried as an announcement by Commissioner of Higher Education Arvo Van Alstyne that public and higher education would join forces in requesting from the legislature $150 million to be distributed between the two according to the existing ratio of 2.5 to 1.

Reportage in the mass media of the regents' meeting of 11 October 1983 was the first public notice of this alliance between education sectors. A careful reading of the minutes of the Board of Regents, the State Board of Education, and the State Board of Education/State Board of Regents Joint Liaison Committee meetings through the preceding spring and summer indicates that the full memberships of these three groups had little more prior notice than the general public of the details of this political strategy of cooperation. The cooperative legislative budget strategy between public and higher education had, in fact, been established months earlier by another group external to either education board as formally constituted. That group, the Utah Education Reform Steering Committee, organized under the aegis of the governor, had worked consistently over the course of the summer and early fall to establish a foundation for an alliance and to implement the strategy.

For the remainder of October and the first half of November the $150 million joint request by public and higher education received some media attention through the activity of people in the higher education community. A prominent leader in this effort was Chase Peterson, the newly installed president of the University of Utah. Speaking before the Salt Lake Kiwanis Club, President Peterson was seriously misquoted in the press as saying that "higher education is in need of a $150 million tax infusion, one that has the support of Governor Scott Matheson and the Republican-controlled Legislature, and now requires commitment from the state's citizenry."[11] The error elicited a nearly instantaneous letter to the editor from President Peterson, indicating that the $150 million was a joint request by both public and higher education.

During this time, the leadership of the public education community was conspicuously silent. Finally, on 19 November, approximately fifty days before the legislature was scheduled to convene and nearly six weeks after the Board of Regents' original announcement, the press reported a meeting of the Utah State Board of Education in which the board "threw its weight behind a $150 million school reform package . . . by generally endorsing proposals made a week ago by the governor's Steering Committee on Education Reform . . ."[12] The board, it was reported, would ask the legislature for an additional $109.6 million for public education, and would "support the State Board of Regents' request for an additional $41 million." Oscar McConkie, chairman of the State Board of Education, urged the board to take the "unified approach" with the $150 million, arguing, "We could justify a need for more than $200 million, but this is a distillation of the political realities." No mention of a "fair shares" rationale for the distribution of the legislative appropriation was made, and the concept of direct cooperation and joint action with higher education was downplayed and tied more generally to "school reform" and the recently published report of the governor's ad hoc committee on education.

In spite of the rather scanty public record, it was clear from the timing of public actions by leaders in both groups (the actions of one group being somewhat premature, and those of the other somewhat delayed), and the language and substance of their public statements (particularly the juggling of $1.5 million between them) that an intense competition underlay the public truce that was early and optimistically characterized by the Board of Regents as a "joint lobbying campaign." Most remarkable was the fact that a degree of public cooperation on such matters—however precarious—had been established between public and higher education.[13] Such a stance by the two groups was unprecedented in Utah politics. Moreover, circumstances prevailing in Utah in 1983 had created a political environment in which the two groups were potentially in a state of heightened competition for public monies. An understanding of this unusual, seemingly contradictory, political alliance requires a consideration of several important contextual factors.

Competition for state monies was particularly strenuous in 1983 because of an extended economic slump in which the governor in two successive previous years had mandated budget holdbacks for all state agencies to cover projected revenue shortfalls. Depressed economic conditions had placed added pressures on the state's human services agencies. Record snows the previous winter had melted into record floods in the spring, which did extensive damage to the state's highway and rail system; costs for mandatory repairs were put at $50 million. In short, concerns for education funding within a highly competitive environment had reached crisis proportions in the minds of education leaders. While it was clear to them, and the governor as well, that substantial and timely adjustments in both public and higher education budgets were essential, it was also evident that other agencies of state government would be making strong claims for additional funds.

Education and political leaders from the governor on down clearly saw education's pressing needs. This general understanding provided the "fertile soil" in which a dramatic and unconventional approach to education funding problems could take root, but it was the conjunction of two unusual circumstances that created an opportunity—a "policy window"—to place the issue prominently on the state's public agenda.[14] The first of these unusual circumstances related to the specific composition and grouping of state-level education policy leaders in Utah; the second, to the development of education issues at the national level.

Individuals within organizations, particularly those at the top, can be of considerable importance in establishing both specific policy directions and more general, subjective orientations of the organization to its environment. The training, capacity, experience, and predispositions that an executive brings to the office are crucial. In 1983 the chair of the State Board of Education (Oscar McConkie), the state superintendent of public instruction (Leland Burningham), the chair of the State Board of Regents (Kem Gardner), the commissioner of higher education (Arvo Van Alstyne), and the president of the state system's flagship university (Chase Peterson) all had assumed their offices within the previous two years. Thus, five of the most important decision makers in Utah education, most of whom had considerable experience and capacity, did not have the encumbrances and inevitable constraints associated with extended tenure and were, therefore, more free to follow an unconventional policy course.

This new central grouping of education leaders was intent on destroying the conflictual and self-defeating pattern of the past, and substituting in its place a pattern of efficient cooperation between education boards. As a former associate superintendent at the State Office of Education put it, McConkie and Gardner decided that "the squabbling was a nuisance" and actively sought to demonstrate cooperation. Oscar McConkie saw himself and Kem Gardner as being both the formal and substantive leaders of their respective boards, and as such able to make a difference. Numerous respondents in the interviews referred to the friendship and mutual respect shared by this central group of decision makers that supported their working relationships. Partisan affiliations were cited as well to explain the harmony and influence among the group: Governor Matheson, McConkie, and Gardner were all Democrats.

The pivotal actor within this group of education board chairs and chief administrators was Oscar McConkie. Governor Matheson, in a continuing effort to elevate the performance of the State Board of Education and place education at the top of the state's agenda, had personally asked fellow Democrat McConkie to run for the board. McConkie, a Salt Lake City lawyer, previously had served twenty years as president of the Utah State Senate. His prior public service and prestige virtually assured his election, which, given the circumstances, came very near to a gubernatorial appointment to an elective board. McConkie recalled that having been elected to the board, he was "determined to be dominant." Prior to taking office he lobbied the board members, securing enough votes to be elected chairman at the first meeting he attended in January—in spite of the fact that the board's bylaws called for the election of the chair to be held in February. Thereafter, he managed the board as an experienced legislative politician would, exercising the prerogatives of the chair to control discussion, and always assuring that he had a "solid block of five votes." McConkie's actions over the course of the two years of his chairmanship of the State Board of Education reveal a complex, integrated, insightful, and deliberate program to establish cooperative rather than conflictual relationships with higher education. When asked if he and Governor Matheson had together established a common political action agenda for the board, McConkie replied that they had not. Clearly, however, they were both competent people with a common understanding of the principles upon which action with the board should proceed.

A policy window for elevating education on the state's public agenda first opened in Washington, D.C., in August 1981. At that time, U.S. Secretary of Education Terrel H. Bell established the National Commission on Excellence in Education, naming University of Utah president David P. Gardner as its chair. Both of these individuals, who would remain in the national education spotlight for some time, had close ties to the Utah education community.[15] Because "Utah people" were playing such a prominent national role, it reasonably can be assumed that the impact in Utah of the commission's work was greater than it otherwise might have been. In April 1983, eighteen months after it had been established, the commission issued its formal report, entitled *A Nation at Risk: The Imperative for Educational Reform*.[16] The publication of *Risk* created the greatest public awareness, concern, and debate over the nation's schools that had been felt since the launching of Sputnik a quarter of a century earlier and spawned minicommissions in states across the country. Utah was no exception.

The political task of education policy leaders in Utah, as elsewhere, was to use the ground swell of popular awareness of education and shape it to meet their very specific needs. There were two major education policy planning efforts in Utah organized in the wake of *A Nation at Risk* that were intended to perform this function. Of particular importance to this study is the fact that *Risk* focused on public secondary education, saying little about higher education except in a peripheral way. This fact placed additional burdens upon leaders in higher education in Utah, who subsequently had to mold and reshape the issues so that they would support the needs of the state's colleges and universities as well as the public schools. This transformation was accomplished through an ad hoc steering committee on education reform established under the aegis of the governor. The second planning effort, which took place simultaneously with the governor's steering committee, was organized by the State Board of Education.

It has been said that people who work for policy change "are like surfers waiting for the big wave. . . . If you're not ready to paddle when the big wave comes along, you're not going to ride it in."[17] Governor Matheson was prepared to ride the big wave created by the National Commission on Educational Excellence. Looking back after a half-dozen years, he spoke with feeling and commitment of the importance of excellence in education programs for the state's future. It was his expressed conviction that "education will make a difference." According to a former chairman of the State Board of Education, Governor Matheson felt that "education was the most important issue in Utah." The governor's proactive stance with regard to the State Board of Education is widely acknowledged throughout the education community. Over the years the governor encouraged several individuals whom he thought capable to stand for election to the board, just as he had with Oscar McConkie. With the election of McConkie at the previous election, Matheson had positioned a strong ally on the State Board of Education.

Two years before the publication of *A Nation at Risk*, Matheson had organized two education task forces that had communicated their findings and recommendations in reports entitled *Solving the School Crisis*. His education advisor during his second term of office, Anna Marie Dunlap, had personally participated in national education planning conferences in which other state governors had taken a prominent role. She had the governor's ear and kept him abreast of developments in frequent personal meetings. In the spring of 1983, as the national commission was concluding its work, Matheson appointed Ms. Dunlap to fill a vacant associate director position in the Department of Community and Economic Development. Her primary assignment, new to the department, was to be education. Matheson's appointment is particularly interesting in view of the fact that two other executive department-level agencies were already charged with this responsibility. The governor's actions created, on a temporary basis, a mediating organizational mechanism between public and higher education, and increased his own influence in education policy decisions without increasing his visibility. Clearly, he was laying the groundwork for action.

The Utah Education Reform Steering Committee was organized early in May 1983, soon after the publication of *A Nation at Risk*, through a cooperative effort by Democratic governor Scott Matheson and Republican state senator Warren Pugh. The behind-the-scenes details of the organization of the steering committee are not only interesting, but instructive of the policy process at the state level. Senator Pugh, when asked how the Education Reform Steering Committee had come to be organized, replied simply, "I organized it." He then proceeded to relate how, having obtained the cooperation of the Republican house majority leader (who would sit on the steering committee), he had written a letter to Governor Matheson proposing the committee and asking that certain individuals be named to it. In this sense, Senator Pugh indicated, he had "used the Office of the Governor" in organizing the steering committee.

The governor's education advisors, Anna Marie Dunlap and Henry Whiteside, indicated in interviews that Governor Matheson was the moving force behind the organization of the steering committee, with the "initiative coming entirely from the executive." Governor Matheson himself, when asked about the organization of the committee, replied initially that he "assumed" Anna Marie Dunlap had pulled the committee together. When informed by the author of Senator Pugh's claims, the governor graciously deferred, saying that he would not deny Senator Pugh the credit. He held the senator in the greatest personal esteem, and previously in the interview referred to his honesty: "What can we do with this man? He has complete integrity!" Several other persons interviewed referred to the close working relationship between Governor Matheson and Senator Pugh. It is most likely that the organization of the Education Reform Steering Committee was a joint effort of several individuals, most notably Senator Pugh (a Republican) and Governor Matheson (a Democrat) with his aides, and that the senator exercised initiative in organizing the committee in the proximate sense. Clearly, the thoughts and intentions of most of these central participants were running along the same lines at this time. This interaction underscores the political hazards associated with organizing the steering committee, which included the partisan issue of Democrats versus Republicans, as well as competition between the executive and legislative branches of state government.

A former local district superintendent with considerable experience in working with the state legislature discussed the continuing need "to establish a balance between public education and higher education interests in the legislature." He continued, "Senator Pugh is 'the balancer.'" As a co-chair of the Executive Appropriations Committee, Senator Pugh had been in a position to play the role of balancing public and higher education interests in the legislature for some years. The steering committee was chaired by Emanuel Floor, a respected and highly influential businessman of considerable energy, charisma, a gift for working with groups of people to get things done, and a flair for public relations. One steering committee member characterized him as "a superb facilitator and motivator." Representing public education were the chair of the State Board of Education (Oscar McConkie), and the state superintendent (Leland Burningham). Representing higher education were the chair of the State Board of Regents (Kem Gardner), the commissioner of higher education (Arvo Van Alstyne), and Regent Neal Maxwell, a member of the Council of the Twelve Apostles of the Church of Jesus Christ of Latter-day Saints. Maxwell was judged by many to have been highly influential in establishing more cooperative relationships between public and higher education, most particularly through his work reestablishing the liaison committee on a more formal basis. Four legislators, one from each party within each house of the legislature, sat on the steering committee. Collectively they held seats on the joint appropriations subcommittees for both public education and higher education, as well as on the Interim Study Committee for Public Education. More significantly, legislative representation included both the house majority leader (Robert Garff), and (as indicated above) the powerful co-chairman of the Executive Appropriations Committee, Senator Warren Pugh. Senator Pugh was characterized by a committee staff member as "the most active member" of the steering committee. Senator Omar Bunnell was a long-time Democratic stalwart who could be relied upon by the governor to support responsible innovation. Representative Ron Stephens was a teacher by profession and brought practical insights on public education to the deliberations of the group. (The fact that Representative Stephens was a teacher allowed Senator Pugh to contend that "teachers were represented on the steering committee." (This was a sensitive point, which will be discussed further below.) Representing the governor on the steering committee was Anna Marie Dunlap, the governor's education advisor. Significantly, Ms. Dunlap was the only member common to both the Utah Education Reform Steering Committee and the Utah Commission on Educational Excellence, which was organized thereafter by the State Board of Education.

Of considerable importance to the case is the fact that the Utah Education Association was excluded from formal representation on the steering committee. Governor Matheson took personal pride in his contention that "special interests were kept out. What we had was a fair, pure approach to serve the public interest." Senator Pugh, as well, was dissatisfied with the abrasive, self-interested stance of the UEA at the time, characterizing in retrospect the executive director as "a Chicago union organizer." In a political culture in which overt conflict is frowned upon, the UEA's abrasive tactics had caused it to lose influence during a critical year.

At the 7 June 1983 meeting of the State Board of Education, board chairman McConkie announced the organization of the governor's Education Reform Steering Committee, the purpose of which was "to develop a package of education reforms."[18] Board member Richard Maxfield objected that the governor had exceeded his authority in organizing the steering committee, for he had had no contact prior to organizing it with the state board, the constitutionally established organization responsible for public education in Utah. Maxfield proposed that rather than a "steering" committee, a "tracking" committee on education reform would be more appropriate. He expressed a desire for a meeting with the governor "to pledge mutual support." A second board member joined Maxfield, saying that the Steering Committee "was not needed." The board proceeded to vote thanks to the governor for his concern and efforts in behalf of public education, with two members voting no. These competitive relationships between the executive and the State Board of Education further complicated legislative-executive and Democratic-Republican divisions.

The board then turned its attention to a request from an umbrella group of public education organizations known as HOPE (Helping Organizations for Public Education), which was asking that the State Board of Education appoint an advisory commission "to explore and make recommendations in response to *A Nation at Risk*." While Chairman McConkie voiced the possibility of overlap with the already established steering committee, he supported the request. Accordingly, in June 1983, the board organized a blue-ribbon commission that it christened the Utah Commission on Educational Excellence. It was chaired by a respected broadcast journalist and administrator, Ted Capener. State Superintendent Leland Burningham sat as a member on the commission, with associate superintendents providing staff support. The membership of the commission followed a well-established pattern in public education, in that it was large —as it necessarily had to be to fully represent the numerous organizational components and client groups within the public education community. Twenty-two individuals were named in the final report as having sat on the commission. They represented more than a dozen organizational entities within the public education community, the business community, the media, the legislature, higher education, and the governor's office.[19]

Given the sequence of events surrounding the organization of the Utah Commission on Educational Excellence as documented in the State Board of Education minutes, it appears that the board was in the position of having to react to circumstances rather than giving proactive direction to them, at least so far as legislative action was concerned. The opening of a policy window had been anticipated and prepared for by those responsible for organizing the governor's Education Reform Steering Committee. The response by the State Board of Education to the same circumstances had been "a day late, and a dollar short," and appears to have been based at least in part on the board's desire to vindicate its constitutionally established responsibility for the public schools. A former associate superintendent at the State Office of Education who was heavily involved in the commission recalled the decision to organize it as being politically poorly advised, saying the State Board of Education "should not have competed with the Education Reform Steering Committee." Governor Matheson initially opposed the organization of the commission and was advised by staff "to invite them on." Looking back, the chairman of the commission recalled that there was "an early decision [by the State Board] for no cross-over" between the commission and the steering committee, again based on the board's desire to assert its constitutional role. He went on to indicate that while the two groups were "not overtly competitive," there was "no coordination between the two" and "no consideration of their separate missions." His comments on the separate missions of the two planning groups are important and require further consideration.

Compared to the Utah Commission on Educational Excellence, the Education Reform Steering Committee was relatively small and compact. With eleven members, the steering committee was half the size of the Utah Commission. However, the big difference between the two lay not in their sizes, but in the substantive composition of their memberships. Just as the membership of the Utah Commission reflected the fragmented politics and diverse client groups of the public education community, the membership of the steering committee revealed a studied regard for the broader politics and power relationships of the executive and legislative policy process within Utah state government. Given its composition, the Utah Commission on Educational Excellence was equipped to produce a thoughtful, comprehensive, and insightful analysis with far-reaching recommendations for improving education in the state's public schools.[20] This it did, but it was beyond its competence to formulate a budget policy package that the legislature could act upon. Its final report reveals that the commission did not even attempt to do so. Given its composition, the Utah Education Reform Steering Committee was equipped to formulate and execute a bold and daring legislative budget strategy linking public and higher education in an unprecedented alliance; it would succeed in adding to the overall state education appropriation more than $100 million. However, the steering committee was not structured to plan and implement a comprehensive program of reform in public education. Rather than considering themselves competitors, the participants could just as well have deemed themselves members of complementary planning committees.

As late as July the State Board of Education was still formally appointing members to the commission, one of whom was Anna Marie Dunlap, who would serve as the de facto liaison with the governor's steering committee. Members of the commission recognized that the steering committee was more politically powerful because of its ties to the governor and the legislature. According to the chairman, the commission tried to insert major issues into the deliberations of the steering committee, relying implicitly on Ms. Dunlap to perform this function. The final report of the Utah Commission on Educational Excellence was received and adopted by the State Board of Education on 7 October 1983.[21] On 18 November, when Oscar McConkie presented the steering committee's final report to the State Board of Education, he characterized it as "a restatement of the Capener [the Utah Commission's] Report."[22] A reading of both reports makes it clear that this assertion by McConkie was something of an overstatement intended to mollify the board and the public education community represented by HOPE. An urban school superintendent recalled that "the Capener Report was buried," that the State Board had been "slow in publishing the results of its commission," and that, consequently, the Education Reform Steering Committee "received all of the publicity." In actuality, the commission's report was published and received by the State Board of Education in early October. It had initially been expected in August. The board waited for another six weeks before receiving, or even discussing, the steering committee's final report and recommendations. It is very likely that the delay between the two events is at least partially explained by the need for State Board of Education chairman Oscar McConkie and State Superintendent Burningham to demonstrate their solidarity with the public education community by waiting an appropriate period after the receipt of the commission's report before considering the program proposed by the steering committee. Clearly both leaders (most particularly Burningham who personally sat on the commission) were experiencing considerable cross-pressures because of their responsibility for and participation in both planning efforts.

The minutes of the Board of Regents meetings held during the first half of 1983 reflect primarily a concern by the regents over a "fiscal crisis" in higher education. Regents chairman Kem Gardner had sought to obtain increased appropriations for higher education through the Joint Appropriations Management Committee, but had failed.[23] These concerns reached a crescendo at the 23 August 1983 meeting of the regents in which it was reported that Governor Matheson had requested a reduction in general fund expenditures of $25 million to compensate for lagging tax receipts. The institutional presidents universally rejected the idea of a cut, one saying simply, "No cut is possible; raise taxes." This view was supported by a regent and former university president who indicated that "higher education has hit rock bottom . . . and cannot take further cuts." The result of the meeting was the passage of a formal resolution reaffirming that higher education was underfunded and could not accept further cuts without incurring "serious, tragic, lasting, and totally unacceptable damage to the system."[24] The regents urged a tax increase, and served notice of a tuition surcharge to meet the fiscal difficulties facing them.

As the governor faced the possibility of a substantial revenue shortfall, this action by the regents put him in a dilemma. While he had budgetary control over higher education because it was funded through the state's general fund, the regents and institutional presidents had blocked any budget holdback. Furthermore, he had no statutory authority to order a budget cut for public education, which was funded through the Uniform School Fund. He had to rely only on moral suasion to urge a voluntary cut. This circumstance provided reinforcement to the state's chief executive to do what could be done to foster a politically viable cooperative solution to problems that would involve the least possible damage to public education and higher education, as well as to himself. In a political battle between education sectors—with himself in the middle—he could only lose political capital.

References to the governor's steering committee do not even appear in the regents' minutes until the July 18 meeting at which Commissioner Van Alstyne, a member of the steering committee, commented on *A Nation at Risk* and simply enumerated the groups in Utah that were addressing the problem of excellence in education. Heading the list was the governor's Education Reform Steering Committee, which was followed by the State Office of Education's "blue-ribbon committee" (the Utah Commission on Educational Excellence). Regent Neal Maxwell, also a member of the steering committee, shared with the regents the fact that "the unintentional focus of the [steering committee] tends to be K-12." He then tied the steering committee's planning effort to the regents' immediate and pressing concerns by asking whether efforts should be made for higher education to develop a student funding-level mechanism similar to the weighted pupil unit (WPU), and whether public education and higher education should share the pain equally on budget cuts. It was not until the middle of September that the Education Reform Steering Committee was mentioned again in the minutes of the regents. At the regents' meetings on September 12 and 13, the board was formally told that Chairman Kem Gardner, Neal Maxwell, and Commissioner Van Alstyne had "been serving as higher education representatives [on the steering committee]." Regent Maxwell was excused from the meetings because he was "drafting language for the report."[25] This is the most detailed reference to the work of the steering committee appearing in the regents' minutes. It is provided so late in the process and in such a way that it is clear that the Board of Regents, as such, had nothing to do with formulating the political strategy to be followed by public and higher education in the 1984 legislature. The same observation is equally true of the State Board of Education. At a meeting of the board on September 30, board member Richard Maxfield and Chairman Oscar McConkie played "cat and mouse." Maxfield asked McConkie if he had any information about his membership with the "governor's reform committee." McConkie responded simply that recommendations on finance reform would be made.[26] He would not be ready to say more to his board for another month-and-a-half.

Wilson hypothesizes that temporary and limited cooperation between organizations results from the interaction and agreement of leaders in which the rank and file play no active role. The unified legislative budget strategy followed by the state's education agencies was exclusively the creation of the steering committee. This ad hoc organizational structure allowed a small number of leaders at the highest levels to meet regularly during the late spring, summer, and early fall of 1983 to work out a comprehensive approach to the legislative budget problems of education, insulated to some degree from the cross-pressures caused by the complex, often contradictory, desires of their constituents. Members of the steering committee met weekly and outside the public eye to establish an approach to the 1984 legislature that would capitalize on the policy window created by the national commission's report. A steering committee staff member indicated that the work of the committee was "consensual; there was little conflict." In his view, 90 percent of the meeting time was spent on public education; higher education leaders bided their time. The steering committee surfaced momentarily in August to report the results of an opinion poll that it had commissioned showing that Utah's citizens were willing to raise taxes and spend more for better schools.[27] The committee would not appear prominently again until the publication of its final report in November.

The relationship between Oscar McConkie as chair of the State Board of Education, and Leland Burningham as the state superintendent, as well as Superintendent Burningham's impact on the other members of the Steering Committee, was important to the working of the steering committee, and requires additional explanation. It has been postulated that "the more practical experience one has had in the arena of electoral politics and that of policy negotiation, bargaining, and compromise, the more pragmatic and instrumental one becomes."[28] In this regard, participant/observers ascribed a particularly influential role on the steering committee to Oscar McConkie. His experience has been alluded to above. He brought to his role an exceptional background of practical political experience that equipped him with a broad public perspective and a highly developed sense of political realities, of compromise, and of the need to balance interests.

McConkie was an outsider to the public education establishment and had never attended a meeting of the State Board of Education prior to the meeting of the board, five months previous, at which he was elected its chairman. In the intervening period, McConkie had established a dominant/submissive working relationship with the state superintendent, Leland Burningham. An associate superintendent indicated that McConkie and Burningham had "weekly four-hour meetings in McConkie's law offices." McConkie referred to these meetings himself, saying that he and Burningham discussed meeting agendas in detail and that he regularly asked Burningham to justify the board meeting agenda items to him. Clearly, public education, politically the more powerful—and having a rank and file less amenable to compromise—of the two groups, was represented most prominently on the steering committee by one of its most politically sophisticated members, who, in the judgment of participant/observers, had sympathy for higher education as well. On the other hand, there was no one on the steering committee, including the state superintendent, to assertively inject the desires of the public education rank and file into the discussions. The state superintendent was characterized by other committee members as "not a strong personality," "secondary and supportive," "one who said yes when needed," "out of his league," and "out of his depth." A former state superintendent indicated that Burningham "was inexperienced in his work with the legislature and in his role generally."

With the major problems of education being defined in terms of inadequate funding, the first step for the steering committee in fashioning a comprehensive funding solution was to identify a bottom-line figure that the legislature might realistically allocate in additional monies for education in total. The prime contribution of the four part-time legislators to the steering committee's work was as legislative critics and judges of likely legislative responses to committee proposals. It is also true that their participation made possible the development of four strategically placed legislative advocates who could defend the committee's proposals before their peers during the legislative session. Having identified a bottom line of $150 million, the steering committee relied on what a committee staff member called "the obvious principle of fair shares" in distributing the sum.[29] One consideration, projected enrollment growth rates, served to complicate the process and created misunderstandings that surfaced in the form of differing figures given by each board in its initial public announcements. The agreement was ostentatiously equitable. In agreeing to request only an additional $41 million, higher education would cut its justified need ($80.5 million) by nearly half. For its part, public education would cut its justified need ($200–225 million) by the same proportion.

At a meeting of the liaison committee on 5 October 1983, Regents chairman and steering committee member Kem Gardner announced to the other members of the liaison committee that the two boards had agreed "to develop a common and unified legislative approach under the auspices of the liaison committee of the two boards."[30] (In actuality the two boards and the liaison committee as well had had nothing to do with the development of the strategy.) Continuing the presentation, State Board of Education chairman and steering committee member Oscar McConkie commented on the need for "unity of the education family to ensure that increased taxes be earmarked primarily for education entities and not lost through the remainder of the state government budget." Both boards would have to work to support the overall budget and not undercut each other.

In spite of the elegant symmetry and practical political wisdom embodied in the steering committee's unified budget request, in each organization (the State Board of Education, the State Board of Regents, and the legislature) leaders who had participated in the committee's deliberations and decision making were faced with the challenge of returning to, confronting, and winning over others in their organizations who had not been personally involved in formulating the unified strategy. Some were very dubious. In each education sector there were voices saying that "going it alone" would be more productive.

At a meeting of the regents a week after the liaison committee meeting at which the joint strategy between boards was announced, Chairman Kem Gardner asked the Board of Regents and the State Board of Education to adopt a unified approach to legislators "in behalf of their interrelated needs." Accordingly, former regents chairman Donald Holbrook made the motion that the appropriations increase proposed be sought in a "joint campaign" by both the education systems for all of education for "not less than $150 million." The motion stated a higher education need of $80 million in additional appropriations. However, "sober consideration of what is possible . . . suggests that the state legislature cannot be expected to provide more than $50 million in new appropriations for higher education next year."[31] The activity reflected in the minutes then became even more specific, modifying the substance of the previous motion. The minutes read as follows:

> A further strategic consideration of what is possible persuades the Regents that an effort should be made where higher education and public education work together for an increase of not less than $150 million for all of education in 1984–1985, to be divided between them on a ratio of 28.3 percent and 71.7 percent, consistent with the current

legislative appropriations ratio for higher education and public
education respectively.[32]

The regents' actions on the funding motion(s) ended with the acknowledgment that the multiple compromises (from $80 million, to $51 million, and
finally to 28.3 percent of $150 million) would not provide for the full
needs of higher education. The actions, in sum, created ambiguity and
confusion within the Board of Regents. This confusion surfaced one month
later at the November Board of Regents meeting just as the steering
committee's final report, which gave hard proposed figures for both public
education and higher education, was being published.

The regents' Budget-Finance Committee chairman, Hughes Brockbank (an outsider to the steering committee's joint budget strategy), was
holding out for an additional $51 million for higher education. In a 1990
interview, University of Utah president Chase Peterson summed up the
steering committee's strategy when he said that "the governor was
committed to raise new money for education; the steering committee
decided on the division in advance." The division of dollars, as well as the
aggregate sum that would be requested of the legislature, had already been
determined before either board received and acted on the proposal. For
Regent Brockbank to insist on the $51 million figure (which had in fact
been passed at one time by the regents) was to jeopardize the strategy.
Commissioner Van Alstyne, a member of the steering committee, came to
the rescue. He reaffirmed that the proposal of the steering committee was
for $150 million additional education appropriations, with $41 million
going to higher education and $109 million to public education. The
minutes then record that Brockbank and Van Alstyne "held firm that $51
million was the justified need," but that "the Board of Regents had agreed
to go arm-in-arm with the State Board of Education to work for the
realistic target of $41 million."[33] In effect, it was Commissioner Van
Alstyne who had taken Regent Brockbank "arm-in-arm" into accepting a
budget strategy that he had not helped to formulate and that he did not
initially endorse. (In a 1990 interview Brockbank characterized Commissioner Van Alstyne as "a real leader." On the basis of this action alone, the
author concurs.)

The cooperative budget strategy created further difficulties within the
legislature, where it forced legislative committee interactions that violated
the established domains of the various education committees in each house.
Legislators on the steering committee, most particularly Senator Pugh, had
to deal with these issues. The problem is exemplified by one disgruntled
senator's testily voiced complaint in a meeting of the Interim Legislative
Study Committee for Public Education that he did not understand why the

committee was concerning itself with a funding measure involving higher education. (In a 1990 interview, Senator Pugh characterized the individual as "a friend who was highly opinionated and ill-informed.")

In mid-November, the steering committee published its final report and recommendations, *Education in Utah: A Call to Action.*[34] The report built explicitly on *A Nation at Risk* while adroitly molding and refashioning the issues so as to tie the needs of public and higher education in Utah together in a single education reform package. Soon thereafter, on November 18, the State Board of Education received and, after discussion led by Oscar McConkie, accepted the steering committee's report. McConkie argued, "If we keep unity among the school family, we will have a good chance of getting the $150 million."[35]

In retrospect, Governor Matheson recalled, "We really marketed our stuff." The governor personally made "six or seven major speeches across the state" in support of the unified education budget request, as well as a televised "White Paper on Education" that he remembered as being "the best speech [he'd] ever given." Regional hearings on the plan were held in ten locations statewide. At some of these, members of the steering committee in attendance recalled fielding questions planted by UEA members in opposition to the report recommendations, most specifically the career ladders (merit pay) proposal.

Relationships between the UEA and the steering committee had been troubled from the beginning. Since he considered the UEA to be a special interest group, the governor had kept the organization off the steering committee. Senator Pugh expressed the same idea in a more sympathetic fashion, saying that the UEA was kept off the committee "to avoid giving it the stigma of being self-serving." The chairman of the steering committee recalled that "the teachers were furious" at not being represented. While there was not formal representation of the UEA on the steering committee, there was informal involvement between committee members, staff, and state and local leaders of the UEA. A steering committee staff member from the governor's office recalled the UEA full-time staff as being "reasonable," but described the teacher-activists as being "locked into their positions like Irish peasants." The chairman of the State Board of Education characterized the UEA as having a "dog in the manger mentality," which prompted them to expect the committee to "clear it with them first." A former state superintendent who watched the activity from the State Office of Education as an associate superintendent recalled that the UEA was "most critical" of the steering committee's activity, and that "public education leaders (knowing they would have to work with the UEA in the future) had to be careful." (This constraint applied in full measure only to State Superintendent Leland Burningham.) The informal communications with the UEA likely had some indirect effect on the work of the committee. The reform most vehemently objected to by the teacher rank and file was the career ladder (merit pay) proposal. A committee staffer indicated that a very detailed career ladder proposal was developed by the committee and then later scrapped for a generic plan. Once the steering committee had completed its work, it held a special meeting in September for UEA officials and teachers. It was thought by the committee that UEA administrators might "buy on, but the lower ranks rebelled." The meeting, which was very conflictual, was unsuccessful in winning any degree of acceptance or cooperation from the UEA. In the words of the chairman of the committee, UEA's response was, "You can't publish the report without us." The UEA never did buy on.

Timely positioning of the steering committee at the head of powerful political forces in a preemptive strategy that excluded special interests (the UEA) allowed it to determine the unconventional shape of the budget package that would be debated in the legislature. Once the legislature had convened, however, the traditional education interest group relationships reasserted themselves, and the steering committee lost control of the process. Higher education leaders, because it was in their perceived interest to do so, continued throughout the legislative session to speak in terms of the "$150 million for education," but public education leaders downplayed the concept of cooperation, speaking in terms of the specific dollar figures of the steering committee's recommendations for public education alone.

While Governor Matheson recalled that "the team never varied," there was still conflict and the continuing possibility throughout the pressure cooker budget session that the alliance would fall apart. At least one incident was serious enough to be commented on by several individuals in interviews. As McConkie explained, State Superintendent Burningham had been approached by a powerful senator capable of delivering his offer, with the proposal that he could have an additional $2 million for vocational education. As the state superintendent began to "waffle," McConkie was approached by a concerned university president who asked, "What is going on? Do we have a deal, or don't we?" McConkie responded decisively to both men that public education would keep its bargain with higher education. It is likely that his action saved the alliance for the rest of the legislative session; it also lost $2 million for public education.

The broad coalition of public education organizations (known as HOPE), which included the State Office of Education, the UEA, the PTA, the School Boards Association, and the Society of Superintendents, lobbied for the specific public education reform measures (as differentiated from the full package) proposed by the steering committee. However, the UEA challenged outright the steering committee's budget proposals for public education as being inadequate, and, having failed by the latter part of the session to sway the legislature, informally withdrew, leaving a letter of "no confidence" in each legislator's mailbox. In a 1990 interview, the UEA associate executive director recalled this gesture as being one required of the UEA administrative staff to demonstrate to the rank and file that they were doing something, even if it would not make any difference in the outcome. A member of the steering committee recalled that by this time the UEA could not actively oppose the steering committee's proposals because of the committee's popular support.

When the dust had settled, the 1984 legislature had allocated an additional $74.5 million to pubic education and an additional $29.5 million to higher education.[36] Unified education interests had been allocated 69 percent of their original request. In these figures, both supporters and critics of the unified approach found ample support for maintaining their positions, and there is no objective way of resolving their differences. Soon after the legislative session, prominent state senator Haven Barlow, who had not participated in the formulation of the joint strategy, spoke before the Utah School Employees Association and rendered his judgment that in cooperation "the only one who gained was higher education; the one who lost was public education."[37] In an interview six years later, Senator Barlow viewed the matter differently, saying that "it was a useful strategy. Money isn't everything." He went on to elaborate that the strategy had resulted in "major reforms, and an awakening of interest and support" for education.

Others gave their retrospective judgments on the joint budget strategy. Judgments from both education sectors were mixed, but tended to be somewhat upbeat. A regent said that "it was a successful strategy, healthy for all entities; we recognized our interdependence." Another regent explained that "in actuality, each system got its own budget. The joint strategy was a political statement to the state." A university president indicated that higher education received "not much out of cooperation in 1984. We can do better on our own. Public education is too big; higher education gets swamped in its wake." An institutional administrator indicated that the joint strategy was "less successful than hoped; more successful than might have been."

A member of the State Board of Education who was critical of McConkie and the joint budget strategy judged that "McConkie cut a deal with the regents who were protecting their fair share of the budget." He continued that the steering committee strategy "was not successful in getting new money, but it did stimulate interaction." A local superintendent said that the strategy was good for public education because it had "influential people talking for it, people who could advance our interests." He concluded that "practically, public education got not a lot." Another local superintendent stated that "collaboration between public education and higher education at the program level was very successful. The money result was not exceptional."

In spite of the mixed reaction among education policy leaders to the unified budget strategy used with the 1984 legislature, the chair of the Board of Regents Budget Committee, Hughes Brockbank, an experienced former legislator, recommended in the September 1984 meeting of the regents that they "continue with the Utah State Board of Education the cooperative approach followed last year."[38] In a formal motion he asked the commissioner to enter into conversations with the state superintendent "to seek and develop further discussions between the Board of Regents and the Board of Education leading to a unified and cooperative approach to the Legislature for adequate funding for education, both public and higher, during the next legislative session."[39] The motion passed the board unanimously. Regent Brockbank continued in an afterthought that the regents ought to make it an objective "to seek restoration of the historical percentage of state appropriations that higher education had enjoyed up to recent years."[40] There is no further mention of the formal motion; the issue of a joint legislative budget strategy with public education never appears again in the minutes of the Board of Regents.

Two months later in the liaison committee a member of the State Board of Education made a formal motion, seconded by another member of the State Board of Education, that both boards work together during the upcoming legislative session "to support increased funding for all levels of education," adding that "each board must recognize the need of the other for increased funding," and concluding that "the traditional division of funds between the two should remain."[41] This motion, too, was unanimously passed. It stimulated no more action than the similar motion previously passed unanimously by the regents.

In retrospect, Mr. Brockbank attributed the lack of implementation of his motion regarding the 1985 legislative session to "a lack of leadership."[42] It is true that the leaders who had been responsible for the joint legislative budget strategy of 1984 had indeed left the scene. Governor Scott Matheson, having completed two terms as one of the state's most popular governors, chose not to seek a third term in the 1984 elections. The chair of the State Board of Regents, Kem Gardner, had run unsuccessfully for governor in 1984 and did not return to the regents after his defeat. The chair of the State Board of Education, Oscar McConkie (who, some say, was "running" for governor in 1984, as well) had been elected in 1982 to a two-year term on the board; when his term expired at the end of 1984, he chose not to run again.[43] The commissioner of higher education, Arvo Van Alstyne, was mortally ill during the fall of 1984 and died during the 1985 legislative session. Moreover, within months of the adjournment of the 1985 legislature, the state superintendent of public instruction, Leland Burningham, resigned his office under a cloud of criticism. The kind of cooperative budget strategy that these individuals (with the help of others) had successfully employed in 1983–84 would not be formally discussed again in public and higher education governing circles for three years.

Perhaps one of the most important results of the steering committee's cooperative legislative budget strategy of 1983–84 was the grand, strategic vision it gave of the strength of the two education sectors in united action. A local district superintendent looking back on the strategy commented that "public and higher education working together are formidable." This view was expressed by policy leaders in both education sectors.

James Moss assessed the steering committee's 1984 cooperative budget strategy from the vantage point of his seat in the Utah House of Representatives. (Reflecting on the strategy in retrospect, he found it to be "an excellent strategy, but artificial; it could not last.") Two years later, in November 1986, he was appointed state superintendent of public instruction by the State Board of Education. Moss, an outsider to the public education establishment, brought to his position a comprehensive vision of the political shortcomings and needs of public education from the legislative perspective. His agenda as state superintendent focused on bringing some discipline and unity to the highly fragmented public education community and establishing productive liaisons with other groups that could help.

In a meeting of the liaison committee held in November 1987, one year after he had been appointed, Superintendent Moss raised for the first time since the fall of 1984 the grand vision of a legislative budget alliance between the two education sectors. He adroitly presented the topic as an orderly smorgasbord of possible cooperative budget strategies; but no one in higher education had an appetite. The sequence in the minutes summarizing the discussion of the liaison committee is so strikingly unusual, so precisely worded, so revolutionary in its implications, that it is quoted here in its entirety.

> Superintendent Moss said he would like to ascertain the liaison committee's interest in a unified budget posture for the two boards.

He said the following might be considered:

1) a percentage distribution between the two systems;
2) mutual support for each system's budget priorities;
3) mutual support of funding levels sought;
4) a unified lobbying effort for educational funds; or
5) an approach toward funding education as a generic whole.

Discussion turned to past cooperative efforts of the two boards during legislative sessions, especially during the Kem Gardner/Oscar McConkie era when there was a remarkable degree of harmony between the two boards. Several of the committee members expressed the opinion that it would be valuable to pursue a course of cooperation, especially in light of the fact that few new dollars will be available for all of education.

Chairman Checketts [State Board of Education] and Superintendent Moss suggested that this be a major agenda item for the next liaison committee meeting. Commissioner Kerr said that his staff would also discuss this issue and be prepared to have dialogue during the next meeting.[44]

The proposal was never heard of again. It was not discussed—as had been mutually agreed by both the state superintendent and commissioner —at the next meeting of the liaison committee. It never appears again in the minutes of the liaison committee. It was as though a cannon had been fired into the Grand Canyon, to be followed by not so much as an echo; there was nothing but silence.

Interviews with participants in the liaison committee meeting at which the state superintendent placed his proposal on the table revealed the differing perspectives of each group. Superintendent Moss reflected that at the time the public sector was facing the strong likelihood of a tax limitation initiative campaign during the coming year.[45] In his judgment, an alliance between education sectors would be needed to weather the storm. He cited his personal concern to build coalitions that would politically strengthen public education and education generally. Finally, he wished to "institutionalize" the personal relationship of cooperation that existed between himself and the commissioner of higher education, Rolfe Kerr. When viewing Superintendent Moss's proposal against his activity of the previous year in organizing the Utah Education Coordinating Council, it appears that he was intent on following through on the implementation of a grand political strategy, even though the public education alliance that he had worked for a year to fashion was collapsing around him. (See the discussion of his efforts with the Education Coordinating Council in chapter 6.) The first step of that strategy had been to unite the public education community. An outgrowth of the strategy, based on his vision of the 1983–84 legislative budget alliance, was to forge a political union with higher education that could successfully oppose the tax limitation initiative campaign, but be one that "would last," as well. Perhaps, too, he was seeking strength to shore up a collapsing effort within public education. There seems to be no other way to account for his astounding proposals in November 1987.

An associate state superintendent viewed the state superintendent's proposal as being based on a recognition of the fact that with diminishing resources the potential for conflict would build. What he was seeking, from her perspective, was "a congenial agreement." The members of the State Board of Education on the liaison committee were strongly cooperative in their orientation. For one, the proposal was "a sharing exploration of future points." Another saw cooperation as being "more productive" and did not envision any particular strategic gain for public education through the various provisions of the proposal. A third saw the proposal as seeking to "maximize the results of education influence." The proposal was "pushed out because of pressure to deal with immediate needs." In short, the proposal was taken seriously by all public education representatives on the liaison committee.

Interestingly, Commissioner Kerr had no sharp recollection of the proposals. Reminded of the provisions, he indicated that while there was "no conscious, deliberate rejection of the proposals" by higher education, there was "no motivation to cooperate in that fashion." The state revenue picture indicated dollars were not available; and besides, it was "too late in the year to do anything." When reminded that he had even failed to include the Moss proposal in his routine summary memo accompanying the liaison committee meeting minutes sent to the regents three days later, he said with a twinkle in his eye, "I guess it didn't make much of an impression on me." The commissioner acknowledged an "informal pact with Moss to communicate," but he sensed as well pressure from the institutional presidents and regents who felt he had already "gone too far" in cooperating with the state superintendent. An associate commissioner—who, once again, had no firm recollection of the proposals—suggested that higher education would "avoid being locked-in" with a formal understanding of the type suggested. A regent indicated that the proposal was judged by administrative staff to be "unworkable" and "unwieldy," and gave it little credence. A second regent, with a background in public education, interpreted the proposal as "an end run by the state board" prompted by "selfish motives." He continued that "they perceive that higher education has greater credibility and prestige"; there is now an agreement "not to cut each other's throat, but higher education will not be involved in public education squabbles." A former associate superintendent at the State Office of Education now serving as a local district superintendent offered the interpretation that cooperation in the early 1980s by higher education was prompted by its desire to obtain the cooperation of public education in amending the state constitution so as to "unload the gun pointed at its head." With that specific goal achieved, there was no further motivation for higher education to cooperate with public education.

An indirect answer to Superintendent Moss's cooperative budget proposals came eventually from higher education, but it took eighteen months. Commissioner Kerr articulated in a March 1989 meeting of the liaison committee a new "spirit of cooperation" the essence of which was, "Let us support each other, but not mingle our fates."[46] The following September in the liaison committee, Superintendent Moss tacitly acknowledged this response—the only one he ever received to his 1987 cooperative budget strategy proposal—when he "suggested that public and higher education assume a joint posture of mutual support as we approach the legislature this year, as we have in past years."[47] The liaison committee then agreed that the separate budget requests of each education board would be discussed at the November meeting of the committee.

DISCUSSION AND ANALYSIS

Looking back, Governor Matheson expressed the rationale of the 1983–84 unified budget stance between public and higher education: "Pull together for strength, and share the benefits." He continued that the Education Reform Steering Committee had set the precedent, but the strategy "was not even *tried* again!" Oscar McConkie, upon being asked why there had not been a joint budget strategy since 1984, replied, "I can't understand why." This case raises two questions of primary importance. First, given the complexity and ambiguity of circumstances, why did a unified budget stance between public and higher education emerge in 1983–84? Second, why has the unified stance—successful when it was first used—not been tried since then, even though members of both boards have asked for it, one board and the liaison committee have voted unanimously for it, and one state superintendent with the support of board members and staff placed the issue very explicitly on the table for discussion? The answers, unlike the questions, are complex.

In the first instance of the unified budget strategy of 1983–84, education agency leaders were confronted by a particularly complex array of circumstances and relationships that potentially could have led either to competition or cooperation. An important initial assertion of the study was that the current structure of state-level governance of public and higher education that has evolved is inherently conducive to competitive relationships between the two, as well as with other agencies within the state budget process. Established practices and procedures within the state budget process were based upon separation between the two agencies in their budget requests. Wilson hypothesizes increased competition in the case of a major allocation of new money above the base. The chronic scarcity of funding for education, coupled with the clear indication that both agencies would seek substantial additional funding to address the problem, supported competitive dynamics between the two.

Wilson further hypothesizes strong incentives for cooperation in circumstances in which the autonomy or resources available to prospective alliance members are severely threatened (as in a crisis), or in which there is an opportunity to augment substantially the autonomy or resources of prospective participants. In this instance, a sense of financial crisis in both education camps was coupled with the opportunity created by *A Nation at Risk* to increase the resources available to education. Nevertheless, it was public secondary education, not higher education, that was highlighted in the report and that was the focus of a dramatically increased national public awareness. It would seem that public education, politically very strong within the state, would have been encouraged to ride the crest of the wave alone in seeking additional funding. Given the ambiguity and ambivalence of these multiple factors, why, then, did education agency leaders follow an explicitly cooperative budget strategy contrary to all past practice?

Many interview respondents saw friendships and personalities as the key. Clearly, the chairs of the two education boards had mutual respect for one another (perhaps even friendship), and both had made active commitments to establishing cooperative relationships between the boards they headed. It is also true that the two chief executive officers of the education agencies had a good working relationship, as was asserted by several respondents. Others said that the political affinity between the governor and the two board chairs (all Democrats) was an important part of the explanation. Those few interviewees who mentioned the productive and mutually respectful working relationship between Democratic governor Matheson and Republican senator Pugh may have come closer to the mark without realizing it.

The unified budget strategy of education interests in 1983–84 provides a textbook example of a Dominated External Coalition. The individuals comprising the coalition included Governor Matheson and Senator Pugh (the core members) and education board chairs McConkie and Gardner. For a brief period all were occupying positions of authority within the External Coalition and were united in a common policy objective: that of obtaining additional dollars for publicly funded activities for which they had interest and held organizational responsibility. The importance of the Dominated External Coalition in providing an adequate explanation of this case is put in sharp relief when one poses the question: Could the chairs of the two education boards with their chief executive officers have decided among themselves to establish a unified budget strategy without the governor and the chair of the legislature's Executive Appropriations Committee being centrally involved? Upon reflection, and in the light of relationships presented in the case, it seems highly unlikely. Success with the unified budget strategy required the prestige and power of both the governor and the key legislative leader to establish the validity of the unconventional policy package in the legislative process.

The impact of the governor and the senator should not be overstated; neither Matheson nor Pugh could have compelled public and higher education to join together against the better judgment of the board chairmen and chief executive officers. The political contribution of the two elected officials was a necessary, though not a sufficient, condition of a successful alliance strategy. There were clear incentives and benefits that justified the alliance in the minds of education policy elites, if not in the judgment of the public education rank and file. Those in a position to make such decisions for the organizations involved found the benefits, on balance, sufficient to justify the alliance.

The major obstacle to the alliance lay within the External Coalition itself, for the UEA, the most powerful voluntary education association in the state, played no role in formulating the terms of the alliance. Wilson argues that ad hoc alliances between organizations can form because they are based essentially upon the actions of leaders and do not involve the rank and file of constituent organizations. Stated another way, ad hoc alliances, which may be in the interests of leaders and members of all constituent organizations, are not possible with the full participation of the rank and file. Given the basic divergence between elected political leaders, education agency board members, agency administrators, and the public education rank and file in their collective judgments of what was politically realistic, it appears that achieving consensus on a cooperative strategy would have been not simply costly, but impossible.[48] This explains the exclusion of the UEA from the formulation of the terms of the alliance. By excluding the UEA, Governor Matheson and Senator Pugh preempted the political space needed by the UEA to effectively divide the External Coalition, thereby shifting organizational power to the public education Internal Coalition.

It may be that the calculation of interest and benefits (the stakes) continues to be the basic consideration supporting cooperation or competition between organizations; the question becomes, Who makes the calculation of interest that makes the difference? Where within the configuration of organizational power is the decision made? The determination of benefits, upon which a cooperative or competitive strategy depended, shifted from persons internal to the education community to persons and bodies external to education. The case gives evidence of the parallel interests of the governor and Senator Pugh in the cooperative strategy that was used.

The total payoff available to winning coalitions is subject to the interpretation of the parties involved and is not an objectively obvious matter.[49] The case highlights the differences between political and agency leaders and the public education rank and file in their views of political reality. In their initial announcements, leaders in both agencies made it clear that in their judgment the cooperative strategy, with the supplemental amounts agreed to in advance for each sector, was politically realistic. The possibility of larger gains in "going it alone" had to be weighed against the possible losses incurred through competition with each other. That which was in the immediate interest of agency leaders in both camps, the single most instrumental accomplishment of the alliance, was the self-imposed and mutually agreed upon maximum dollar amount that each agency would request. Each side successfully had induced the other to limit its request of the legislature; for either camp, the additional money requested by its nearest competitor (public or higher education) would very likely come from the money potentially allocated to itself. Clearly, minimizing potential losses through a cooperative strategy that reduced conflict and competition, rather than maximizing potential gains through direct competition (with the attendant risk of relative loss) was judged by agency leaders in both camps to be the more prudent and politically realistic course. Thus, even prior to the convening of the legislature, agency leaders had received payoffs in the form of mutually agreed-upon budget request limitations. Furthermore, on the basis of the fair shares principle it was established that any degree of success by the alliance would result in a proportional benefit to both parties.

The public education rank and file placed a negative value on these payoffs, which were very significant and real for agency leaders. The rank and file of public education, represented by the UEA, held a much different view of political reality.[50] From their perspective, the alliance was a "high investment/low return" proposition in which no possible gains through cooperation could equal what the UEA projected to be the immediate benefits to public education of acting alone. Even had the joint request been fully funded, the monies going to public education as its "fair share" ($109.5 million) fell far short of what the public education rank and file represented by the UEA thought to be their justified need ($225 million).

The alliance strategy of the steering committee focused unprecedented attention on education and sensitized elected officials and the public alike to the critical needs of education. In the words of an associate superintendent at the State Office of Education, "Public education had important and influential people speaking for it." Unquestionably, the galvanizing effect of the strategy carried over into subsequent legislatures, and this was a benefit to leaders in both camps. As for higher education, the alliance strategy had allowed it to maintain its then-current budget position vis-à-vis public education during a year when its financial needs were particularly great and national concern over secondary schools, and public education generally, threatened to upset the balance.

The role of mediating organization structures was crucial to this case. In form, there were three such structures; in substance, only one. While it is true that the Utah Commission contained individuals from both the higher education and public education communities, those representing higher education were organizationally based within the higher education Internal Coalition and had no authority to represent higher education regarding system commitments. The real impetus for the Utah Commission came from within the public education establishment and, as such, reflected essentially the needs and interests of the public education sector. The liaison committee, through the public actions of the chairmen of the two state education boards, was used as a means of symbolically validating political decisions previously made elsewhere, and of mustering support for those decisions once they had been made. Nevertheless, it is clear that the liaison committee per se was peripheral to the formulation of the strategy. In fact, it is most likely that the formulation of such a strategy exceeded the political competence of the liaison committee in the sense of having sufficient means to meet its ends. It was through the Utah Education Reform Steering Committee that the Dominated External Coalition established and implemented a unified budget strategy that addressed the needs of both education communities. This ad hoc decision structure allowed peak decision makers in each education sector to step away from the pressures of rank-and-file interests and priorities, and take political actions that accommodated two very different organizations.

Judgments of participants and education officials as to why the unified budget strategy has not been used in Utah since 1984 primarily center on the stakes and a calculation of organization self-interest. Accordingly, a former gubernatorial education advisor suggested that "there have been inadequate incentives" since 1984 for a unified strategy. "Each can do as well on its own; there is no need to 'hook' the money together." The commissioner of higher education echoed this theme, saying, "There was no money." A university president said, "Too much energy is required for not a strong result. We can do better on our own." A former state superintendent felt that "an ongoing effort of this type is not beneficial; it is too cumbersome and costly." A local superintendent said that "higher education is successful in appropriations, and has no need for an alliance with the State Board of Education."

Comments on the relationship of dollar incentives to cooperation in this specific instance are interesting for two reasons. In the first place, the dollars allocated—and even the amounts requested—through the 1984 unified budget strategy generally were not judged by education policy leaders, in retrospect, to be great or exceptional. Second, more than one legislature since 1984 has allocated more additional dollars to education than did the 1984 legislature. (The 1985, 1987, and 1990 legislatures all allocated more additional dollars to education than did the 1984 legislature.) A consideration of the relationship of dollar stakes to cooperation, when used alone without other factors, gives confused and conflicting explanations of this cooperative action.

One participant attributed this to organizational structures. In the words of an insightful university president, "Public education is hard to work with. Who is the leader? Higher education can't work with forty-one heads." That the two organizations would have difficulty working together because of differences in their inherent structure suggests a more adequate explanation. It is in the changing configuration of organizational power surrounding the state's education policy structures during these years that we will find a fuller answer to our question. The influence of the Dominated External Coalition, anchored by two highly popular elected officials, made it possible for public and higher education through the steering committee to transcend the organizational differences between them and establish a unified budget strategy. Likewise, the almost immediate dissolution of the Dominated External Coalition, with the majority of the central actors leaving the public stage, provides a persuasive element in an adequate explanation of why such cooperation was not used again in the subsequent legislative session. The politically preemptive strategy adopted by the Dominated External Coalition in 1983–84 bore fruit in the form of an aroused and reassertive UEA. Five years later, the organization's leaders were meeting directly with a new governor delivering the demands of the public education Internal Coalition for a major budget increment for public education alone.

James Moss, as chief executive officer of the State Board of Education, sought to take control of a highly fragmented public education community by asserting the authority of his office. This personal effort was clearly manifested in his actions in reorganizing the internal decision and authority relationships at the State Office of Education and the Utah Education Coordinating Council, and in the remarkable cooperative budget proposals that he made to the liaison committee. The reasons given above by education policy leaders may account for the failure of the Moss budget proposals to be taken seriously by those in higher education. The proposals were seen by them as being both unworkable and self-serving. Objectively speaking, they may have been both. But there may be another reason, unspoken because it colors all other considerations and judgments. A Dominated External Coalition, anchored by two popular and powerful elected state officials and two equally powerful education board chairs, accounted for the success of a unified budget strategy four years earlier. It was clearly the case that the proposals placed on the table by the state superintendent emerged exclusively from within the public education Internal Coalition—more specifically, from the political mind of James Moss, a dominant member of that coalition. It was undoubtedly the judgment—unspoken though it was—of those in higher education that the source of the proposals lacked both the organizational and political resources that would have been required for them to take the proposals seriously.

5. Competing for Domain

Vocational Education

Primary factors that lie at the root of intergroup conflict include interdependencies and shared resources, and intergroup differences in goals, values, and perceptions.[1] The potential for conflict depends on "the extent to which resources are shared, the degree of interdependence, and perceived incompatibility of goals" between groups.[2] Enforced organizational interdependence can give rise to considerable conflict. Leaders, seeking to reduce the dependence of their organizations upon other organizations, work to extend and define administrative control over activities of interest to the organization, the often unattainable goal being the definition of an area of exclusive authority and control—a domain. Disagreements over domain—turf issues—are often the basis of the most conflictual relationships between organizations because parties expect to gain only at each other's expense. In the political relationships between the public education and higher education sectors, the function area of vocational education presents classic conflicts over domain.

The multifaceted concept of vocational education has come to be closely associated with the economic well-being and development of the community, as reflected in economic productivity and an increasing tax base.[3] From this perspective, it is the purpose of vocational education to prepare people to enter the work force so they can buy homes and pay taxes. Perhaps this explains why vocational education is often a priority for legislators, and why in some education circles it has been a stepchild, if not an outcast.[4] The commonsense case for vocational and technical education is illustrated by the fact that in Utah, for example, only 19 percent of the jobs require a four-year college degree, while 81 percent do not.[5] Thus, it is not so much higher education, but vocational education, that is needed to put the greatest part of the population productively to work.

VOCATIONAL EDUCATION ISSUES IN UTAH

In the early 1960s the Utah State Board for Vocational Education established three area vocational centers (AVCs) to meet the vocational education needs of high school students in various areas of the state. In the late 1970s and early 1980s state funds going to vocational education were significantly increased, as two additional AVCs were established through a concerted effort by legislative leaders and the direct legislative lobbying of vocational educators and AVC directors. This building effort was made at the expense of traditional public education programs and skewed the budget allocations of the State Office of Education. Because of the direct political relationships between AVC boards, directors, and the legislature, vocational education has been a wild card that administrators at the State Office of Education could not always predict or control.[6] Vocational education administrators developed political clout that required public education administrators at the state level to pay attention to them. A former state superintendent recalled that "vocational educators created demands on the state board" that were "tougher" in the 1970s than in the 1980s.

The Search for a Principle of Division

A close observer of Utah education politics has characterized vocational education as "a no man's land . . . in which there is wealth to be extracted." The implication of his comment is that vocational education fits neatly and comprehensively into neither public education nor higher education, yet there are strong incentives—as well as justifications—for both education sectors to establish claims upon it. At one point, as the liaison committee worked to complete the 1984 Master Plan for Vocational Education, the task force was seeking to establish a definition of vocational education so that the finance committee could address the question of funding. With dollars riding on the definition, the state superintendent argued that the definition was too narrow because it did not include any instruction before the eleventh grade. At the same time a regent, a former university president, expressed concern that the definition was too narrow in that it might not recognize "the significant amount of vocational education being conducted at the state's colleges and universities."[7]

In 1990, the state of Utah funded instruction in vocational education offered through five area vocational centers, one skills center, high schools across the state, two community colleges (formerly technical colleges), and other colleges and universities.[8] Given the dispersion of these programs through diverse organizations in both education sectors, coupled with the interests of the state in economy and efficiency, there has been an endless effort to define a logical principle that would reasonably establish a division of vocational education governance roles between public education and higher education. Traditionally, instruction given to secondary students in noncredit/nondegree programs has been deemed the domain of public education, while instruction given to postsecondary students in programs issuing credits and degrees has been the domain of higher education. But these divisions have blurred in the face of technological change and demographic evolution. A former state superintendent voiced the judgment that vocational education in high technology is considerably different from what has historically been referred to by that term and often requires a higher education context to be accomplished successfully in spite of the noncredit/nondegree status of the instruction. By this view, both public and higher education will appropriately offer noncredit/nondegree instruction, which each sector should govern and control.[9] The demographics of the work force have blurred the secondary/postsecondary criterion. The populations served in the state's vocational educational institutions, which have been governed by public education, have shifted from a predominance of secondary students to a predominance of adults. By 1982, only 30 percent of the enrollment in the state's area vocational centers consisted of secondary students; the remainder were adults.[10]

Thus, the actual application of these criteria as traditionally associated with one another would cause each sector to lose control of activities that have become important to it. Each sector would now support the use of a simplified dividing criterion that gives itself an advantage. Specifically, public education would focus on the nondegree/noncredit criterion, while higher education proposes the use of the secondary/postsecondary criterion to divide the turf. Each of these criteria would give to the other much of the activity that is now governed by one sector. The following example places the issue in context.

In the midst of controversy over the governance of the AVCs and the skills center, the State Board of Education set its hand at fashioning a principle that would serve effectively as a demarcation line between public and higher education in vocational education governance. The proposal was to "give full governance authority to the State Board for Vocational Education for all noncredit offerings . . . regardless of where the classes are held," the rationale being that the regents had traditionally exercised governance and control of curricula in all areas that culminated in a degree.[11] The chair of the state board opined that higher education would be concerned at such a broad delegation of authority to the State Board for Vocational Education. More to the point, a regent with much experience in public education indicated that "the regents finally realize they are funding much short-term intensive training, more even than public education." In his opinion, public education leaders downplay the higher education role in this area in order to facilitate their own funding. He went on to suggest that all postsecondary education should be governed through the regents. As has been stated, the implications of such an arrangement for public education are far-reaching, for the AVCs, which are funded and controlled through public education, are now serving predominantly postsecondary (adult) students rather than high school students as originally intended.

The division of governance in vocational education continues to be an issue with major implications for cooperation between education sectors. One local superintendent asked the rhetorical question, "Do the regents *want* a connection with public education and all of its problems? They have what they want now with constitutional status.[12] The only thing left is a clean cut in vocational education." He continued to explain that if this were achieved, higher education would have less incentive to cooperate with public education. In the meantime, there is a strong incentive for continuing cooperation in order to keep vocational education off of the legislative agenda, for administrators lose control when the legislature becomes involved.

Mutual Perceptions of Commitment and Performance

Judgments of board members and administrators regarding the performance of the opposing (complementary) education sector in vocational education are another basis for conflict between the two. A former chairperson of the Board of Regents expressed the opinion that the State Board of Education had served primary education well, but had "missed the issues and the vision" of secondary and postsecondary education. In her view, public education had "dropped the ball" and should now "let it [postsecondary vocational education] go" to a Board of Regents that is fully committed to meeting its responsibilities. She acknowledged the "possible neglect [of vocational education] of the 1960s and 1970s" by higher education, but was confident that the regents "are now fully committed."

By contrast, proponents of vocational education in the public education community argue that the commitment to vocational education of those in higher education is low and unreliable. An assistant commissioner with the Utah System of Higher Education indicated that public education has rightfully questioned and doubted the commitment of the higher education community. In his mind, higher education historically "has not been a champion of vocational education." These doubts were reemphasized in the late 1970s as the presidents of the University of Utah and Weber State College, both influential leaders in higher education, voiced their opinions that vocational education has no place in higher education. Their strong opinions made a lasting impression. Those in public education see a consistent institutional drift away from vocational programs given over to the administration of higher education. Weber State College at one time was considered the ultimate vocational school in Utah, but now goes by the name of "university" and emphasizes an academic curriculum. A successful effort by the regents in the late 1980s to change the names of the state's two "technical" colleges to "community" colleges revealed again the distrust of higher education, at least where vocational education is concerned, by those in public education, as well as by those in the legislature. That interaction merits further consideration here in that it shows in sharp relief many of the political relationships surrounding vocational education in the state.

The state legislature had established at both technical colleges the statutory requirement that 75 percent of the courses had to be in vocational education, with no more than 25 percent in general education. The provision was intended to fix in law the curriculum of these institutions in order to prevent the drift toward an academic focus. In one of the first formal discussions that the newly appointed state superintendent James Moss had with his board (in November 1986), he indicated that the technical colleges were a "thorn" to both higher education and public education, and that the regents were moving to control them and pushing for a name change. (Two-and-one-half years previously, college presidents had approached the State Board of Education as petitioners with a similar request to change the name "technical colleges" to "community colleges.") He indicated that the 75:25 vocational education course requirement rule was routinely flaunted by higher education because "99 percent of the sections [as opposed to courses] are in general education." He continued, "We need to seek real protection for vocational education which is a funding formula to ensure that dollars flow to the need." He concluded by expressing a preference for the name "technical college" over "community college."[13] Two months later, in the liaison committee, Superintendent Moss, having received assurances from the commissioner of higher education that funding for vocational education would be preserved through a funding mechanism at the community colleges, reported that the State

Board of Education had voted to support the name change and to delete the statutory 75:25 vocational education requirement. The State Board of Education's action was opposed by one member of the board, Richard Maxfield. The legislature took action and the two technical colleges became community colleges.

One year later, two powerful senate advocates of vocational education met with the regents at the Utah Valley Community College (formerly known as Utah Technical College at Provo) to voice their strong dissatisfaction with the lack of attention higher education was giving to vocational education. Senate President Arnold Christensen and Senator Haven Barlow spoke on behalf of vocational education in their capacity as members of the Utah Council for Vocational/Technical Education. Senator Barlow's message was that the Utah System of Higher Education should give priority to programs that help prepare Utahns for jobs, "for their life's work, whatever that might be." Senator Christensen was more pointed in his criticism. Said he, "The expansion of general education at the state's former technical colleges is a matter of concern to the vocational council." He recalled that the name changes were supported by lawmakers on condition—a condition that had not been met. "Frankly, we [the state legislature] are concerned that the new community colleges may lose their . . . vocational thrust long before a realistic funding mechanism is in place to encourage vocational-technical education."[14]

Program Review and Approval

Another point of contention between education boards has been the issue of who has the right and responsibility to review and approve vocational education programs. The position taken by the State Board of Education, and actively reasserted by State Superintendent Moss in August 1988, has been that the State Board of Education is the only state-level board for vocational education in the state, and therefore it has the legally established responsibility to review and approve all vocational education programs in the state. In asserting that prerogative in a board meeting on 16 August 1988 the state superintendent warned the board that "there may be resistance from the regents."[15] His comments came in the context of board actions "approving" curriculum changes at five institutions of higher education. An associate commissioner with the Utah System of Higher Education responded immediately that the proposal had not been submitted to the State Board of Education for approval, "but so board members might ensure against duplication of programs in high schools and vocational centers." He explained further that the law allows review to eliminate overlap and duplication, but does not allow the State Board of Education to either approve or disapprove certain changes.[16]

State Board of Education decisions on the accreditation of vocational education programs have raised even deeper conflicts between the two boards. At the same meeting cited above, while the vocational education program of a university was granted full accreditation, a junior college program was granted only conditional accreditation pending the correction of deficiencies. Some members of the board suggested that a letter to the regents "expressing concern that the vocational emphasis at Dixie College and its ability to honor the AVC functions of the institution is weakening and needs attention by both boards." While one member of the board suggested that simply referring the matter to the liaison committee would be more appropriate than a letter, the board chairman raised a more important issue when he indicated that the college was in trouble on the issue *because* the regents had directed that more funds be spent on academic programs.

Meditating the Conflict

One of the primary purposes behind the establishment in 1983 of a very formalized joint liaison committee between the State Board of Education and the State Board of Regents was to create an organizational structure that could achieve coordination and planning between the two sectors in vocational education and put an end to the seemingly endless conflict between them in this area. The liaison committee was a political priority for both boards because of legislative dissatisfaction with contention between them. Major accomplishments of the liaison committee since 1983 include the formulation of two vocational education master plans for the state—the first completed in 1984, and the second in 1989. Conflict over the adoption of specific provisions of the 1989 master plan culminates the dynamics of this issue area case.

The Salt Lake Skills Center

The preceding discussion has described in some depth the most important contextual political relationships that surround vocational education in Utah. Vocational education issues are so vast and complex that they defy comprehensive analysis in a study of this scope. The intent of this issue area case is to isolate and follow over time only a single thread in the broad tapestry. That thread is the interaction between the State Board of Education and the State Board of Regents over the Salt Lake Skills Center during the 1980s.

Using federal funds, the Salt Lake Skills Center was established in 1947 in downtown Salt Lake City in a building that had been previously used as a laundry. Vocational instruction courses were directed toward the educationally and economically disadvantaged. One higher education administrator characterized the skills center as "the last resort for the unemployed." Courses were open entry/open exit, with the specific intent of moving students as quickly and directly as possible into jobs. The skills center has been influential in Utah's approach to vocational education. The area vocational centers (AVCs) grew out of the skills center concept and federal dollars, but moved away from the focus on the disadvantaged that characterized the skills center.

As skills center programs grew and federal funding proved to be inadequate and unreliable, administrators sought budget stability with state dollars. According to a former director of the skills center who is now with the Utah System of Higher Education, the skills center has always been "a hybrid." State dollars were originally appropriated through the Higher Education Appropriations Subcommittee of the legislature and instructional programs were coordinated through the State Office of Education. In the late 1970s the funding channel was shifted to the Public Education Appropriations Subcommittee, with instructional programs administered "by default" by the Utah Technical College at Salt Lake. At this time, the skills center was a stepchild wanted by neither education committee of the legislature. Ironically, the skills center has provoked intense turf wars between public and higher education. The persisting division between both education sectors of budget and programming control raised the issue of accountability. One director, who had administered the skills center successfully for eighteen years, pushed hard to move it completely to the Utah Technical College at Salt Lake, an effort that was strongly and successfully opposed at the time by those in public education.

Competition and conflict over the Salt Lake Skills Center in the late 1980s was characterized by one interview subject as "a hot flash point" in the continuingly difficult interrelationships between public and higher education regarding vocational education. A former chair of the State Board of Education said that the skills center issue generated "more heat than light. It was a child of the preceding decade of conflict between state-level education boards." The interaction analyzed here, extending over a period of five years from the spring of 1984 to the spring of 1989, was something akin to a stylized three-round boxing match in which each succeeding round becomes more turbulent and conflictual than the one preceding it.

POLITICAL DYNAMICS

"He intended to pull the AVCs *and* the skills center."

Oscar McConkie recalled that in January 1983, upon assuming the responsibilities of his office as newly elected member and chair of the State Board of Education, he was astonished at the depth of the schism between public and higher education. He found that the basis of the continuing daily conflict between the two education boards was not funding, but vocational education. Following close on the heels of the successful cooperative budget strategy used in the 1984 legislature, and as part of his personal agenda to establish a new foundation for cooperation between the State Board of Education and the State Board of Regents through the removal of points of conflict, McConkie proposed in a meeting of the liaison committee in May 1984 that higher education assume budget responsibility for the Salt Lake Skills Center.[17] Relationships surrounding the administration of the skills center were perfectly calculated to incite and sustain turf warfare, for the instructional program was administered by one education sector and the budget by the other. McConkie sought a clean cut. "It makes sense to have the budget for the Salt Lake Skills Center transferred to the administration which is already functioning well in operating the programs," he argued. The minutes of the meeting show that a vote was taken in which a lone State Board of Education member, Richard Maxfield, voted against the proposed transfer. McConkie returned to the liaison committee at its next monthly meeting in June to report that the State Board of Education wanted "to discuss the skills center proposal."[18] At the liaison committee's July meeting State Superintendent Burningham reported that the State Board of Education would use a contract between the State Board of Education and the Utah Technical College at Salt Lake, which "will operate the skills center through State Board of Education budget channels and procedures."[19] A local superintendent then serving at the State Office of Education explained that the state superintendent, on the basis of staff discussions to identify options, instigated the concept of the contract to support the chair of the state board in his initial proposal. In effect, the State Board of Education would become a "National Science Foundation-type" contractor, technically preserving control of federal dollars as required by statute, yet still acknowledging only a perfunctory role in the skills center. The regents would continue to exercise real authority. By contrast, an official at the Utah System of Higher Education questioned the interpretation of the technical budgetary requirements regarding federal funds that was used to justify the contract arrangement through the State Board of Education. In any case, apparently all parties were satisfied that the matter was decided, at least temporarily, for better or worse; round one was over.

These interactions between education sectors in the spring and summer of 1984 appear to have been limited to the membership of the liaison committee and senior administrative staff, in that no formal reference is made to these problems in the minutes of either board's meetings during this time. The issue of the skills center was put to rest for the remainder of Oscar McConkie's two-year tenure on the State Board of Education. There was no further controversy over the skills center for nearly a year-and-a-half, by which time there was a new cast of central players.

The skills center issue resurfaced peacefully enough in August 1985 when the liaison committee reviewed and heard proposals on the construction of a new skills center building presented by an administrator of the Utah Technical College at Salt Lake, who also served in the state legislature. As an advocate of vocational education in higher education, and one with power because of his position in the legislature, some influential individuals in public education (including a former state superintendent) distrusted him. He was viewed by some policymakers in public education as an individual who could take what he wished from public education. One interview respondent felt that this individual intended "to pull the AVCs *and* the skills center." The meeting reemphasized the complexity of the compulsory interrelationships between the State Board of Education and the State Board of Regents in the administration and operation of the skills center. The new chair of the State Board of Education, Richard Maxfield, asked the regents to give the matter of the new skills center facility high priority in the coming legislative session, even though the facility was requested through the State Board of Education. The new commissioner of higher education, Rolfe Kerr, responded that the regents would support the effort as a priority item.

The skills center issue bubbled up again, somewhat less peacefully this time, in the liaison committee later in the fall. A joint staff subcommittee was named and directed to study the issues of skills center governance and administration and prepare options and recommendations to resolve "current difficulties."[20] At its December meeting the liaison committee received and discussed three options for resolving the skills center issue submitted by the staff subcommittee.[21] Option one would transfer both funding and governance of the skills center to the State Board of Regents; option two would place the skills center under the control and management of the State Board for Vocational Education (comprised of the same individuals sitting on the State Board of Education); and option three would delay any movement or transfer of the skills center pending further study. It should be noted that options one and two required legislative action at one point or another in implementation.

The discussion in the liaison committee following the presentation of the subcommittee's options revealed an interesting division between the prime actors. The commissioner of higher education reaffirmed an earlier stated concern, saying, "Regardless of who governs or administers the skills center program, we must be certain that this unique program is protected to serve the economically and educationally disadvantaged students."[22] His expressed concern was that the liaison committee had not yet evaluated the pros and cons of the various options so that it could determine where skills center services could best be provided. Essentially, his comments came down in support of the subcommittee's third option. The president of the Utah Technical College at Salt Lake, while explicitly indicating his preference for option one, asked that the liaison committee "not do anything this year that would leave the skills center without adequate funding."[23] The view of the state superintendent, a man who had come up through the public education ranks, was that "the skills center and its basic purposes would more properly be placed with the State Board of Education," and he invited committee members to seriously consider whether this position was logical.[24]

While the three primary administrators involved had each expressed a preference for a different option, they were united on one point: that governance and funding of the skills center should not be fought as a turf battle before the upcoming state legislature. At the conclusion of the discussion, it was the consensus of the liaison committee that the state superintendent and the commissioner should meet together and be prepared to propose a resolution of the issue to the committee at its meeting three weeks later on 6 January 1986. Committee members in both education sectors expressed the hope that the needs of students could be served through an arrangement agreeable to both boards.

At the appointed time State Superintendent Furse and Commissioner Kerr returned to the liaison committee with their joint recommendation on the skills center; the recommendation was presented by the state superintendent, whose preference (option two) had prevailed. In an interview, he indicated that "public education held a long-standing view that the skills center was public education domain." Their joint recommendation was "to assign the skills center to the State Board for Vocational Education with the stipulation that the skills center not become an area vocational center."[25] In order for this recommendation to be implemented, legislative action would be required. Additionally, they made transitional recommendations on facilities, and urged the establishment of a skills center board that would maintain communications among service providers (the Utah Technical College at Salt Lake) and users (local school districts).

The commissioner related to the liaison committee his personal efforts to assess the real needs of the situation. He emphasized that "skills center programs are not incompatible with the role and mission of the comprehensive community college," but that he "and the state superintendent agreed that skills center activities more nearly relate to those of schools and centers governed by the State Board for Vocational Education."[26] With potential future developments clearly in mind, the commissioner differentiated circumstances in the Salt Lake Valley from those in the Ogden area, where "it seemed to make sense to establish an area vocational center." However, to have the Salt Lake Skills Center evolve into an area vocational center would be inefficient and counterproductive in that it would "directly compete with the role and mission of the Utah Technical College at Salt Lake."

The policy proposal of the superintendent and commissioner went to some length to define the unique characteristics of skills center programs (to provide educationally and/or economically disadvantaged students with entry level skills and to place them on the job in the shortest time possible through open entry/open exit, individualized, self-paced, hands-on instruction) and to differentiate them from those of area vocational centers. In effect, having agreed to concede the issue of budget control of the skills center to public education, the commissioner wished to be assured that it would not grow into a direct competitor with higher education programs in the form of an area vocational center. It was clear from the joint statement of the state superintendent and commissioner that such assurances had been given, and that the process had involved give-and-take between the two administrators. (Even four years later, in 1990, the issue of an area vocational center in the Salt Lake Valley was still alive and well in the thoughts and plans of some legislative advocates. One powerful senator indicated that he was simply waiting for the "right time" to join with Salt Lake legislators to "get their AVC.")

In interviews with both administrators, the commissioner recalled his need "to establish trust and confidence as the new man on the block" with those in public education who clearly had very strong emotional commitments to resolving the skills center issue in a particular way. For his part, the state superintendent expressed his concern that the commissioner might have thought that he (the superintendent) "was taking advantage of him because he was new." He clearly recognized that the decision placed the commissioner "in an awkward position with the regents," and that he received criticism from them for giving in.

The jointly agreed-upon recommendation of the two peak administrators for public and higher education for the resolution of the skills center governance and funding issues was sent to the 1986 legislature, where it was killed. Round two was over. Once again the existing relationships would continue. The issue of the skills center subsided; public manifestations of conflict were gone, but an undercurrent of contention remained. The issue of skills center governance and funding would not surface again for another two years, by which time there would be a new team of leaders in public education and a major new cooperative planning initiative between public and higher education for vocational education.

At a meeting of the liaison committee in June 1987, members discussed the 1984 master plan and determined that an update of the vocational education master plan was not only desirable but necessary.[27] The previous April the legislative fiscal analyst assigned to public education had met with the State Board of Education and expressed legislative concern with the role of vocational education, and "the battle of higher education and public education with accreditation, financing, and governance, including the issue of the Salt Lake Skills Center, the governance of the AVCs and their role, and a concern that the AVCs' primary goal does not relate to public education and high school students," in that the majority of AVC students were actually adults.[28]

Feeling pressure from the legislature, four days later in a meeting of the liaison committee, the state superintendent and commissioner proffered to the committee a "principle of cooperation" in facing the legislature. Together they reaffirmed, "[We] must promote cooperation between boards so we do not work at cross purposes in addressing study items of the Interim Education Committee. We must work together through the liaison committee to maximize joint efforts on all common issues and to be supportive to the maximum extent possible on issues of concrete concern to a single system."[29] The statement added refinements as well as substance to an informally established cooperative stance between the two boards.

At a joint meeting of the State Board of Education and the State Board of Regents with the Interim Education Study Committee of the legislature in August 1987 the commissioner of higher education pointedly addressed cooperation in vocational education. "Both systems of education can either cooperate or duplicate," he said, and then reaffirmed that higher education did not intend to absorb the area vocational centers, only eliminate duplication, which was a high concern.[30] He continued, "All programs are needed, but not at all institutions. The Salt Lake Community College and Skills Center can meet the training needs in the Salt Lake Valley." He concluded by touching a sore spot for public education: he expressed concern that the "major focus of the AVC is high school students, but the majority of students at the Salt Lake Skills Center are postsecondary." The newly appointed state superintendent, James Moss, responded that "closer cooperation with postsecondary issues is imminent." The groundwork had been laid for reassessing the organizational relationship sustaining the skills center.

At the liaison committee meeting in November 1987, six months after it had originally been proposed, the commissioner and state superintendent organized a Vocational-Technical Education Master Plan Task Force. The new planning effort was "to identify issues in the current vocational education master plan needing revision or updating and prepare recommendations for consideration of the liaison committee and the two state boards."[31] The task force would be co-chaired by an associate commissioner of the Utah System of Higher Education and an associate superintendent at the Utah State Office of Education. The two would work closely together over the next fifteen months to draft and obtain final approval of the plan. In interviews with them it was made explicit that they developed a close and trusting working relationship, and a particularly strong personal commitment to each other and to their shared task. Said one of the other, "I would go anywhere with him." This personal commitment would be fully tested before the plan was adopted by both state boards.

By May 1988 a draft of the proposed master plan was produced. The major thrust of the plan was a regional planning concept in which education service providers from secondary schools, institutions of higher education, and vocational education facilities within a single geographic region (nine throughout the state) would collaboratively plan and coordinate vocational education programs so as to avoid duplication and make the most efficient use of existing facilities through cooperative use. On page 21 of the draft was a listing of specific actions that should be accomplished during the time frame of the master plan. Point 6 in the list was to ignite a firestorm and potentially jeopardize the adoption of the plan when it was presented to the State Board of Education for initial review. It read as follows:

Appropriations for the skills center shall be transferred from the State
Board of Education to the Salt Lake Community College. However,
the skills center budget shall be maintained as a line-item and a
separate entity. The role and mission of the skills center will not be
changed.[32]

In late September, hearings on the final draft of the master plan were
held at seven sites across the state, with a statewide hearing transmitted
over the state's telecommunications system originating at the University of
Utah and received at six other academic institutions. With regional hearings
completed, during the first week of November the liaison committee held
a major discussion of the plan prior to its formal submission to the two
boards for their initial consideration. No mention was recorded in the
minutes of any anticipated or potential points of conflict. Four days later,
the two co-chairs of the task force presented the draft master plan to the
Board of Regents for its review. The associate commissioner indicated that
the plan had established "a better understanding of the mission, role, and
governance of vocational education on the part of both boards and their
staffs."[33] The associate superintendent expressed the primary purpose of the
new plan as being "the elimination of the conflict that has existed between
the State Board of Regents and State Board of Education regarding area
vocational centers." He assured the regents that regional planning mechanisms were then in place to handle these difficulties.[34]

Curiously, the minutes of the State Board of Education meetings
contain no record of the initial review of the vocational-technical education
master plan. In an interview, the chairman of the board suggested that the
review could have taken place in executive session, in which minutes were
not kept. It would likely have occurred in conjunction with a regularly
scheduled meeting; he could not recall precisely when it actually occurred.
In any event, the reaction to the plan was stormy. One faction of the board,
led by the board's former chairman Richard Maxfield, was adamantly
opposed to provisions of the plan. He specifically objected to the provision
transferring the budget of the skills center to higher education. In the
words of one board member, Maxfield "came out of the woodwork . . . he
was in bitter conflict at the conceptual level with higher education."
Another board member recalls that Maxfield "came unglued," and that he
and another member were "vociferous in their objections," feeling that the
State Board of Education was giving away something significant. Matters
became even more ugly. In an interview, a member of the Board of
Regents recalled that at one point, board member Maxfield "threatened
Superintendent Moss with the loss of his job if higher education [got]
funding for the skills center."

With one faction of the board having made it clear that they were prepared to go to any length in opposing specific provisions to which they objected, the public education representatives on the liaison committee were faced with the prospect of losing everything. A compromise was required to save a positive plan. The obvious solution, proposed by the chair of the board and fully supported by the other board members of the liaison committee, was to excise the controversial element that was jeopardizing the full plan.

Once again, there are no minutes of any liaison committee meeting reflecting the committee's response to the blow-up at the State Board of Education. There is, however, a document dated 4 January 1989 that indicates changes to the master plan "recommended by the SBR/SBE Liaison Committee and approved by the State Board of Regents and the State Board of Education at their first reading."[35] The provision transferring the skills center to the Salt Lake Community College was simply deleted. An introductory paragraph explaining briefly the history of the skills center noted that the current administrative relationship between public and higher education "does not accommodate effective and efficient budgeting or accountability." It concluded with the statement that "control and supervision of the Salt Lake Skills Center should be *maintained as is and functions studied for one year to make a determination where the Center should be* assigned by Statute" (emphasis in the original). Thus, the compromise agreed to by the liaison committee reaffirmed the undesirability of the established relationships between education sectors, but postponed the resolution of the problem for one year. At the 6 January 1989 meeting of the State Board of Education, the associate superintendent who had co-chaired the master plan task force distributed the changes recommended by the liaison committee. A member of the board faction so opposed to the transfer of the skills center (Neola Brown) reaffirmed her opposition and formally moved that the offending paragraph be removed from the document and the issue considered for a year. The motion was seconded by a member of the liaison committee who had supported the skills center transfer, and it was passed. The associate superintendent concluded the board's consideration of the issue by indicating that "this point is not the main thrust of the document. The regents felt it important enough to be included, but they did not feel it would jeopardize the overall direction of the document itself."[36]

At the meeting of the State Board of Regents on 27 January 1989, it was reported that the State Board of Education had put aside "for further study" the section of the master plan dealing with the Salt Lake Skills

Center. With this refusal to approve the master plan with the skills center provision, the regents and the state board were at loggerheads. The response from the regents was one of anger. One regent suggested, "If the State Board of Education rejects the plan, then resolve the issue through the legislature." While the regents considered a formal motion to this effect, an experienced regent urged that the matter be allowed to proceed without a formal motion because, he argued, "the issue may be resolved without a confrontation." Commissioner Kerr recommended that the regents pass the master plan as originally prepared and presented with the skills center provision intact.

With the two boards on a collision course and the master plan itself in jeopardy, a meeting with legislative leaders and the liaison committee was held and reported in the press on 29 January 1989. Legislative dissatisfaction with the continuous battling between the two boards was highly apparent. The legislators asked many pointed questions on the purpose and function of the liaison committee itself. The house majority leader suggested that both boards be stripped of their responsibilities in vocational education and that the governance of vocational education be assigned in its entirety to the liaison committee, which would be given some teeth to enforce coordination. An "education" senator indicated that a simpler—and potentially better—way to run education services would be to have only one education board for both public and higher education; another option was to establish a third co-equal board for vocational education. Having reviewed the legislative history in which such options had been considered and rejected, he concluded encouragingly, "We decided to work together and coordinate. You have a way to go, but take on the problems and deal with them. . . . You're far better off than you were a few years ago."[37]

In the face of these criticisms and exhortations, liaison committee members unitedly expressed confidence in the relationships established in the new master plan, which, coupled with the coordinating role of the liaison committee, could resolve the conflicts. Commissioner Kerr then put the concrete issues on the table, expressing concern at the fact that the State Board of Education had "pulled things out of the new vocational education master plan before the board had tentatively approved it this month."[38] With the spotlight focused on him, the chairman of the State Board of Education, Keith Checketts, acknowledged that items had been deleted from the master plan in order to achieve board consensus. Then he added significantly, "But if a decision needs to be made, I am sure the majority would approve it."[39] The meeting concluded with the legislative leadership agreeing to give the master plan, and the liaison committee, a chance to work. However, the legislative directive was unmistakably clear: there was to be cooperation.

The ball was now in the State Board of Education's court, with the Board of Regents having accepted the master plan as it had been originally presented. The public education representatives on the liaison committee were embarrassed before their higher education colleagues on the committee because of the "eleventh-hour" concerns expressed by their two colleagues on the State Board of Education. (Significantly, Richard Maxfield as chair of the State Board of Education had participated on the liaison committee during earlier considerations of the skills center transfer that had resulted in keeping it with public education, but he had surrendered his seat on the committee to the new chairman, Keith Checketts, who had presided over the most recent negotiations over the skills center in the liaison committee.) More importantly, the last-minute crisis brought on by the intransigent stance of board members Maxfield and Brown was clearly threatening the common legislative strategy of both education boards. A primary purpose of the master plan was to persuade the legislature that the two boards could, indeed, work together cooperatively in a single turf area, thereby making unnecessary precisely the kinds of undesired legislative modifications of education governance relationships that had been alluded to by the legislative leadership in the meeting.

During the following week, one of the two individuals opposing the skills center transfer, Neola Brown, was taken to the center for an on-site visit and orientation to the programs as administered by the Salt Lake Community College. This last-ditch lobbying effort was successful in taking the sharp edge off of her opposition to the skills center transfer, apparently persuading her that the programs were not being slighted under higher education administration. As indicated indirectly in the State Board of Education minutes for 7 February 1989, Brown's modified stance was communicated to at least one other member of the board. Interestingly, however, she did not attend the meeting of the state board at which the issue was finally resolved (contrary to her initially strongly held position), and the final vote on the master plan taken.

The meeting of the State Board of Education held at the Hilton Inn in Salt Lake City on 7 February 1989 was the setting for the culmination of the action in this issue area case. Participants in this last confrontation were all within the public education family. As the board agenda moved to the master plan, the associate superintendent and co-chair of the master plan task force had to justify to an angry board member, Richard Maxfield, actions taken by the board's liaison committee representatives that were contrary to Maxfield's understanding of the way such things were to be done.

Following the associate superintendent's explanation, board members who sat on the liaison committee came forward in the discussion to give their own personal justifications of their actions.The dialogue reported in the minutes is of such central interest and importance in describing and explaining the dynamics of this highly conflictual decision process that it is reproduced below at some length, with explanatory information or highlighting comments in brackets.

> Associate Superintendent Bruce Griffin provided a status report on the Master Plan. He reported that staff was given the responsibility to make the suggested recommendations by the Board in the draft document regarding the Skills Center and the Strategic Plan. Those recommendations were taken to the Liaison Committee for their review. In addition to that action, it was very obvious that during that time frame that circumstances changed a little bit. [Legislative leaders intervened.] There was, as a result of the dialogue, considerable concern as to whether or not the State Board of Education and the State Board of Regents working cooperatively could resolve the issues of Vocational Education. Some people [state legislators] have interpreted those in ways that have resulted in questions and concerns that need to be alleviated.
>
> As the Liaison Committee reviewed the suggested changes, it appeared from the dialogue [with legislative leaders] that it was felt that the State Board of Education and the State Board of Regents needed to send a very strong message to the constituency [the state legislature] that the State Board of Regents and the State Board for Vocational Education can and will resolve vocational issues and have a capacity to handle those issues in a positive and constructive way.
>
> The Liaison Committee reviewed the suggestions that were made and after some dialogue it was concluded by the Liaison Committee and unanimously recommended that the best way to serve vocational education and the interests of the State Board for Vocational Education and the State Board of Regents would be to accept the Master Plan as presented with the eight changes recommended by the Liaison Committee at the January meeting. . . . Mr. Griffin reported that the changes the Board had recommended at the January Board meeting [to delete the skills center transfer item] were not drafted into the document based upon the discussion and decision of the Liaison Committee. . . .
>
> Member Richard Maxfield voiced concern that the Liaison Committee, which included members of the State Board of Education, had voted to accept the Master Plan without the inclusion of the

recommendations made by the State Board of Education. He questioned why the Board was not polled or some action taken by the Board regarding those issues.

Member Valerie Kelson responded that she was on the Liaison Committee and had made the proposal to accept the Master Plan based on input from Board Members [Neola Brown] who had previously supported those issues [deletion of the skills center transfer from the plan] and had changed their minds and felt good about the direction the Master Plan was taking.

Member Keith Checketts stated that as you sit on these committees it is important to maintain the position of the body . . . you represent. Sometimes you are put into positions where you have to make some other kind of decision. Member Checketts indicated he had also received enough phone calls from Board Members to know there was a majority of the Board that favored the other stance [accepting the master plan with the skills center transfer to higher education] and felt it was politically expedient that the Committee take that stance in the meeting.

Member John Covey indicated that the other issue besides the Skills Center that the Board had recommendations on was the Strategic Planning on a statewide basis and he was one of the main proponents of that, and his fears have been eliminated and what is contained in the document will move this forward. He indicated he supported the unified approach.

Member Richard Maxfield stated that he felt the Board should have been polled formally on the issues so Liaison members are not put into an untenable bind.[40]

The motion to accept the master plan carried, with six members present voting in favor, and one, Richard Maxfield, abstaining. On 21 April 1989, nearly five years after the action had been originally proposed by Oscar McConkie as chairman of the State Board of Education, the board formally requested of state officials that funding for the Salt Lake Skills Center be transferred to the State Board of Regents. The transfer was to be effective for the 1990–91 fiscal year. Included in the board's motion was the recommendation to the legislature that future appropriations for funding the skills center be made directly to the regents. Round three—and the match, at least on this specific issue—was over.

DISCUSSION AND ANALYSIS

The original expectations and intentions for a reactivated liaison committee were that it should serve as a continuing forum in which a few members from each board (including the chairpersons) and senior administrators from each state-level education office (including the chief executive officers) could resolve the ongoing conflicts between the two boards in the area of vocational education so as to avoid unwanted legislative involvement in education governance. Looming over the actions of education boards and administrators throughout this interaction were the legislative presence, legislative concerns, and legislative expectations. Education leaders had to avoid controversy because with conflict and contention the legislature would get involved and education boards and administrators would lose control. Cooperation could forestall legislative intrusions into education governance.

The fact that the organizational locus of most of the activity in this case was the liaison committee can be read as confirmation that the committee was filling its intended purposes. The two education boards were involved in important, though less visible, ways in the case. Important actions were taken by both boards in response to decisions made within the liaison committee.

Over the course of the five years studied, there were three "sets" or "teams" of leaders representing public education on the liaison committee, sets corresponding roughly to rounds one, two, and three, respectively. With some change of higher education representatives as well, there was a different mix of leaders for each "round of the match." The case, as it traces activity over five years, describes an extended political interaction in which public education ultimately "lost" an organization that it had controlled at the beginning of the case, and higher education ultimately "won." Given this fact, it is of particular interest to look at the public education "teams" on the committee (a team being defined as the chairperson of the board and the state superintendent, although there are other members as well), and to identify briefly the relationships between the public education representatives, the public education establishment, and the analogous higher education team.

In round one, the public education representatives were Oscar McConkie, board chair, and State Superintendent Leland Burningham. McConkie was clearly an outsider to the public education establishment; Burningham, while not an outsider, was new to his job, was not popular within the public education community, and was under the sway of a very strong personality in McConkie. Their higher education peers on the committee were State Board of Regents chairman Kem Gardner and Commissioner Arvo Van Alstyne. Allusion has been made in the previous case to the friendly personal and working relationships that existed between these leaders. The political dynamics of round one were in the direction of accommodation, though no major change in the status quo was made.

In round two, the public education representatives were board chairman Richard Maxfield and State Superintendent Bernarr Furse. Maxfield had served several years on the board and led a faction of the board that viewed themselves, in the words of another board member and former chair, as "champions of vocational education." State Superintendent Furse had come up through the public education ranks, having served as a senior administrator at the State Office of Education in the 1970s during times of the highest conflict between public and higher education. In an interview, he expressed his judgment that Maxfield was "bright" and "most knowledgeable of governance issues." Because Maxfield "understood the principles" he was a "strong support" to public education. Both were insiders with the public education establishment. Their peers representing higher education on the committee were State Board of Regents chairperson Sue Marie Young, and Commissioner Rolfe Kerr. In the words of a former State Board of Education chairman, "There was no chemistry between Young and Maxfield." Kerr was new to his job and felt he needed to establish cooperative and congenial working relationships with the public education leaders. The dynamics of round two firmly reasserted and confirmed the status quo in which public education maintained budgetary control over the skills center.

In round three, the public education representatives on the liaison committee were State Board of Education chairman Keith Checketts and State Superintendent James Moss. Checketts had come to the state board as a university professor. State Superintendent Moss, as well, had come from higher education. Moss was a newcomer to public education and was unpopular with the public education establishment. With the election of Checketts to the chairmanship of the board, Maxfield left the liaison committee, though he was still a member of the board. Thus, both primary representatives of public education were outsiders to the public education establishment. (A former state superintendent who had come up through the public education ranks, commenting on the final results of the case, said that Checketts "could not understand the issues because he was from higher education." He was further "amazed that the board would go against Maxfield.") The dynamics of round three were in the direction of accommodation, with an explosion at the end of the political interaction within the State Board of Education.

In an interview, the chair of the regents made indirect reference to the important role played by staff in the interaction of round three. On the basis of clear directives from the state superintendent and commissioner to establish cooperative solutions to common problems, two second-level administrators had developed an extraordinary level of mutual trust and confidence in each other, with no need to protect turf. Rather, they were able to address and to clarify issues and solve problems. This relationship sustained the liaison committee in its decisions and actions.

The liaison committee in round three moderated interactions and accommodated conflicting organizational stances. It effectively established emotional distance between public education members and firebrands on the State Board of Education, who were willing to go to almost any length to defend their perspectives. (It must be stated as well that the presence on the liaison committee in round two of individuals with territorial, highly ideological approaches to their responsibilities served to preclude accommodation.) The feelings of solidarity among public education and higher education members of the liaison committee in round three were revealed in interviews. Each viewed the other—in the words of one member—as "sincere, reasonable, and positive." Another said that public education and higher education representatives on the committee "were listening to each other." The chairman of the State Board of Education indicated that he believed that "higher education was trying to get the job done." He viewed the state board faction opposing the transfer as "expansionist." Another member who was to serve as chair of the State Board of Education indicated that "over a year's time there had been much discussion of the skills center issue and the at-risk students." She continued that some members of the board were "highly defensive of this role." Ultimately, all of them were persuaded that the Salt Lake Community College was redefining its role and effectively integrating the skills center. These individuals representing the State Board of Education on the liaison committee were sensitive to the political realities of the circumstances, open to change, and nonterritorial in their orientation to the issues. The minutes of the State Board of Education meeting at which the action of the case reached its culmination exemplify the personal feelings, cross-pressures, and interpersonal dynamics associated with participation in a mediating organizational structure.

The stakes in this case were different for various groups and individuals at different times. Viewed at one level, public education and higher education were playing a zero-sum game. The winner would claim the skills center. For several public education leaders, there was the implicit assumption that the stakes were not simply the skills center, but the AVCs in their entirety. State Superintendent Moss shared his opinion that the skills center issue "became inflamed because of the greater fear that higher education was actually grabbing for the governance of the AVCs." In his judgment, the skills center had become a power issue based on territoriality. A regent shared his opinion that public education "gave up the skills center in hopes of keeping the AVCs." For that faction within the State Board of Education that saw itself as the sole defender of the vocational education programs of the state, the statutory charge to the State Board for Vocational Education itself was at stake. For them, losing the skills center would seriously erode that charge. Furthermore, in the judgment of this group, by assigning vocational education programs to a higher education community that had no real interest and commitment to them the students ultimately would lose.

The commissioner of higher education had more riding on the issue than was readily apparent. He recalled using the skills center issue to buy time with an irritated and impatient State Board of Regents who were ready "to take over the AVCs" as competing and duplicating organizations. The proposed threat voiced in the regents meeting to "resolve the issue in the legislature," in effect, would have pulled out all the stops, in that it would have risked all in a full-blown political battle. Commissioner Kerr was persuaded that higher education would lose a political battle over the AVCs with public education. In effect, as he wryly put it, he "was invited to show up at the Battle of the Little Big Horn in the role of General Custer." It was an invitation he chose to decline.

While the commissioner wished to avoid a losing battle with the State Board of Education over the AVCs urged upon him by the Board of Regents, he still sought to maintain the full confidence of the regents. He could not lose the skills center in round three and achieve this result. Having bought time with the skills center issue, the Regional Vocational Education Councils that were proposed in the 1989 master plan could be established and begin functioning in their coordinating and decision-making role, thereby solving the problem of conflict and duplication in the future.[41] Thus, the stakes were great for the commissioner.

The meeting with legislators in late January 1989 changed the stakes, or more accurately, made explicit to education policymakers (administrators and board members) what the implicit stakes involved in their contentious interactions had always been. The stakes were not budgetary control of the skills center by public education or higher education (a zero-sum game, which inevitably sparks sharp conflict), but a grant of authority to existing policy bodies (the State Board of Education, State Board of Regents, and their joint liaison committee) to make comprehensive decisions on vocational education. Members of the liaison committee had developed a mutually shared commitment to what they viewed as a reasonable solution to a specific problem; that reasonable solution and the decision process by which it had been established were at stake in the continuing conflict. Unless a reasonable solution could be arrived at and peacefully implemented by these bodies, the legislature had threatened to withdraw that grant of authority and create new organizational structures and relationships to exercise it. Thus, at a higher level, there were important incentives for leaders to cooperate so as to maintain established authority patterns and levels of organizational autonomy. Defending the prerogatives of the established education governance structures was a supcrordinate goal upon which all participants of the liaison committee in round three agreed, for it provided benefits for all.[42]

The public education External Coalition in this case was divided up through the closing minutes of round three by a faction of the State Board of Education that represented strongly held commitments of the public education establishment. The power relationships that accounted for this division were dramatically changed by the informal meeting of the liaison committee with legislative leaders in February 1989. The active involvement of legislative leaders established a Dominated External Coalition that mandated a timely resolution to the conflict. That solution had already been outlined by the liaison committee. Members of the State Board of Education who originally had opposed, or questioned, that solution were persuaded that the broader stakes discussed above justified a course of action that otherwise they may not have followed.

6. Managing a Crisis

Opposition to Tax Limitation Initiatives

Thomas Hobbes argued that money is to the body politic what blood is to the living, organic body; as the blood nourishes "every Member of the Body of Man," so money, which flows to the coffers of the commonwealth in the form of taxes, sustains and makes possible the continuing existence of the state.[1] It is through the process of what is referred to by some scholars as "extraction" that personally or corporately held resources in the private sector are appropriated for public use.[2] Taxes make possible the services that governments are organized to provide. For Hobbes, an outright refusal to pay taxes would have constituted an attack on the life of the body politic to be punished in the most severe fashion. In more modern times, and within the framework of a democratic political theory, efforts by the populace to limit the level at which governments may tax and spend have been likened—to change the metaphor—to an effort by some taxpayers "to change the rules of the game in terms of state-local finance."[3] In the American experience, the popular establishment of such limitations is within the accepted rules of the game, and is accomplished either through action by the legislative body or through a mechanism of popular legislation: the initiative.

Tax and expenditure limitations on state governments are not new; such limitations were widespread in the 1930s. For various reasons closely associated with the fact of progressively increasing government spending in the face of inflation, rapidly rising energy costs, and the declining real income of many American families, there was considerable interest and activity in this area nationwide in the late 1970s. Between 1976 and 1980, more than twenty states adopted general limitations on taxing that applied to state governments and most or all local governments within the state. One-third of these limitations were established through the use of the initiative. The limitations were evenly divided between statutory and constitutional measures.[4] During the same period a dozen other states considered and rejected tax limitations.[5]

119

Two successful tax limitation initiative campaigns that have received considerable attention and analysis are California's Proposition 13, which established constitutionally based tax limitations on state and local government, and Massachusetts's Proposition 2½, which limited by statute the level of state and local government taxation. In each case, education interests were prominent in the coalitions opposing their passage. Each measure had an important impact on the education service sectors in its state. In 1978, in California, the coalition opposing Proposition 13 consisted of teachers and professors (public and higher education), the PTA, the League of Women Voters, labor, and elected officials. In spite of the dire pictures of service cutbacks that were painted by the coalition, the projections lacked credibility, because the opponents were "people and groups associated with state and local government (officials, employees, and beneficiaries of service programs)."[6] Somewhat ironically, as Susan Hansen reports, "The probability of cutbacks in education was not emphasized by opponents of the initiatives in the campaign because of recent controversy over bussing, teachers' unions, discipline, and 'back-to-basics' teaching."[7] In the aftermath, school districts were the unit of local government most severely hit by Proposition 13, because they were so highly dependent on property taxes and had few options for raising revenues from alternate sources. Mary Williams asserts,

> Another consequence of Proposition 13 was that it changed the politics of education and school finance in the state legislature. Before education had been considered in isolation; the only concern was what did education need. It then became a zero-sum game, and all functions were considered in relation to one another. More aid for education meant less for someone else.[8]

In Massachusetts, Proposition 2½ was opposed by a similar coalition of education groups, good government organizations, public employees, and local government officials. Interestingly, the Massachusetts Teachers Association had placed on the same ballot its own property tax limitation proposal that would have increased state aid to education. The proposal was defeated, and Proposition 2½ was passed. Support for Proposition 2½ at the polls was linked to hopes for increased government efficiency and greater voter control over school spending by eliminating the fiscal autonomy of local school committees. In the aftermath, education and recreation agencies were cut disproportionately, while police and fire protection agencies were the least affected.[9]

Williams concludes that unsuccessful tax and expenditure limitation campaigns share two characteristics: they are typically sponsored by narrowly based groups, and are opposed by a broad-based coalition of groups that draw on personnel, treasuries, and memberships of organizations to mount a statewide campaign. She finds further that compared to a variety of public services, voters on tax limitation initiatives during the late 1970s peak interest period were more likely to say that school services should be increased and less likely to say that if cuts must be made they should be in education.[10]

It is asserted by several individuals and groups who have studied tax limitations that because of the variety and complexity of circumstances and structure of the measures themselves, one cannot generalize about their effects across states.[11] In actual implementation the results of such limitations have often been different from those intended. Placing the analytical, retrospective viewpoint of the scholar aside, there is no question that tax limitation campaigns viewed prospectively by those holding responsibility for providing government services most often constitute a "crisis." The brute fact facing the administrators of all service agencies in such circumstances is that the resources made available to them would decline under tax and expenditure limitations. Depending on the service sector, this may or may not be true, but in the heat of battle such must be the operating assumption held by those politically and administratively responsible for publicly funded government services, including education.

POLITICAL DYNAMICS

> "Work up from the base; then set priorities up to the maximum realistic figure" for budget increases.

The seeds of the Utah tax limitation initiative campaign that culminated with the general election of November 1988 were sown more than two years before by leaders in public and higher education in their powerful efforts to increase their own state funding. In a meeting of the State Board of Education in April 1986 the state superintendent called for a tax increase in spite of the unfavorable political environment. A month later, during two days of meetings, the board heard the director of the governor's Office of Planning and Budget discuss Utah's fiscal capacity (which was not great), and the majority leader of the House of Representatives, who affirmed that "the money is not there." Utah, he argued, could not raise $120–30 million in taxes to add to the education budget. He urged the state board to "do something different."[12] The meeting progressed more affirmatively with a message from the president of one of the state's colleges who stated that "taxes for education are an investment," and exhorted the board to "maintain educational quality." Even the absentee director of the Utah Symphony delivered, via video, a message that he would "support a tax increase for education." The second day's meetings were less glamorous and more in earnest. The executive director of the Utah Education Association pushed the board for more money in a thinly veiled threat: "There will be no business as usual without money."[13] The State Board of Education concluded its meetings by formulating general responses to "an education funding crisis" that included, predictably, more revenues, program cuts, and a restructuring of education delivery systems. Understanding what they were getting in for, board members even discussed potential responses by taxpayers, including the possibility of a tax limitation initiative campaign.

The governor had been listening. Faced with shrinking state revenues, all state agencies in the summer of 1986 had been directed to prepare and submit budget requests at 94 percent of the base. This highly publicized budget exercise would partially justify a tax increase in the 1987 legislature; having cut the fat out, voters would—it was hypothesized—support increased taxes.

In a State Board of Education/State Board of Regents Joint Liaison Committee meeting in September, discussion centered on strategies to increase taxes for education. A regent asked that "staff from the respective boards work together to develop complete strategies." A month later, in October 1986, the liaison committee heard the chairman of the governor's ALERT Committee (a group organized to address and marshall support for education issues) solicit letters to be sent to the governor in support of a tax increase for education. The governor's education advisor indicated to the committee that the governor would request $130 million in new taxes, 80 percent of which would go to education. In response, the commissioner of higher education urged the governor to "set his sights higher," for "$90 million gets higher education back to square one." For his part, the state superintendent responded that without more funds, the team relationship between educators and the governor "would soon fall apart."[14] Later that fall, the regents heard an influential university president remind them of the necessary effort to support a tax increase to fund education and assert that a tax increase for education was "an investment in Utah's future."

The governor, having been forced by declining state revenues to make successive budget cuts and even call a special session of the legislature in November 1986 to deal with funding issues, requested $206 million in additional taxes from the 1987 legislature. The results of these combined efforts by education policy leaders in both public and higher education, coupled with those of the governor, were gratifying to education interests.

The 1987 legislature enacted the largest one-time tax increase in the history of the state of Utah: $150 million in additional income, sales, motor fuel, and cigarette taxes.[15] In response to the tax increase, a newly appointed state superintendent (a former legislator) meeting with his board characterized the legislative session as "the most difficult I have ever seen . . . we received as much as possible given the economic realities."[16] The commissioner of higher education commended the governor and the legislature for the tax increase "to finance both public and higher education."[17] Earlier, the liaison committee had passed a resolution to commend the governor on the "significant tax increase to support education as the first and highest priority for economic development and a healthy, prosperous Utah."[18]

The proposed increased tax rates elicited immediate and angry protests from many citizens who descended en masse on the capitol during the legislative session to shout their disapproval. Passage of the tax increase by the legislature provided the impetus for the organization of the Tax Limitation Coalition of Utah, which would spend the next twenty months placing three tax and expenditure limitation initiatives before the Utah electorate in the 1988 general elections.[19] Drawing inspiration from Parkinson's second law—that expenditure rises to meet available income— the tax limitation proponents sought to put a lid on the taxes made available to the insatiable agencies of government, which always, in their view, seek budget increases. The initiatives constituted what was judged by education policy leaders to be the greatest single threat to the education service sectors of the previous decade or longer. During the campaign, the chair of the Board of Regents said that "the initiatives would affect the higher education system more than anything that has taken place since the founding of the University of Deseret in 1850."[20]

The responses to the tax limitation initiative campaign by each sector came in two phases. Phase one consisted of preliminary organization efforts by both education boards during the summer and fall of 1987, during which the severity of the problem was assessed and acknowledged, and basic approaches and principles were established to meet the challenge. Phase two consisted of the actual public battle; it lasted for six months through the late spring, summer, and early fall of 1988, culminating in the general elections in November. The minutes of the two education boards show a concerned attention to the tax limitation initiatives during meetings held from April through October of 1987.

At the 9 April 1987 meeting of the State Board of Education the state superintendent voiced his opinion that the "tax protesters seek a significant decrease in state funding" and asked the board to oppose them.

The following October the board responded and formally went on record opposing the passage of the tax limitation initiatives and discussed strategies to involve the "education family" in a consolidated campaign. (The phrase "education family" in this instance—as in most cases involving public education—referred to the numerous organizations within the public education sector.) The superintendent responded that the initiatives would not appear on the ballot for one year, that the staff of the State Office of Education was "moving appropriately," and that he had affirmed with the governor that the governor would take a firm position against the initiatives "at the appropriate time." As for unity of the education community, the recently organized Education Coordinating Council, which the state superintendent himself would chair, would ensure a unified stance opposing any threat to public education. More will be said of the Education Coordinating Council below. Phase one had begun.

In August 1987, in the face of public opinion polls showing popular support for the tax limitation initiatives, the Board of Regents organized a Tax Limitation Task Force with one of its members, an advertising executive, serving as chair. A principle initially articulated by the new chairman was that the task force "must be perceived as a general movement, not just higher education."[21] Beyond this point there was no mention of potential coalition partners, the most obvious of which was public education. In September 1987, the liaison committee, with representatives from both education sectors, received from the state budget director initial budget projections that indicated that passage of the initiatives would result in the loss of $200 million in tax revenues, $55 million (28 percent) of which would have gone to education.[22] Following these initial symbolic organizational actions, the issue of the tax initiatives does not surface again in the minutes of the education boards or liaison committee until the spring of 1988, at which time the actual battle for votes had begun in earnest and continued through October under the direction of the umbrella organization Taxpayers for Utah.

In the latter part of March 1988, leaders of the Tax Limitation Coalition of Utah announced that the number of signatures collected on petitions then exceeded the 62,964 required to place the initiatives on the ballot in November, but that they would continue to work up to the mid-June deadline to collect additional signatures as a hedge against invalid signatures.[23] Ninety days later, in early July, the lieutenant governor formally confirmed that initiative petitions had been signed by thirteen thousand more registered voters than were required to place them on the ballot.[24] This announcement formally culminated a more than year-long effort by tax coalition leaders and twelve hundred petition carriers across the state and served as the starting gun for the public battle for which both proponents and opponents had been preparing for months. Phase two had begun.

The threat posed by the tax initiatives to programs of all agencies of government at the state and local level provided more than ample motivation for those charged with providing government services to be actively involved in opposing their passage. The difficulty with such participation is that all people on the payroll are liable to the charge of acting in self-interest as "tax-eaters," and consequently have low levels of credibility. In this regard it is difficult for publicly funded service providers to defend themselves directly; they need others who have more credibility to speak in their behalf. Those in public and higher education were no less vulnerable than others on this score.

Taxpayers for Utah was the organizational vehicle established by a powerful group of concerned government, business, and civic leaders for effectively opposing the initiatives. Two former Democratic governors (Calvin Rampton and Scott Matheson), a former Republican United States senator (Wallace Bennett), and a former Republican state senator (Warren Pugh) served as co-chairs of Taxpayers for Utah; they constituted four of the most popular, respected, and influential politicians in the state's history. The incumbent Republican governor (Norman Bangerter) and his Democratic challenger in the upcoming general election (Ted Wilson) were listed prominently on the Taxpayers for Utah literature and signed an open letter from the co-chairs to voters urging them, "Vote No on all 3 Initiatives!" At least two of the four co-chairs (Matheson and Pugh) were far more than figureheads; they played very active and visible roles throughout the campaign. Those staff members charged with central organization and fund-raising were highly competent individuals with experience in politics, government, and business.[25] Taxpayers for Utah had been working quietly for several months before it was formally announced in the press in mid-July that the campaign opposing the initiatives was underway. Fifty government, business, and civic leaders met to discuss and "unveil strategies for thwarting the tax limitation initiatives."[26] The issue of economic development was the primary and recurring theme of Taxpayers for Utah. During this first public meeting co-chair Scott Matheson indicated that the tax limitation initiative vote was more important to the state than the contests for governor and the United States Senate, which also would be decided in November. Speaking later in the fall to the Utah Public Employees Association General Council, he expressed the hope that voters would not listen to "the siren song of the pied pipers" promoting tax rollback and limitation, for passage of the initiatives "could dig an economic black hole for Utah that would take years to crawl out of, if ever."[27] Taxpayers for Utah provided the umbrella under which many organizations and groups opposed to the initiatives could work together for their defeat. The groups opposing the passage of the initiatives under the aegis of Taxpayers for Utah were described by one centrally involved regent in an interview as being "the most broadly based political coalition in the history of the state."

The Taxpayers for Utah steering committee (to be differentiated from the four high-profile co-chairs) was characterized by one individual participating on the committee as a "rump committee," in the sense of there being no officially designated leader who consistently conducted its weekly meetings or set direction for the group. The organizational relationships between participants on the steering committee were informal and undefined. The two individuals charged most specifically with fundraising for Taxpayers for Utah most often played the role of informal chairpersons. Referring to meetings of the steering committee, one participant expressed the judgment that "no one specifically was in charge; it was a group of peers sitting around a table brainstorming proposed future actions, or reporting the activities of the previous week." The primary function of the steering committee meetings was information exchange and loose coordination of activities. Organizational representatives were not directed by the steering committee, but rather volunteered what their organizations would or could do. In addition to representatives from the Utah Association of Cities and Counties, and the Utah Public Employees Association, education interests were central participants and well represented on the committee. In addition to the full-time liaison person from the Utah System of Higher Education and one individual sitting on the Board of Regents, there was important involvement from two individuals serving on the institutional councils of two higher education institutions. A former president of the state PTA served on the staff, charged with the logistical concerns of the committee. One participant not in the professional education ranks noted "not much activity from the Utah State Office of Education" on the steering committee.

With the announcement in July that the initiatives would be on the ballot, a prominent leader of the Tax Limitation Coalition, a radio talk show host, renewed his call to effect major tax savings by consolidating local school districts and by "eliminating the Utah State Office of Education."[28] Previously in April in an address to a Salt Lake civic group, the chairman of the Board of the Kearns-Tribune Corporation and a behind-the-scenes force in the organization of the Taxpayers for Utah, characterized the initiatives as "disastrously destructive" and shared his belief and judgment that "the hope of finding very significant savings in public education is . . . faint."[29] In May, Taxpayers for Utah published a widely distributed flyer detailing projected budget impacts of the initiatives on state programs; total loss in revenues was placed at $349 million. The two most prominently featured service areas in the flyer were public education (which was projected to lose $125 million) and higher education (which would lose $33.9 million). The two education sectors combined would account for a total of almost $159 million in lost revenue, equalling more than 45 percent of the total projected loss.

In late June 1988, at a meeting of the Utah Advisory Council on Intergovernmental Relations, representatives of the state's departments of social services, public health, transportation, and the Utah System of Higher Education presented assessments of the impact of the initiatives on their services. The higher education representative received most of the press attention as she described the loss of ten thousand students to higher education and a 25 percent increase in tuition to maintain even this reduced student body. Public education would lose $135 million (a figure $10 million higher than that previously published by Taxpayers for Utah). She took care to tie higher education to the theme of economic development, relating how fifty-seven new companies and forty-two hundred new jobs had directly resulted from activities at the University of Utah in recent years. At the same meeting, a Republican businessman running for governor as an Independent, a strong proponent of the initiatives, responded to what he had heard from the state's administrative elite by saying that he would protect programs in social services, health, and transportation, but would achieve tax savings by reducing administrative costs in public education and achieving greater efficiency in higher education instruction by moving "University of Utah professors" up to a minimum eight hours per quarter class load.[30] Three weeks later, in mid-July, he elaborated on this theme by specifying that as governor he would "eliminate the State Board of Education," and reduce waste in the Utah State Office of Education by $34 million, and "modify higher education teaching loads" to save $28 million.[31]

Having first determined to "keep his head down" in the controversy, under repeated attacks from tax limitation leaders in which the University of Utah was used as a "whipping boy," President Chase Peterson led in countering their attacks, defending not only his institution and higher education, but education generally. In an early speech to the Salt Lake Rotary Club in mid-July he warned of the extreme danger posed by the initiatives to highly productive education programs at the university. "It took decades to get where we are at today, but that can change in one day in November." He went on to outline the economic benefits that the university brought to the state. "The state gets twenty cents on the dollar for its investment in the university."[32] President Peterson's speech elicited a personal attack by the tax limitation standard-bearer and gubernatorial candidate, who discounted his claims as "wildly exaggerated" and urged that in future he "should speak out on his own time, not state time."[33] He went on to blame all of the faults of higher education and public education on the administrators. The university president continued to draw the fire (and in some cases, the abuse) of the tax limitation leaders throughout the summer and fall as he made more than fifty speeches in various counties statewide in opposition to the passage of the initiatives.

By mid-July both proponents and opponents of the initiatives had fired their initial salvoes and struck the themes that would be followed throughout the campaign. On the basis of public statements made by the central organizers and leading proponents of the initiatives and much of the content of the campaign opposing their passage, it appears that public and higher education were the primary focus of the tax protesters and at the center of the conflict—in spite of the fact that all agencies of state and local government were threatened. Each education sector made a very energetic response in opposition to the initiatives using the organizational forms and structures available to it. The approaches in each sector were different. In a phrase used in an interview by a regent who was central to the campaign, it was a case of "playing to your strengths."

In higher education, the regents determined that it was important for the commissioner, in spite of the potential problem of conflict of interest, to work actively to alert the people to the negative impact of the initiatives on higher education. Of more importance to the organizational structure of the opposition campaign was the fact that the commissioner's assistant for government and media affairs (to avoid those same charges of conflict of interest) took a formal leave of absence from the commissioner's staff to work full-time with Taxpayers for Utah. The higher education plan for informing Utahns of the initiatives called for a Taxpayers for Utah Committee to be formed in each county, with the resident college or university president actually organizing it. It was suggested that the composition of the county committee, which would be a local version of the state committee, include

> business and public service leaders, public officials, such as the institutional president, mayor(s), county commissioners, superintendent(s) of public instruction, PTA leaders, legislators, Regents, Institutional Council members, and student leaders in public and higher education.[34]

It is interesting to note that while some components of the public education community appear on the list (local school boards are conspicuously absent), public education is not designated as a special partner; it is simply one of several interests and perhaps not considered to be the most important of the group.

The purpose of the local county committees was to publicize through news conferences, local and regional newspapers, newsletters, and the distribution of flyers the damaging impact of the initiatives within the local county. Institutional councils were directed to take a formal position against the initiatives in September or October as the campaign would reach a crescendo. Each individual institutional council member was asked to personally discuss the impact of the initiatives on higher education with at least ten individuals. Institution presidents were directed to work with student leaders to organize student voter registration, and student speak-outs on the initiatives. There was even an effort to arrange contacts with the parents of high school and college students to discuss the impact of projected enrollment cuts.[35]

One of the most successful of the county Taxpayers for Utah committees was headed by a rural college president with an unusual talent for public relations. He organized a highly effective slide-tape presentation that he delivered personally by invitation to numerous school, civic, and professional groups throughout the state. He indicated that public education administrators were sometimes in the audience. His organization published a "Citizens Alert" newsletter and exchanged materials, data, and information on contacts in rural counties with the Taxpayers for Utah steering committee in Salt Lake City and other county organizations. On his campus, the higher education/public education connection came through the academic vice president, whose wife was the president of the PTA. He judged his efforts to have been effective given the fact that voters in his county defeated the initiatives with the highest margin in the state.

An important participant in Taxpayers for Utah, who was not a professional educator, judged that participation by college and university presidents gave credibility to the campaign, perhaps because they were able to "paint the broad picture." Higher education institution presidents tapped into the strengths of the PTA. As a non-tax supported organization, the PTA sponsored speakers against the initiatives. It was noted by one state PTA official that "presidents came to the PTA faster than school superintendents." Interview subjects in both education sectors consistently expressed the judgment that University of Utah president Chase Peterson was the earliest and most visible defender of education interests: first higher education, then education generally. The president of the state PTA determined to pull her organization actively into the fray in order "to draw the fire from Chase Peterson and the University of Utah," both targets of abuse from tax limitation proponents. Student body officers at the state's colleges and universities were also judged by this individual to have played an important role in getting the message out and getting opposition voters to the polls.

The response by public education to the initiatives was more politically complex than that of higher education, in that it became entwined with the politics surrounding the new state superintendent of public instruction, James Moss. Moss, a public education outsider, took the helm of the State Office of Education having observed from the vantage point of the state legislature the disunity of the public education community. From that perspective, the divisions and conflict within the public education community were a cause of political weakness in the legislative process. Having assumed his responsibilities at the State Office of Education, it was also his judgment that weak predecessors in his office had inappropriately delegated decision-making authority to second-level administrators. His personal agenda upon taking office included not only reasserting and consolidating of leadership and accountability within the state superintendent's office, but also asserting the office of the state superintendent as a unifying force within the fragmented public education community. The tax protest movement added urgency, as well as a publicly defensible rationale, to his agenda.

Anticipating a battle over taxes, the state superintendent had conceived and embarked upon an ambitious plan to unify the diverse public education community in its own defense: the Utah Education Coordinating Council. It was formally announced by the state superintendent at the State Board of Education's meeting at the close of the legislative session during which the tax increase had been passed (February 1987). The state superintendent would chair the council himself; as such, it would be his group, and he said as much. The council included at least sixteen different organizational entities (depending upon how one counts each organization) and resembled in this respect a naïve textbook exercise in education interest groups divorced from the political realities of the public education community.[36]

The intended purposes of the council were fourfold: 1) to serve as an umbrella organization for communication between groups interested in public education, 2) to provide a unified posture in legislative concerns and governmental actions affecting public education, 3) to provide feedback and evaluation of proposals coming from one constituent group to another, and 4) to share resources. Complaints about the council surfaced immediately, directed first to the substantive composition of the group, and later to the state superintendent. The education community's substantive objections to the composition of the council were directed to the fact that all component member organizations regardless of size, influence, and responsibility were given equal weight. The council did not recognize differential power relationships among participants: the Utah Home Schools Association was equal to the Utah Society of School Superintendents, and the Elementary School Principals Association had as much standing as the Utah School Boards Association. Perhaps the most galling breach with tradition was the inclusion of both of the teachers' unions (the UEA with seventeen thousand members and the AFT with one thousand members) on the same footing. While the UEA was incensed and forced the superintendent to make concessions, such as holding separate meetings for the UEA and AFT representatives, in an interview he defended his decision on the grounds that "the AFT is a force to be reckoned with." One local superintendent identified the political error in this approach to the council when he said that "informal power and influence are more critical in this area; you get agreement from the major actors to define the legislative agenda." Another observed that the council was "too broad, large, and diverse to be an effective decision and lobbying body."

The state superintendent worked throughout 1987 to effectively implement the new council. At the end of the year it was clear that there were problems deeper than simply the structure and composition of the council. The Education Coordinating Council had been universally interpreted as a vehicle for the new state superintendent to empower himself and the State Board of Education, and thereby gain control of the public education agenda for the state. Many saw the state superintendent as being arrogant, abrasive, and untruthful in his dealings with others. These behavioral characteristics led ultimately to what one local superintendent characterized as "a total lack of trust" by the public education community. In the spring of 1988 the superintendent apparently still hoped that he could make the council work effectively in opposing the initiatives, but he failed in this organizational effort. By that time the Education Coordinating Council had fallen apart with the formal withdrawal of two of its most powerful constituent organizations: the Utah School Boards Association and the Utah Society of School Superintendents. The superintendent remained in the fray and established high personal visibility in fighting the initiatives, but it was not the battle he had envisioned. Ultimately, public education fell back to an old, symbolically established organizational pattern to fight the initiatives.

In the spring of 1988 public education leaders outside the State

Office of Education—working around (rather than through) the state super-intendent—decided that HOPE (Helping Organizations for Public Education) should be rejuvenated. HOPE was a coalition of the major organizations in public education that had been organized some years before to defend and lobby for public education interests. Component organizations in HOPE included all of the core establishment organizations in public education that would have been expected to participate through the defunct Utah Education Coordinating Council. The state superintendent was initially invited to participate, but declined to do so; later in the campaign, his presence on the committee would not have been welcomed. Even the commissioner of higher education was invited to participate, but little or nothing came of this proposed relationship.

A recently retired urban school superintendent, a trusted member of the old guard, was pressed into service as the coordinator of the effort. Scott Matheson, as co-chair of Taxpayers for Utah, tapped directly into the informally established power structure in public education by personally recruiting this former superintendent to sit on the Taxpayers for Utah steering committee representing HOPE. The public relations officer of the State Office of Education participated centrally in HOPE, serving as the source of financial and operational data on public education for the committee. HOPE members so distrusted the state superintendent that she sat on the HOPE committee without a vote.[37] The membership did not want the state superintendent's preferences felt—even indirectly—in decision making. They sometimes asked the State Office of Education representative not to report the details of the committee's deliberations to the superintendent.

Considerable care was taken to see that HOPE's activities took place on private time, and that the writing, printing, and distribution of informational brochures were accomplished with private resources. The UEA was responsible for most of the writing, printing, and delivering of HOPE brochures to local schools around the state. The PTA organization then took the baton and saw that the brochures were delivered to the homes by students. Thus, in contrast to the ad hoc higher education county commit-tees, public education's HOPE committee relied on already established organizations and relationships to get its work done.

The activity levels of local school superintendents and boards varied, as did—no doubt—the activity of the presidents and institutional councils in higher education. One local superintendent reported that he had not spent a great deal of time coordinating efforts, though he had worked to "make the local case" and had worked with other superintendents. In contrast, another local superintendent reported that he had been "consumed by the issue for months," meeting with school and community groups. Some local district boards played a very active role in educating the public and leading citizen committees. During September and early October local school boards formally went on public record as opposing the passage of the initiatives in much the same way that the State Board of Education had done earlier and as the institutional councils in higher education were doing at the same time, according to the higher education plan. In an interview, the state superintendent indicated that there had been some conflict between the State Board of Education and "the locals who wanted both control and credit" for the opposition campaign.

Based on early meetings with a consultant from the National Education Association (NEA) Denver office, the UEA, according to organization officials, took a deliberately low-profile stance throughout the campaign. It was recognized that highly visible identification of the teachers' union with opposition forces would not help the cause. However, the UEA made major contributions to the campaign: it provided substantial sums of money (both from its own coffers and from the national parent organization, the NEA), as well as in-kind contributions such as telephone banks and the delivery of brochures to schools throughout the state. A UEA official sat on the Taxpayers for Utah steering committee, and the organization provided staffing support for the opposition campaign. In retrospect, it appeared to the state superintendent that the UEA used the campaign as an opportunity to recruit members.

In mid-August, the startling results of an opinion poll showing that 40 percent of the state's teachers at the time planned to vote for the initiatives were made public.[38] An official of Taxpayers for Utah, who had considerable familiarity with both public and higher education, expressed the opinion that one of the major contributions of the UEA was in rallying its members to oppose the initiatives at the polls where such a substantial proportion had supported their passage earlier in the campaign. While its influence was initially underestimated by the state organization, the UEA proved that through its focused approach to the issues and high level of organization at the employee level it could wield considerable influence on its members.[39]

The Parent-Teacher Association, as a private organization, sponsored meetings and presentations opposing the initiatives. The state PTA president recalled proponents of the initiatives entering these meetings, demanding equal time, and using strong-arm tactics (using bullhorns to drown out presentations, videotaping participants, and threatening lawsuits) to intimidate local PTA officers. Quoted in the press, she indicated that in twenty-seven years of civic activity she had never before encountered such bullying tactics, and urged local PTA officers throughout the state to "stand firm in [their] opposition."[40]

During the latter half of August, retired state senator and Taxpayers for Utah co-chairman Warren Pugh met with the Interim Education Study Committee of the legislature, the State Board of Regents, and the State Board of Education. It was his judgment that the use of public forums to educate voters about the impact of the initiatives on education had been ineffective because proponents of the initiatives "do not address the issues in the debates. Instead . . . they make irresponsible statements."[41] Pugh called for a grass-roots campaign to get the word out. The PTA, with its nineteen regions, 516 local units, and 144,000 members statewide, provided the grass-roots organization that is credited by board members and senior administrative officers of both education sectors with the defeat of the initiatives. In the words of an associate commissioner with the Utah System of Higher Education, "It was the PTA mothers going door-to-door that turned the situation around" and changed peoples' minds on the initiatives. This sentiment was repeated numerous times in the interviews.

In a meeting of the State Board of Regents held the week following the defeat of the tax limitation initiatives at the polls by a two-to-one margin, the chairman of the regents voiced his opinion that "the vote indicated . . . people believe in our institutions [colleges and universities] as well as in the public schools."[42] At a similar meeting of the State Board of Education held the same day, the board first passed a resolution thanking those who had helped to defeat the tax limitation initiatives and then proceeded to a discussion of the political prudence of requesting budget increases in view of the battle just concluded over taxes. The chair of the board got down to business by suggesting that they "work up from the base; then set priorities up to the maximum realistic figure" for budget increases.[43]

DISCUSSION AND ANALYSIS

The stakes involved in this case transcend every other factor. The stakes are not only "what we can win" (both tangible and intangible benefits), but also "what we can avoid losing." The threat to education interests posed by the strong possibility of major reductions in resources through tax limitations was of the highest magnitude. Wilson hypothesizes that such crises provide a strong incentive to organization elites to cooperate with one another. In this instance, by successfully opposing the passage of the initiatives, each education sector would win substantially; and the benefits would be equitably distributed between the participants by force of circumstance. Should the initiatives have passed, each sector would have lost substantially.

Interview subjects within both education sectors expressed enthusiasm for the cooperation they observed and experienced between higher education and public education during the campaign. Their words best express these feelings. A PTA leader indicated that "there were the best interrelationships possible between public education and higher education. There was a sense of comradery throughout the campaign." A member of the State Board of Education saw the initiative campaign as fostering a "sharing of values" between higher education and public education. A local school superintendent observed that there was "much interaction in planning" between public education and higher education. A regent said that there was "high cooperation between public education and higher education . . . a temporary uniting of diverse interests." He continued that "there was no one-upmanship; the initiative campaign was a uniting crisis in which there was bonding." A university president indicated that he "worked well with people in public education." An official at the State Office of Education responded that "there was no competition, but strong mutual support" between public education and higher education.

Ultimately, however, the feelings of unity and comradery were based more on a common opposition to a very serious common threat than on organizationally integrated activity. In contrast to the observations of cooperative interactions cited above, one university administrator characterized the cooperation between public and higher education opposing the initiatives as being "more apparent than real." Another indicated that there was cooperation "only in the sense of joint meetings." Potentially, each education sector was for the other the most powerful ally it could acquire. Yet each sector was ineffective in structuring any formal, operational cooperation with the other. Certainly there was no formal organizational relationship between the two education sectors in structuring and implementing their activities. Each sector essentially "did its own thing in its own way." Actual cooperative interaction between education sectors was either highly informal and limited in time and space, or highly symbolic, as in the instance of the liaison committee's meeting in which the board chairs and chief administrative officers of each state education agency were quoted together in the press as opposing the initiatives. Clearly, the real action took place outside the established state-level education governance bodies. Given the ephemeral nature of cooperative interaction between individual leaders in public and higher education, there were no organizational maintenance costs entailed by the effort.

In this issue area case, experienced players in the External Coalition understood the history and prevailing political relationships—most particularly those within public education—and did what they could to support and sustain those established organizational relationships that could get the job done. They required no more of cooperative interaction between education communities than was realistically achievable. An initial principle, which we broaden here to include all of education, was that opposition to the initiatives should be perceived to be broader than just education. Both sectors were vulnerable to the charge of self-interest in opposing the passage of the initiatives. It was, however, beyond the capacity of either education board or the administrators in either sector—or even both boards acting together in concert—to establish the broad-based coalition needed to fight the initiatives. Each sector took action separately within the scope of its competence and on the basis of historically proven and trusted relationships and established capacities to organize opposition. Ultimately, efforts by public education and higher education policy elites to formally involve representatives from the other sector in their tax limitation opposition programs were awkward and failed to yield results. It was only at the informal level of interaction that cooperation occurred under the umbrella of Taxpayers for Utah.

The organizational constraints on the actions of leaders, as well as the impact of personality on organization actions, are primary themes of this study. The political mini-drama in this issue area case between an energetic state superintendent and the public education establishment demonstrates the constraints on a leader created by the distribution of power in and around an organization. State Superintendent Moss was characterized by one experienced local superintendent as "an excellent legislator, who could not implement in public education." He brought important legislative experience and a broad view of the political problems facing public education in the legislative process. Ironically, he seriously misjudged the structurally based distribution of power within the public education community. He sought to establish, in Mintzberg's terms, a Personalized Internal Coalition in public education, but failed to recognize that the prevailing distribution of power within the administrative and governmental environment in which he worked would not allow such a consolidation of authority and influence as he had envisioned.

7. Building the Infrastructure

Bricks, Mortar, and Libraries

Governments organize and support different types of libraries to meet the diverse and changing needs for information that their citizens will have over the course of their lives. Libraries are organized as ends in themselves (as with public libraries) and as information support agencies for other more comprehensive social endeavors (as with academic libraries found in institutions of higher education and in the public schools).[1] There are important differences in the socially defined purposes, goals, and institutional settings of different types of libraries. School and public libraries, because of the purposes and clientele they serve, maintain collections that do not necessarily grow in size beyond a certain optimal point. The emphasis of the collections is on currency, and "outdated" material will be systematically withdrawn. For school libraries, the problem of physically housing the library is solved in the construction of the school building itself. The library will not be a building apart; consequently, library capital facilities are not typically an issue in public education.

At institutions of higher education, the library is most often a separate building located at the physical center of the campus, and intended —by librarians at least—to be the intellectual "heart" of the college or university. Its collections, particularly those supporting graduate programs, are intended to grow almost indefinitely and contain both the most current scholarly contributions to the field and works of historic importance to the discipline, which will be held indefinitely. The size of the academic library's collections in number of volumes has been a measure of its adequacy. Such an approach to collections creates a recurring problem of how to find room to house them. Over the decades, academic library collections fill the buildings that house them and additions to buildings must be made or new library facilities constructed in order to accommodate collections, students, and staff.

The physical plant (bricks and mortar) is of fundamental importance to both public and higher education, but there are major differences between the two education sectors in the political and administrative processes whereby each is enabled to construct new facilities. The political and administrative center of gravity of the capital facilities construction process in public education in Utah is at the local district level. Local boards are charged by statute with constructing and maintaining all new schools. This is not to say that the State Office of Education does not exert considerable influence in the construction of new school buildings in the local districts through the administration of state regulations and the allocation of supplemental state and federal funds. However, the need to build a specific school in a specific district does not compete directly within an integrated administrative process with other building needs outside of public education. The most important decisions in the process are made at the local level.

The political and administrative processes through which higher education in Utah is enabled to construct new buildings are centralized at the state level and involve significantly the Department of Facilities Construction and Management, the State Building Board, and the General Government and Capital Facilities Appropriations Subcommittee of the state legislature. Each of these organizations in turn works with, oversees, and authorizes the construction of new buildings for all agencies of state government. Within this integrated administrative process, higher education is literally in direct competition with all other agencies of state government for capital construction dollars. Interviews with higher education officials, most particularly those at the Utah System of Higher Education, underscored the importance of interactions with the Division of Facilities Construction and Management and with the State Building Board. Higher education policymakers are very sensitive to the fact that the capital facilities process is "highly politicized." No such concerns were voiced in the interviews by individuals in public education.

Because there are also organizational and functional commonalities among libraries (for example, all libraries use essentially the same resources of personnel, books, and journals to provide information services to their patrons) the general public and elected officials at all levels of government have been encouraged to seek savings of tax dollars through multitype library cooperation.[2] Organizational cooperation is never so fervently discussed and considered as when there is a shortage of money. The fact that in the spring and summer of 1987 no fewer than three state organizations initiated studies of multitype library cooperation attests to the shortage of funds in Utah. Significantly, the Interim Education Study Committee of the legislature was studying the service implications of school and public library cooperation as a means of reducing tax expenditures. The most prominent and important library study was the Utah System of Higher Education's Statewide Library Study. It provides an informative example of the political uses of the symbols of cooperation and highlights important differences in the functional definitions of the public and higher education sectors.

POLITICAL DYNAMICS

> "We can recommend anything we want on resource
> sharing so long as everybody gets his building."

On 4 August 1987 a memo from two associate commissioners of the Utah System of Higher Education went out to a "statewide library committee" consisting of the library directors of the academic libraries in the state, a representative named by the Utah State Office of Education (an individual of long experience, recently demoted in a reorganization of the state office and slated for imminent retirement), and the director of the State Library Division. The group had met the previous month for a "roundtable sharing of library concerns/information." The memo confirmed an August 13 date for a teleconference of the committee and set the agenda for the meeting. Included with the memo was a copy of a report dated in June 1987 to the Higher Education Appropriations Subcommittee of the legislature from the Office of the Legislative Fiscal Analyst, entitled "Utah System of Higher Education Current Status of Libraries."

The directors of the libraries of the state colleges and universities were requested particularly to review the institutional library holdings figures and volume equivalency standards, which troublingly showed several of the state's academic libraries, including the University of Utah, to have volume equivalencies that exceeded the standards of the Association of College and Research Libraries. The last page of the report analyzed the current distribution of assignable space at each of the libraries and the percentage of the student body that could be accommodated in study space. The report concluded unobtrusively with the point of it all: a summary of proposed capital facilities construction projects intended to bring the state's academic library buildings into conformity with the standards, all with a price tag of just over $150 million. The figure that would actually be used by the Utah System of Higher Education in its 1988 budget request to the legislature for new buildings and additions or renovations to existing libraries—$170 million—was even higher.

The 13 August meeting, co-chaired by the joint authors of the original memo, initially addressed the issue of library collection statistics in the legislative fiscal analyst's report, which clearly undercut the arguments the system would put forth in support of an academic library capital facilities request and for additional collection development funds. The major item on the agenda, however, was firming up plans for a statewide library inventory. As presented in concept by the associate commissioners, the inventory would provide data on the holdings, acquisition rates, space, staff, clientele served, available technology, and the current automated linkages and networks of the state's academic, school, and public libraries.

Procedures for the inventory easily fell into place for the academic libraries. As discussion turned to the integration of school library-media centers into the library inventory concept, the representative from the State Office of Education indicated that the total number of school library locations was so great, the level of professional staffing and collections support so low, and the implementation of automated networking relationships so limited that he could see little benefit—but much pointless work—in involving the school library community in the inventory. His judgment was corroborated by the State Library Division representative. The meeting concluded with a consensus among the academic library directors on the approach they would follow in the library inventory, but with the potential involvement of school and public libraries unresolved, though by no means dismissed. It was made clear in the course of the meeting that the inventory would be used to support a budget request by the Utah System of Higher Education for $150,000 to $200,000 to conduct a study of the state's libraries that would give direction in solving some of the major problems that the group had discussed.

The statewide library committee did not meet again prior to the 1988 legislature. The System of Higher Education staff worked throughout the fall with individuals and groups of academic library directors building a case for the authorization and funding of a formal and comprehensive statewide library study. No major efforts at generating new data on school and public libraries for the library inventory were attempted. Near the close of the 1988 legislative session, on 18 February 1988, the Executive Appropriations Committee of the legislature passed an appropriation of $150,000 for a study of higher education library needs in the state of Utah. Prior to the actual vote of the committee, the proposed study was defended by an associate commissioner of higher education as a means of potentially paring down a request by the Utah System of Higher Education for $170 million for academic library facilities construction and renovation. He argued that the expenditure of $150,000 could certainly be justified if the study could reduce capital facilities costs "by even a few million dollars."

A dissenting member of the Executive Appropriations Committee prior to passage voiced the proposal, "Why not simply spend the $150,00 on books?" Ironically, this sentiment was duplicated in a comment made privately by the director of one of the larger academic libraries who, upon hearing several days later of the appropriation, asked, "What do they hope to accomplish? Why don't they buy some books instead?"

The legislative intent language of the bill authorizing the study placed first priority on academic library capital facilities planning, which precisely matched the intentions of the Utah System of Higher Education staff, institutional administrators, and library directors. The second and third provisions of legislative intent gave what was apparently satisfactory expression to the interests of some legislators in the potential economies of technological innovation and multitype library cooperation, as well as giving scope to the issue of library systems development, an area of genuine interest to academic library directors. Public education remained linked with higher education in point three of the legislative charge defining the study, in spite of the informed judgments of state-level library and public education administrators that it was unprofitable, in a practical sense, to do so.[3]

The scheduling of the study called for the national advertisement of the study with the request for proposals by the state's Division of Facilities Construction and Management in early April, and the selection of the consultants in early May, with the final report to be presented to the Statewide Library Study Steering Committee by 1 September 1988. The schedule of the study itself was deliberately compressed into less than four months, for it was intended to provide the recommendations to support legislative budget requests in the legislature convening in January 1989.

With the study authorized and funded by the legislature, and public school libraries explicitly named in paragraph three of the intent language defining the purposes of the study, it was necessary to name a new representative from public education to the Statewide Library Study Steering Committee because of the retirement of the previous representative. Once again, the decision by State Office of Education leaders was to reach down into the fourth level of the administrative ranks and appoint an individual who was regularly assigned as a language arts curriculum specialist and who exercised no organizational authority. At the 22 April 1988 meeting of the regents it was reported that $150,000 had been appropriated for a consultant study of libraries to be conducted between May and September of 1988. No particular mention was made of any involvement with public education and school libraries, or public libraries.

Division of Facilities Construction and Management staff, along with a reconstituted steering committee, reviewed several study proposals in April. In early May a contract was granted to a consulting team consisting of two organizations: an architectural firm based in Salt Lake City and a nationally recognized library automation and system consulting firm head-quartered in Chicago. Academic library building specialists working in con-junction with the architects would address the issue of library buildings. The library automation and technology firm would focus on the issues of library technology and resource sharing.

An introductory meeting with the full team of consultants and representatives from the academic institutions and the system office was held early in June at the capitol to gain mutual understandings about the background of the issues giving rise to the study and the ways in which the consultant team would carry out their charge. Institutional representatives were questioned in turn by the full panel of consultants. At one point the senior consultant leading the facilities study team—a respected, nationally known academic library director—addressed a pointed question to an institution administrator who had been instrumental in formulating the original $170 million facilities request. His question, preceded by a troubling statement, was, "I believe I could build all of these libraries for *far* less than has been requested. How were the figures arrived at?" The response was enlightening: "The figures were derived from a system-wide study in which institutions used maximum formula requirements." Clearly, the goal of the system study had been to generate the largest defensible request possible. The result was an academic library facilities construction request that substantially exceeded the state's entire annual capital facilities budget. The study and resulting budget request had been calculated to gain the undivided attention of the state legislature, as well as executive agencies controlling capital facilities construction.

The study process proceeded with site visits and data gathering across the state throughout the months of June and July. With the academic library site visits completed, a member of the consulting team assigned to the library technology and resource sharing component of the study, when asked how things were progressing, remarked drily, "We can recommend anything we want on resource sharing, so long as everybody gets his building."

On 18 August 1988 the steering committee met with the Board of Regents and members of the Interim Education Study Committee of the legislature to provide information on the processes used and progress made on the study. Every academic library in the state had been visited on site by a team of consultants who had collected and compiled pertinent data and compared them to state and national standards. Individual recommendations for each campus had been determined and it was made clear that the final report would present a priority list for academic library construction and remodeling, in addition to recommendations on interlibrary cooperation and technology.

On August 19, the day after the regents met with the Interim Education Study Committee, the State Board of Education accepted a report from the State Office of Education staff on the status of Utah's school library media centers; the report detailed why only 9 percent could meet accreditation standards. In response, the board directed that an action plan to address the problem be formulated and presented at its October meeting. The chair of the board indicated, "We have a crisis in libraries only because we have focused the light there. We have actual crises in other areas as well." Within the context of circumstances, it is clear that the Statewide Library Study was the primary reason for focusing on school libraries at this particular time, but there was no mention at all of the study in the minutes of the board meeting.

Previously in August, public library directors and school library media coordinators at the school and district levels had met to hear and comment upon the consultants' draft recommendations for interlibrary cooperation and technology. The director of the State Library Division had had to press the consulting team hard to receive even this half-day "workshop" for the other two library constituencies named in the legislative intent language. Reactions in this meeting had been mixed, with concerns expressed privately after the meeting by influential members of the public library community that the recommendations of the study not deflect or impinge upon policy directions and established programs of the State Library Division in support of the state's public libraries. Another concern raised by the public and school librarians at this time was the shadow that was being cast over all government services by the tax limitation initiative movement, whose proponents were gathering strength for the November elections.

As late as the second half of August a joint meeting of the Board of Regents, State Board of Education, State Building Board, and State Library Board remained on the schedule for 15 September to receive and endorse the study's findings and recommendations. This meeting was intended to be the highly publicized culmination of the study process. Then, during the first week of September, the Statewide Library Study bandwagon was brought to an abrupt halt by the commissioner of higher education and the Board of Regents, who asked the governor to delay consideration of the state's capital facilities budget (in which they had such interest) until after the November elections. The fear was that discussion of capital facilities needs would add fuel to the fire kindled by proponents of the tax limitation initiatives. Accordingly, the formal presentation of the results and recommendations of the study to the State Board of Regents, the State Board of Education, the State Building Board, and the State Library Board was postponed until after the election. Predictably, proponents of the tax limitation initiatives picked up on this point as well, arguing that publicly funded organizations were conspiring to hide relevant information on their activities from the taxpayers of the state.

The delay in formally receiving and accepting the *full* findings and recommendations of the study did not extend to the consideration of the library facilities recommendations. By the time the commissioner felt free to send the executive summary of the report to the regents (3 November 1988) with his recommendation that it be fully endorsed, the capital facilities recommendations had already been fully discussed and endorsed by the Utah System of Higher Education's council of presidents, library deans and directors, and the Board of Regents's Capital Facilities Task Force. The findings and recommendations of the Statewide Library Study were never formally presented to the State Board of Education, as had been planned.

An associate commissioner of higher education who served as co-chair of the steering committee recalled with frustration the difficulty with which the committee received requested information on school libraries through the public education representative. (At the same time, she admitted that there was nothing in the policy package for public education.) By late summer of 1988 the State Office of Education representative on the steering committee was sharing with the committee data and information describing serious problems facing the state's school library-media centers, among the more sobering of which was that "it would require $14 million to fully staff school-library media centers with certificated personnel so as to meet accreditation standards." This point was elaborated later in the fall by others in public education who exercised considerably more organizational authority than the steering committee representative. In November, an associate superintendent of the State Office of Education reported to the State Library Board the "catastrophic conditions" prevailing in the state's school libraries. Only 9 percent (57 of 644) of the state's schools then met accreditation standards. An average Utah school with a student body of five hundred had a library media budget less than one-fourth that of a comparable "good" national school. Amid the devastation, the State Office of Education cited findings of a national education consulting firm that "of all expenditures that influence a school's effectiveness—including those for facilities, teachers, guidance services, and others—the level of expenditures for library and media services has the highest correlation with student achievement."[4] The associate superintendent concluded his comments by announcing that in order to meet the crisis the State Board of Education had set a ten-year goal of increasing the state's school library-media budgets by $25 million, and would request of the 1989 legislature an initial installment of $2.5 million toward that goal.

None of the descriptive data highlighting the neglect of school libraries were particularly new or unexpected to anyone who had followed the state of school library-media centers through the 1980s. Over the decade, local district administrators across the state had repeatedly reduced library book budgets and substituted library aids with no formal library education for credentialed librarians. With tight budgets libraries had been judged to be an appropriate place to cut. In October 1988 the State Board of Education passed a motion to assert itself into local decisions on school libraries by including library skills in the core curriculum, by clarifying and reinforcing certification standards for library personnel, and by issuing a warning status to schools whose accreditation was in jeopardy because of library deficiencies.

With the defeat of the tax limitation initiatives, the full findings and recommendations of the Statewide Library Study were finally made public. The argument that had been used by an associate commissioner of higher education to justify the initial funding of the study before the Executive Appropriations Committee of the legislature nine months earlier proved—predictably—to be well founded; the projected cost for library facilities was reduced by more than just a "few million dollars." The consultants recommended the construction of new library buildings or renovations on each of nine campuses in the system at a total cost of $73 million, rather than the originally requested $170 million. It was carefully explained that this embarrassingly large difference was attributable to the adoption of tighter standards for calculating the requirements for square footage, uniform construction cost estimates, and the deletion of estimated costs for renovating vacated library buildings for other institutional uses, as well as the recommendation of different (presumably less costly) solutions to building needs. The estimated construction costs were listed by institution in order of relative priority as recommended by the consultants. The report validated the serious inadequacy of academic library operating budgets and collections, citing the fact that while national standards indicate that 6 percent of an institution's educational and general expenditures should be allocated to the library to provide adequate support, library budgets in Utah ranged from 1 to 3 percent. The study recommended that institutions internally reallocate their budgets so as to meet this standard percentage and specified that the University of Utah library should receive at least 3.6 percent, which was the average level of support provided members of the Association of Research Libraries. While affirming that technology cannot substitute for library floor space, the consultants recommended finally that a statewide automated library system to support resource sharing be funded to involve initially only the state's academic libraries and the State Library Division.

On the basis of the recommendations of the Statewide Library Study, the Utah System of Higher Education and the Division of Facilities Construction and Management requested and received from the 1989 legislature $300,000 to develop plans for new or renovated library facilities on each of nine campuses. Further, the regents received $800,000 of a $1.3 million budget request in supplemental funding to address academic library collection needs.

What about school and public libraries? The study validated as well the very serious deficiencies in funding and collections in the state's public and school libraries and concluded that "areas of concern expressed by public and school libraries identify needs which are very acute and preclude immediate active participation in statewide resource sharing programs."[5] The State Office of Education's request for $2.5 million in increased funding for school media coordinators was denied. However, the legislature did pass House Joint Resolution 21, which concluded with the following words:

> *Now, Therefore, Be It Resolved* that the Legislature of the state of Utah strongly encourages the State Board of Education to determine adequate size standards for elementary school media centers in Utah.
>
> *Be It Further Resolved* that the Legislature of the state of Utah encourages efforts to establish an adequate media center in every elementary school of the state.[6]

Clearly, hortatory resolutions are easier to obtain from the legislature than dollars.

Perhaps the last word spoken (or not spoken, in this instance) on the results of "cooperation" between higher education and public education in the Statewide Library Study was during hearings before the Higher Education Joint Appropriations Subcommittee in the 1990 Legislature. In testimony before the committee, the director of the State Library Division made general reference to important benefits accruing to the state's academic, public, and school libraries as a result of the Statewide Library Study. An experienced and powerful senator, who was returning to the legislature after an absence of several years, broke into the testimony and asked very pointedly, "Would you please explain to me how libraries in the public schools benefitted from this study?" It was obvious that he already knew the answer to his question. To the relief of a momentarily flustered state librarian, the senator was instantly and forcefully gaveled into silence by the chair, and he reluctantly let the issue pass.

DISCUSSION AND ANALYSIS

Compared to other issues that consumed the energies of policy leaders in public and higher education during this period (notably the tax limitation initiatives and vocational education), the Statewide Library Study was relatively much less important. This issue area case is of theoretical value because it so clearly demonstrates the importance of several specific factors that condition the cooperative or competitive relationships between organizations.

Senior state-level administrators within both education sectors described "crisis" conditions in the libraries of both public and higher education.[7] Yet because of fundamental differences in the structure of library services and resources in each sector in 1988 there was no possibility of practical cooperation (as implicitly required by the legislative intent language and the publicly cultivated image of the study) between libraries in Utah's public schools and the state's colleges and universities. This point was understood by those participating in the study very early in the process. Why, then, should public and higher education staff members have been associated in the study at all? More pointedly, why were higher education system administrators so persistent in seeking the involvement of public education?

The characteristics of the leaders involved in the Statewide Library Study and their placement within their organizations provide a key to understanding these political relationships. Activity in the library study was centered at, and emanated from, the administrative level of the Utah System of Higher Education. Neither the Board of Regents nor the Board of Education played an active role. References in the minutes of the two boards to the study, its progress, and its recommendations were minimal. The real impetus for the Statewide Library Study grew out of the need of senior administrators within the Commissioner's Office of the Utah System of Higher Education to respond energetically and effectively to serious system-wide needs at the institution level. At stake for them was their credibility with institutional administrators. The library study was a policy package specifically constructed to meet the needs of the higher education sector within its own political and administrative environment. The political problem facing the System of Higher Education staff was to find a way to dramatize and dress up the need for library capital facilities so as to receive a favorable hearing in a highly centralized, highly competitive policy process centered in the State Division of Facilities Construction and Management, the State Building Board, and the General Government and Capital Facilities Appropriations Subcommittee of the legislature.

One of the most important results of the 1983 joint lobbying strategy —however troubled and tenuous the alliance was in fact—was the vision of a politically powerful (because united) education community. The political strategy that was adopted by higher education system administrators to address the system's library facilities needs was to simulate a cooperative study process to identify solutions to a presumably closely integrated need shared by two of the most powerful policy actors in state government: higher education and public education. This symbolically cooperative approach added legitimacy and played on legislative interest in library cooperation as a means to economize. The political strategy developed and implemented by higher education leaders to address those needs was articulated by individuals wholly within the higher education Internal Coalition. It was administrators within the Utah System of Higher Education who provided the initial and sustaining leadership for the political strategy of which the Statewide Library Study was the active vehicle.

The reason for the persistence of higher education system administrators in involving public education was the political advantage to higher education of having public education involved. Higher education leaders constructed a policy package that gave the appearance of broad-based support across several library service sectors. By implication this planning effort could tap the political resources of two (not simply one) of the most powerful interests within state government. From the beginning, higher education leaders perceived and sought the political value of cooperation (or, rather, the visible symbols and trappings of cooperation) with public education. With public education represented nominally on the steering committee, the study carried the form of cooperation, if not the substance.[8]

A second factor of major importance in an explanation of this interaction between education sectors was the stakes involved for each. The stakes in the Statewide Library Study—as structured by higher education administrators—were never such that they could be divided equitably between participating organizational interests. In terms of the costs of new library buildings alone, the dollar stakes for higher education were actually quite substantial (potentially $73 million over the years). Yet regardless of the level of success that might be achieved by cooperation through the study, there was simply no way for public education to realize any direct and tangible benefits. State Office of Education leaders had come to this conclusion very early in the process. Throughout the study public education was a reluctant partner, making the minimum commitment of time, staff, and organizational authority. Given a realistic assessment of potential benefits to the interests they represented, this response was rational. The primary contribution that public education made to the study was the use of its name before appropriate committees of the legislature.

Nevertheless, given the clearly pronounced legislative interest in libraries and library service generally, State Office of Education administrators saw an opportunity and chose to take advantage of it. They created their own legislative funding package—$25 million in ten years, with $2.5 million in 1989 to start things off. Not buildings and networking, but staff and books were their need. The steering committee was used by public education leaders as a platform from which to begin to build a case to be used in subsequent years to request added funding for staff and materials.

One measure of the comparative importance of the stakes associated with the Statewide Library Study within each education sector is the downward penetration through organizational levels of awareness of the study. The Statewide Library Study as a separately identifiable policy package failed to penetrate public education policy ranks below the State Office of Education. The local district superintendents interviewed were essentially unaware of the existence of anything called a "Statewide Library Study." (One local superintendent reported that he had "seen the cover of the final report.") By contrast, their organizational analogues in higher education, the institution presidents, had been intensely involved over an extended period and were fully informed on at least the facilities recommendations of the study and their implications for their individual institutions. The point to be taken here is not that one group of respondents was well informed and the other ignorant. Rather, it is that the Statewide Library Study related directly to the organizational needs of one group of leaders but had little or no relationship to the needs of the other.

Looking back, State Superintendent Moss indicated that he had viewed the Statewide Library Study from the beginning as an effort to increase higher education funding. He particularly admired the use of outside consultants, whose recommendations made the difference with the legislature by adding credibility to higher education requests. The benefits to higher education system administrators of using outside consultants were, in fact, twofold. First, the outside consultants established much-needed credibility with the legislature. Second, the consultants were required as part of their final report to recommend a priority listing and sequential scheduling of library facilities needs and construction for all institutions in the system. The fact that the final report of the study gave this priority listing would forestall future conflict among the component institutions of the system over the division of the rewards and the scheduling of building construction. The steering committee was used by system administrators to validate and establish compliance by the component institutions of the system with the findings and recommendations of the consultants.

Active proponents of school library service working within the public education community can argue—correctly—that the study provided an opportunity to focus attention on a serious problem that they had tried unsuccessfully to address in previous years. However, this result could not have been an incentive to public education decision makers to participate in the study because, given the prevailing funding relationships in public education, the only long-term solution (reallocating already appropriated dollars to school libraries) would necessarily create heightened levels of conflict within public education as established priorities were readjusted to meet the study recommendations.

8. Political Strategies in Education

Principles of Understanding and Action

The American federal system has been characterized as a great laboratory of government in which both structural and cultural diversity among the fifty states coexist within fundamentally important common patterns. Such has been our national experience with the governance and funding of the public schools and of public higher education. There has been an active evolution in the relative responsibilities borne by the separate levels of government: local, state, and federal. Since the late 1960s, state governments have moved to a central position in the governance and funding of both education sectors. Power has gravitated from local school districts and individual institutions of public higher education to the states, largely through the mechanism of separate, centralized, state-level governing agencies for each sector. This ascendancy in the role of the states has important implications for the education policy process and responsible policy leaders. It is this circumstance, common to all of the fifty states, that established the theoretical focus and starting place of this study and that justifies our attention to the political relationships between public and higher education policy elites within state government. In effect, the relationships between Utah education policy elites reported in previous chapters are only one of fifty different variations on a theme. The broad outlines of the Utah variation are summarized briefly below.

With the legislative establishment in 1969 of the Utah State Board of Regents and the Utah System of Higher Education, the institutional context of education policymaking in the state was significantly changed. The political relationships surrounding the education policy process would not be the same again. From that point on there would be two analogous governing boards and administrative agencies within the focused policy arena of Utah state government, each charged to establish policy, to administer programs, and to defend and foster the organizational interests, respectively, of the public and higher education sectors in the state.

The legislative charge given the fifteen individuals named initially by

151

the governor to the Board of Regents imposed a complex political agenda that was daunting.[1] On the one hand, the regents, with their new commissioner of higher education and his administrative staff, were required to establish effective and credible administrative and political control over nine previously autonomous institutions of higher education that for years past had cultivated and cherished direct channels to the legislature. In place of these bilateral political relationships, the law interposed a single administrative and political channel, the Board of Regents, between the separate institutions of the system, and the governor and legislature. While budgetary controls and procedures have been consolidated within the regents and the Office of the Commissioner of Higher Education, nearly a quarter of a century later there is still tension within the system generated by conflicting regional and institutional interests that surface at times in the legislature.

Simultaneously with this demanding political task, the regents and commissioner were required to establish a political and administrative presence within the policy arena of state government as a coordinate agency for establishing education policy for the state. Operating at a presumed disadvantage to a constitutionally established State Board of Education that had exercised its prerogatives in behalf of public education for years, the regents and senior higher education administrators—and their successors in the system over the years—expended great energy in the first two decades of the new board's existence in extending and establishing an authoritative definition of the statutorily defined higher education domain vis-à-vis the long-established public education board and administrative agency. The most satisfying and ardently sought-after resolution to their anxieties—constitutional status for the Board of Regents—has consistently eluded them.

The legislature's imposition of a second governing board into the education policy process of the state posed equally serious and threatening political problems for the eleven individuals then sitting on the State Board of Education.[2] The board established policy for an increasingly powerful State Office of Education that in the years since the end of the Second World War had exercised ever-growing influence over local districts through the administration of a state foundation formula program, as well as increasing federal funds made available through Great Society legislation. The initial response by the State Board of Education and its aggressive state superintendent of public instruction to this supreme political challenge was to exterminate the competition. This effort in the courts consumed two years; while it ultimately failed in its intended purpose, it created a watershed of ill-will and mutually negative perceptions that colored the interactions between the members of the two boards and their administrative staffs for more than a decade.

For the policy elites involved, the more than two decades since the legislative rearrangement of the education policy landscape have been turbulent. Political relationships between the two groups have ranged between the two extremes of the fight-to-the-death initial conflict and a cooperative legislative budget strategy engineered by education policy elites little more than a decade later. Time, experience, and the personal commitments of several leaders representing both education sectors have smoothed the relationship in recent years. The administrative and political challenges facing each group of policymakers have, in several fundamental ways, been parallel. Each sector has experienced enrollment growth that has far outstripped the resources allocated to meet it. The pressure of ever-increasing numbers of students has strained the administrative and political capacity of each sector. It is also true that over the last two decades each board has experienced ups and downs in the confidence of the legislature. A point of interest for both education boards, which has been the basis of cooperative interaction between them, has been to maintain and protect from legislative incursion established levels of autonomy and delegations of authority over education policy. Each group of policymakers has had to reach its own accommodation with the new neighbor living right next door, and do so in such a way that the legislature would not be encouraged or required to intervene.

Even though the two groups share status as coordinate education agencies within state government, the political constraints confronting each group of policymakers (as compared and discussed at the conclusion of chapter 2) are quite distinctive. These constraints are associated with the organizational structures of governance and the resulting distribution of formal and informal power within each sector, the interest group activity surrounding each sector, and priorities attached to both public and higher education in the public mind. Each group of policy elites must work within a different and characteristic pattern of organizational demands and constraints that have been made apparent through the case studies.

The issue area cases presented in the previous chapters are political dramas whose common cast of characters consists of two groupings of education policymakers interacting within several different policy contexts, none of which is central to the primary work of either education sector, but each of which appears importantly at the organizational interface between the two and the broader environment. It was this characteristic that made each issue area case relevant to the problem at hand. The focus of interest has not been the cognitive decision process associated with education policymaking, but the dynamic political interactions between public and higher education policy elites. Collectively, the cases open to public view important aspects of the political culture of education policymaking at the state level and the interactions of education policy elites seeking, through the use of political strategies of competition and cooperation, to defend and strengthen the organizational interests for which they hold responsibility. Through a thoughtful consideration of the political relationships reflected in the cases and the theoretical concepts and perspectives used to describe and interpret them, we can identify principles of understanding that help to explain why public and higher education interests in Utah compete—and sometimes experience open conflict. We can find as well principles of organizational action that effectively supported productive and cooperative political interaction between the two.

The political strategies employed by public and higher education policy leaders facing each other within the policy structures of state government emerge from the complex and subtle interplay between organizational structure (an expression of the principle of rationality), the configuration of power within and around the organizations that is based on shifting coalitions of policy actors (the political element emphasized by the open systems perspective of organization), and the personal characteristics and interactions of specific individuals occupying positions of authority within the decision structure (the human element). Each of these components will be discussed below in reference to the issue area cases.

ORGANIZATIONAL STRUCTURE: THE RATIONAL FRAMEWORK OF POLICYMAKING

The legislature is at once the symbol and physical embodiment of rational deliberation in our public affairs. The legislative process is intended—at least in part—to inject rationality into our public institutions by establishing appropriate public means to reach agreed-upon public ends. The creation of a formal organizational structure in which roles and policy expectations for the organization and the individuals within it are prescribed, relationships are defined, and procedures are specified is, in itself, an expression of the rational principle. The Utah state legislature (as is the case with almost all state legislatures nationwide) has formally established and empowered two policymaking bodies that serve as peak organizations for education policy in the state. In the area of funding, as well as in other essential areas of education policy, individual school districts and separate institutions of public higher education are ranged hierarchically beneath the two state-level organizations. Administrative interpretation and action have added procedural substance and specification to the general legal framework.

A rational response to the state's need to effectively administer state foundation formula programs and federal dollars in funding public education has been the gradual and progressive establishment since the end of the Second World War of a powerful and efficient state education agency to do the job. Similarly, the more recent creation of a centralized and powerful state-level policy structure to govern public higher education is a rational response to the state's economic need to impose an orderly growth and development upon higher education programs, the costs of which have dramatically escalated along with popular demands for expanded services. These education policy structures, and the reformed structures of state government of which they are a part, are intended to foster rational public action toward achieving proximate goals that relate—at least indirectly—to ultimate civic purposes. In the policy area of education, these purposes include extending liberty and opportunity to the individual, and establishing culturally and economically productive community within the body politic.

Popularly held expectations of the education policy process in state government look to the education policy boards as the central and predominant actors. According to this view, with the assistance of their administrative staffs, these boards establish goals for public and higher education in the state and exercise rational decision and choice in establishing policy to support these goals. The comprehensive rational planning model upon which such assumptions are implicitly based identifies discrete and sequential steps in the process by which policy is established.[3] First, a broad range of alternatives (if not all possible alternatives) is elaborated, and for each alternative the likely consequences are predicted. The alternatives with their projected consequences are then evaluated, and a priority ordering is established among them in light of the broader goals previously established for the organization. On the basis of this essentially cognitive process, the policy alternative is selected that most efficiently and effectively supports the organization's goals. The board makes decisions and establishes policy within an atmosphere of order and reason. Once the authorized body makes a formal decision, the common understanding assumes its implementation (the final step in the policy process), as though the decision alone were equivalent to organizational action.

There are important differences between these expectations and the empirical reality. At the most basic conceptual level, the political dynamics inherent in formal organization assure a continued tension between related organizational entities, regardless of the structural arrangements for controlling and coordinating them. The functional and structural differentiation implied by complex organization is itself a source of conflict, for as subunits develop autonomy and distinct functions, individuals within them develop their own distinctive values, norms, goals, and role perceptions that emphasize differences that will lead them to compete even while they must also cooperate.[4] If we apply this theoretical insight on organization to the education enterprise, broadly conceived, we are better able to understand the organizational tension between sectors within which policy elites conceive and implement the political strategies of organizational competition and cooperation that have been the focus of this investigation.

The cases present an unwieldy, unpredictable policy process in which the mobilization of political power and influence through strategies of competition and cooperation rivals or exceeds in importance the rational aspects of policymaking. The decisions made and actions taken by policy elites are not clean and sharp and motivated by highly rational considerations, but, rather, "subtle, confused, foggy, and complex."[5] This complexity and ambiguity is revealed in the activity of policy elites in the issue area cases. While the popular conception of education policy looks to the two policy boards as the central actors, the number of important policy actors in fact extends well beyond them. The formation of state education policy is influenced directly by a broad range of participants and interests. The impetus for various policies, and enabling as well as constraining factors in the policy process, can come from various locations both within and outside the organization. The cases present circumstances in which seemingly important formal decisions made by authorized policy bodies were never acted upon; indeed, the "decision," once made, was never even referred to again. Conversely, political strategies supporting policy goals of basic importance to both education sectors were formulated and implemented without the primary involvement of either state education board, as such.

The hierarchical model of the rational organization, with its emphasis on the cognitive aspects of decision making and problem solving, does not fit well the political dynamics of education policymaking at the state level. By normative standards the process may appear to be irrational; it is clear that rationally conceived policy structures cannot impose order on an inherently complex and disorderly process. The education policy structures of state government create a technical (or procedural) rationality that identifies some of the important actors and invests them with public responsibility, formal authority, and position power, while imposing procedures and channels on the policy process that serve to some degree as a mechanical means (an instrument) to get the work done. At the bottom line, the formal policy structures of state government integrate the activity into a decision process that authoritatively allocates public resources.

While the rationally conceived structures of formal organization make the behavior of policy actors more amenable to conscious design through the definition of roles and the consequent expectations of behavior, they cannot rationalize the politically ambivalent relationships between the education sectors that are based on their status as functionally interdependent yet co-equal competitors within the policy community of state government. Moreover, organizational structure cannot control and freeze in place the ever-changing configurations of organizational power within and surrounding education governance organizations, nor remove the human element from the policy process.

THE OPEN SYSTEMS PERSPECTIVE

The open systems perspective provides numerous important insights into the political activity of organizations and the policy elites guiding them. A basic concept of open systems theory is that of the interdependence of the organization with other organizations in the environment. It is the organizational exchange relationships between separate, related organizations that define a community of interest that requires ongoing relationships between them. These relationships are structured in part according to the changing configuration of formal and informal power within and surrounding the organizations that is based on shifting coalitions of organization actors. The related concepts of the elite and the rank and file help to explain the tension between various groupings of actors in the organizations. The responses of the rank and file are an important constraint on the actions of organization elites. Elites, who are directly charged with regulating the exchange relationships between their organizations and the wider environment, conceive and implement political strategies of competition or cooperation with other organizations in order to assure that these exchange relationships are favorable to the interests they represent. Their judgments on the stakes of political action help to structure organizational responses to specific circumstances in the environment. One common response by policy elites seeking to engage other organizations in the environment in the favorable resolution of problems facing their own organizations is to form mediating structures that are then used to achieve their focused purposes. In all of this activity the behavior of individuals within organizations is importantly affected by organizational ideologies that serve to consolidate their thinking about the organization and its environment, and to motivate their actions. Each of these closely interrelated conceptual areas, all deriving from the open systems perspective of organization, will be discussed in more depth below as it relates to education policymaking at the state level.

Functional Interdependence of the Education Sectors

Previous discussion has noted the separation between public and higher education in Utah, a separation that is characteristic of education policy structures nationwide. There are several salient characteristics of each education sector that differentiate it from the other and that serve to justify the formal separation between the two in public policy.[6] Yet even if there is a reasonable basis for this separation, from an organizational perspective there is also a functional interdependence between them in which the needs and interests of both intersect at numerous fundamental points. To state simply the reciprocal organizational exchange relationships between public and higher education, we would say that Utah's public schools provide the primary resource for the state's institutions of higher education, that is, students whose prior education in the schools has equipped them to function at levels implied in the term *higher education.* They must have mastered the basics. For their part, the schools rely upon Utah's colleges and universities (and those of other states) to train and certify elementary and secondary school teachers and administrators who can bring about the difficult results expected of them.

The organizational issues raised in this relationship of mutual dependence center on efficiency and the division of labor. While it can be argued, for example, that remedial course work at the college or university is necessary to support the public value of equity, the provision of such remedial work at this educational level, viewed equally from the perspective of the public interest, is organizationally inefficient if it is provided as a response to the systematic failure of the public schools adequately to prepare students for college work. The educational issues raised here that simultaneously impact both the public schools and higher education are as basic as curriculum planning, academic standards, and teacher education and certification. The point to be drawn from these simple and commonly understood examples is that the needs and interests of both public and higher education are closely interrelated. It is this intimate functional interrelationship that assures the continuing necessity of interaction between the two education sectors and that adds irony to the fact of competition between the two for limited dollars within the state government budget process.

The functional interdependencies described above are broad and systemwide and assure continuing interaction between the two sectors that can take the form of either competition or cooperation. By contrast, the administrative definition of obligatory operational interdependency in a specific circumstance in which, for example, funding and operational responsibilities for a program are divided between the two sectors will inevitably engender conflict. There is wisdom in the poet's admonition, "Good fences make good neighbors."[7] As analyzed within the cases, rational efforts at resolving such an awkward administrative relationship through a focused, though potentially far-reaching, redefinition of organizational domains generated progressively increasing levels of conflict over a period of five years until it was finally resolved. Ambiguities and overlaps in the definition of organizational domain in the area of vocational education—in which both sectors have a well-developed and continuing interest—hold continuing potential for conflict. This potential is heightened as technology and the demographics of the work force progressively alter circumstances on which there was some agreement in years past, but which now require new understandings between public and higher education.

Configurations of Organizational Power

While organizational structure creates and allocates formal authority and power, we have seen that individuals and groups at all levels of the organization form coalitions that exercise effective informal power and influence over organizational outcomes. The configuration of organizational power within and around the organization relates directly to the political strategies of competition and cooperation that emerge in the relationships between education policy elites. The institutional system of each education sector at the state level consists of a governing board of directors charged with integrating the activity of the organization into the general public good. The broader concept of the External Coalition (the prime component of which is the governing board) has great utility in explaining the political dynamics between education sectors because it accounts for other central actors in the policy process, including the governor and selected members of the legislature, the policy elite of the complementary education sector (a prime competitor and collaborator), and the powerful teachers' union representing the interests of the rank and file who are politically impotent within the closed structure of the organization.

It is within the External Coalition that broader public interests are articulated and made binding on the Internal Coalition of the organization. Political strategies of cooperation between the education sectors—if they are to come about at all—are associated with a configuration of power in which the main actors in the External Coalition are united in their policy goals, at the same time that the Internal Coalition experiences a dependence upon them. Strategies of cooperation between public and higher education in circumstances of potentially conflicting interests require such a configuration of organizational power. A consensus on focused and limited policy goals among powerful members of the External Coalition (the governor, influential legislators, the chairmen of both state education boards, and the chief executive officers of each state education agency) was achieved in one important instance in the cases by excluding from policy deliberations one powerful member of the External Coalition—the Utah Education Association. This unity and consensus of influencers in the External Coalition supported a remarkable strategy of cooperation in education funding that could not have come about otherwise. In the absence of this Dominated External Coalition (an unstable configuration of power that evaporated in this case soon after achieving its purpose when the central actors left the stage), identical strategies of cooperation between sectors were proposed and even unanimously approved by policymaking bodies, but thereafter they simply were not implemented.

While the External Coalition speaks for the broader public interest, the Internal Coalition (the technical and management systems) speaks for the narrowly construed, immediate interests of the organization. Because of this fact, it is unlikely that effective strategies of cooperation will be based on the policy initiatives of individuals organizationally placed within the Internal Coalition. This is true if for no other reason than that they have little motivation to accommodate their organizationally defined needs to those of other organizations in which they have no stake. More importantly, a dominant member of the Internal Coalition, even should he seek to establish cooperative political strategies, lacks the organizational and political resources needed to implement such a program alone, even should he occupy the powerful position of chief executive officer in the organization.

We conclude that the organizational placement of leaders associated with any given circumstance is a key variable in determining the nature and quality of the political relationships that will form between the education sectors. Strategies of interorganizational cooperation and accommodation in circumstances that are potentially conflictual are associated with a Dominated External Coalition.

The Elite and the Rank and File

Organizational structure is established to meet specific, limited social purposes that in its absence would not be achieved. The public education and higher education sectors are complex bureaucracies, each with its own work to do and its own mechanisms for getting it done. In this sense, each sector is highly insular in its organizational perspective, and single-mindedly pursues its own narrowly defined purposes and interests. The primary impetus within each organization is to accomplish these centrally defined functions. It is the rank and file (the Internal Coalition) of each education sector that actually accomplishes these functions. For the rank and file the be-all and end-all of policy is the immediate support of its closest, parochially defined needs. Such behavior lies within the rational basis of organization. Yet, because the organization must exist within a larger world, policy elites have the dual task of looking simultaneously to the internally defined need as well as to its externally defined constraints—a circumstance that often places organization leaders in conflict with their rank and file. The relationship is disorderly and potentially conflictual.

In this study the complementary concepts of the elite and the rank and file have been implicitly defined according to function rather than simply organizational placement. In analyzing the political dynamics of individuals acting within the context of organizational structure, the focus has been on functional interaction within specific circumstances. Reaching an accommodation with the neighbors—or with two potentially conflicting sets of priorities or perspectives—is a useful element in defining the organizational function of elites. Accordingly, organization elites are those who exercise authority and responsibility in specific circumstances to decide and act in terms of two perspectives: one reflecting priorities internal to the organization, and the second reflecting often conflicting externally imposed priorities. These persons live (at least temporarily) in a world of ambiguity, complexity, and cross-pressures in which they hold decision responsibility to accommodate conflicting viewpoints. Conversely, the rank and file consists of those persons in the organization who, by virtue of their specific circumstances, have freedom (at least temporarily) to view circumstances and act in terms of one internally consistent, simplified perspective. This differentiation in function and perspective is the basis of tension and conflict between elites and the rank and file.

The cases have exemplified different sets of elite/rank-and-file relationships. Generally speaking, members of education policy boards, the chief executive officers of education agencies, elected officials, and legislators have been termed elites, while teachers, professors, and lower-level administrators have been considered the rank and file. Within the microanalysis of the case studies, however, the broadened concepts of the elite and the rank and file helped to clarify the political dynamics among smaller groups of policy actors, all of whom by a conventional definition would be treated as organizational elites. Mediating organizational structures immediately define new elite/rank-and-file relationships in the sense used here. Thus, selected members of both policy boards with the chief executive officers of each state education agency sitting on a liaison committee comprise a new set of elites, while their more numerous peers remaining on the policy boards, but excluded from the activity and decision making of the representative liaison committee, become in this context the rank and file. Whether in the conventional meaning of the term as used to refer, for example, to public school teachers, or in the circumstance of board members who are excluded from the deliberations of a representative liaison committee, the responses—both anticipated and actual—of the rank and file were a constraint on the freedom of action of the elites. Elites were always compelled to give serious thought to the desires of their rank and file, even if they did not always accede to their wishes.

The Stakes of Political Action

That aspect of the political interactions of organization elites that appears to fit best the rational model of decision making was the evaluation of the stakes associated with specific circumstances in the environment and the selection of various political strategies that were adopted to respond to them. In each of the issue area cases there was a different relationship between organization leaders and the stakes. Circumstances both of crisis and opportunity prompted leaders to adopt a cooperative budget strategy in an effort to optimize legislative allocations in a difficult year. The stakes, which supported cooperation in this instance, were specific and tangible, and a fair-shares decision rule was established between the parties in advance. The lack of subsequent cooperative activity along these lines in the aftermath of the joint lobbying strategy was conventionally explained by the lack of sufficient dollar benefits to justify in the minds of education leaders any cooperative approaches. This explanation focusing on the dollar stakes was partially justified, but ultimately inadequate in explaining the full organizational dynamics in either circumstance. A more compelling explanation was found in the configuration of organizational power within the specific circumstances of the case.

As leaders in the two sectors competed for domain in vocational education, the stakes, as perceived by education policy leaders, changed over time. At first, the stakes appeared to be very specific and tangible. The decision rule controlling the initial interaction was winner-take-all. This zero-sum game, with the control, operation, and funding of an only peripherally important educational program as the prize, was the basis of the most heated and focused conflict that occurred between the two sectors during the period studied. The zero-sum game engenders conflict. With the entry of very specific legislative influence into the relationship, the stakes were changed. It became clear to those education policy leaders charged with making the decision that what was actually at stake was the established authority relationships and autonomy of both sectors. The threat to the autonomy of each sector implied by legislative intrusion into the conflict justified accommodation to a policy decision that previously had been judged to be unacceptable by some public education leaders. In effect, the abstract—though very real—benefits of cooperation in this instance would be distributed equally to both sectors as legislators withdrew, leaving educational administrators to implement the decision that their own policy body had already prescribed.

A popular tax limitation initiative campaign created a major crisis entailing huge stakes measured in dollars lost for both sectors. Hypothetically such stakes should have promoted cooperation between public and higher education; in fact, it did not materialize. While there was cooperation of sorts, the most striking point about the response of education interests to this crisis was that there was so little substantive cooperation within the organizational structure of the two sectors; only the minimum of organizationally integrated cooperation resulted. Instead of organizationally based cooperation, the interaction between public and higher education was carried on in the personal efforts of individuals. Both education sectors are highly insular.

Finally, a statewide study of academic library facilities presented a circumstance in which an ostensibly cooperative policy initiative was structured in such a way that only one party to the shared political labor could reap direct benefits; higher education interests alone stood to gain from the study. The stakes for state-level higher education administrators were substantial, affecting not only their personal credibility with institutional administrators as they "brought home the bacon," but providing substantial concrete benefits to the system by building the infrastructure. The stakes for their administrative peers in public education were low, and the benefits available to them and the organizational interests they represented were few. Consequently, substantive cooperation between the two sectors was minimal. Public education policy leaders were completely rational in their assessment of the benefits available to public school interests through the study and in their polite lack of interest in this one-sided policy initiative. In summary, we conclude that the underlying policy considerations of the stakes by organization leaders were complex, but not so rational, precise, and calculated as relevant hypotheses in the literature imply.

Organizational Ideologies

An important aspect of organizational thinking and action that relates directly to the political strategies employed by organization elites is organizational ideology, which is "the tendency of people belonging to the same organization to think similarly about the organization and its environment."[8] All successful organizations develop ideologies to support themselves. Strong organizational interests inevitably mold the thinking of organizational actors along lines supportive of the interests of the organization. The depth and intensity with which such views are held appear to be associated with the length of time actors have spent within the organization, their past experiences, and even their personality characteristics. With strong organizational interests, we commonly expect members of the Internal Coalition, in particular, to hold limited perspectives of wider organizational interests in the environment.

There is a strong ideological component to the education policy process in the state of Utah that has had an important impact on the interaction of policymakers and on policy outcomes. It is most apparent in the public education sector, particularly in the teachers' union, which has effectively used ideology to put in concert the actions of teachers in defense of their own economic and professional interests. The cohesive political presence of the union is a major constraint on the actions of public education policy elites; in some circumstances the policy elites in both sectors had to pay serious attention to its actions. In a more subtle fashion, the ideological component in education politics becomes apparent in comparing the actions and responses of some administrators and governing board members who had extended tenure and narrow career experience in public education (organizational insiders), with those who were new to the public education community and brought broad (or different) career experience to their assignment (organizational outsiders). The practical impact of organizational ideologies on the political activity of policy leaders is placed in sharp relief in their activity in mediating organizations. In several instances, outsiders brought an instrumental orientation to their role that supported political strategies of cooperation and accommodation with complementary education interests, but which placed them immediately in conflict with insiders and with their rank and file. Insiders, indoctrinated with the ideology of the organization, more often were territorial in their stance, with the result being conflict and competition with the complementary education sector, but harmony with their rank and file and the public education establishment. Individuals can play a determining role within the small group dynamics of a mediating organization. Participants who hold position power and are ideologically motivated (rather than being pragmatic or instrumental in their personal orientation to their responsibilities) can obstruct or nullify the dynamics of accommodation and cooperation within the small group.

Mediating Organizational Structures

Over the course of the seven years during which the action of the four issue area cases was played out, there were established several state-level organizational structures having representatives drawn primarily from the public and higher education sectors for the ostensible purpose of establishing cooperative approaches to common policy problems facing the two sectors. Four of the organizations discussed in the case studies were ad hoc; one was permanent. Such publicly established structures were deemed by organization leaders to be an essential, instrumental component of cooperative interaction between the two sectors. They did provide a legitimized forum within which representatives from each sector could interact for specific purposes. The dynamics analyzed in the issue area cases show that mediating organizational structures were necessary for achieving an accommodation between organizations at least potentially in conflict; they were also in place in circumstances in which there was little substantive, active cooperation between the two sectors, as such, but simply passive participation. Thus, some of these structures had substantive value in mediating real conflicts between the sectors, while in others the mediating structure had only symbolic political value based on legislative predispositions in favor of cooperative approaches. In the latter case, policy elites from each education sector used the organizational symbols and rhetoric of cooperation to create a positive legislative perception of broad-based needs and efficient (because cooperative) solutions. Obtaining these potential benefits was clearly a consideration of political strategy.

If the purpose of the structure is to mediate genuinely conflicting interests between the sectors, then its membership must include those who exercise organizational authority and political influence commensurate with these purposes. The competence of a mediating organizational structure to deal with any given issue is a function of the structure of the organization, the members involved, and the organizational interests represented. For example, a permanent liaison committee between the two education boards was competent to deal with the technical issues surrounding vocational education, but was not competent to deal with the politically demanding issue of cooperative funding strategies between sectors. On the other hand, a committee consisting of education board chairmen, peak education administrators, representatives from the governor's office, and strategically placed legislators was competent to deal with a cooperative legislative funding policy initiative, but would not have been competent to deal with the technical issues of vocational education or with the operational substance of education reform in the secondary schools.

The case studies show the Utah Commission on Educational Excellence and the Statewide Library Study steering committee to have been similar to each other in the sense that each was organized to address politically a major problem from the organizational perspective of only one of the participants. Representation on each of these committees failed to include those organization leaders (from one sector or the other) who could exercise organizational authority at the highest level within the sector. Actually, public education membership commitments and participation in the Statewide Library Study steering committee reflected the prior rational judgment of policy leaders that there was little to be gained through the effort. Rather than mediating conflicts between sectors, leaders used each of these structures to address the needs and interests of the Internal Coalitions: the Utah Commission served the public education Internal Coalition, and the Statewide Library Study served the higher education Internal Coalition.

By contrast, other mediating bodies dealt with issues in which the interests of each sector were genuinely in conflict. The membership of each of these structures included those individuals who held decision-making authority at the highest levels for their organizations, in addition to other key actors in the External Coalition who exercised great political power in the given circumstances and were united in their specific policy goals. These mediating structures were organizationally and politically competent in the sense of having means sufficient to the proposed ends assigned to them. They provided leaders from each sector with psychological distance from their rank and file within which they could foster the small group dynamics of communication and accommodation, discuss and establish cooperative policy decisions, and form mutual personal commitments between participants based on a shared experience. Representatives from both public education and higher education boards formed perspectives and personal commitments that conflicted in many cases with those of their peers and organizational subordinates (their rank and file in the broader sense discussed above). These elites had to return home and defend unconventional policy decisions that were not initially accepted—if ever accepted—by their rank and file.

THE IMPACT OF PERSONALITY: THE HUMAN ELEMENT

Within the rational framework of organizational structure, the human element emerges in the decisions and actions of real people bearing personal strengths and weaknesses; exercising formal authority as well as the power of their personalities; and playing roles, defined and specified by the organization, that are either enriched or impoverished by their own capacities, past experiences, and vision of the future. Specific personalities have had an important impact on the political relationships between education policy organizations, which has ultimately been reflected in public policy.

Much of the interaction of the cases called not simply for professional competence within the policy process, but required even more fundamentally the personal commitment of policy actors. The charismatic personal power of a board chairman who brought extensive practical political and legislative experience to his position allowed him to take control of a fractious State Board of Education and implement a complex, integrated agenda of cooperation with higher education that was unprecedented. Personal feelings of friendship, mutual respect, and trust supported decisive action by governing board chairs and chief executive officers of both public and higher education in burying a hatchet that had carved jagged edges in the relations between the two education boards for more than a decade. Their determined and concerted action placed the political relationships between the two boards on a new foundation. The expressed motivation of a state PTA president for jumping into a bruising political fray over tax limitation initiatives was to succor a courageous university president, who, she felt, was being personally abused because of his highly visible role in defending education interests from their critics. The statewide grass-roots action of her organization was judged to have made the difference in a successful effort to defeat the initiatives.

Important decisions on the allocation of organizational resources are often determined through the interactions of small groups of individuals in which personal feelings and relationships, rather than simply rational policy considerations, are the determining factor. The feelings of mutual commitment and loyalty to a common effort inspired through their inter-action on a liaison committee between the two policy boards allowed public education participants to transcend the organizational and ideological boundaries that separated them from higher education representatives on the committee, and to stand together against the angry and imperious demands of an influential peer on the State Board of Education to do other than they had mutually agreed to do. Personal enmities—as well as loyalties—can be reflected in organizational action and policy. Small group deliberations involving two board chairpersons between whom "there was no love lost" generated a conflictual dynamic in their interactions that served to maintain the lingering conflict of the status quo rather than resolving the problem. A belligerent personality at the head of a teacher's union excited sufficiently negative feelings in elected officials to assure the exclusion of the union from important policy deliberations during a critical year. Five years later, that same union, under the administration of a more moderate personality, was negotiating directly with a new governor whose personal approach to the problem of dealing with teachers' demands was different from that of his predecessor. The perceived personal arrogance and self-aggrandizement of a state superintendent, an outsider to the education establishment who was inexperienced in the internal practical politics of public education, doomed his ambitious—and possibly well-founded—political agenda and policy initiatives to failure because of the lack of confidence and trust from other policy actors in his own community. Rather than presiding over a politically integrated public education community, he found himself personally excluded from important policy circles in his own ranks during a time of crisis and was distrusted by many in higher education as well.

The confidence in the realization of expectations that some leaders inspired was an enabling factor in important instances of organizational cooperation. It was feelings of confidence in each other's integrity that allowed two highly visible elected officials (a governor and a state senator) to transcend partisan differences and the built-in competitive relations between the executive and the legislative branches of state government to politically anchor a highly creative and cooperative political strategy between education sectors. The very human elements of loyalty and honor sometimes transcended in importance such policy considerations as organizational interest measured in dollars or in turf. For a dynamic chairman of the State Board of Education, maintaining the trust on which a focused alliance on education funding was based exceeded in importance some millions of additional dollars allocated to his own interests in violation of the previously agreed-upon distribution rule, thereby jeopardizing the broader strategy of cooperation between public and higher education. Mutual trust and confidence between an associate commissioner of higher education and an associate superintendent of public education came about through their joint efforts at resolving lingering contentions over domain between their organizations. This trust and confidence allowed the completion and adoption of a vocational education master plan in the face of angry opposition from a small but influential group of State Board of Education members.

Common sense, intuitive understandings dealing with the personal characteristics of leaders, and the interpersonal relationships among leaders in related organizations are of importance in explaining the competitive or cooperative dynamics between organizations. Instances of cooperation in the cases were associated with the activity of leaders who held an instrumental orientation to their function within the organization and positive interpersonal relationships with their peers in the other organization. Competition was associated with leaders who held an ideological, territorial orientation to their roles, and who did not have relationships of trust, confidence, and friendship with their peers in the complementary organization, or even within their own community.

SUMMARY

The discussion in the preceding sections is not intended to argue that the state-level education policy process is irrational. It may be as rational and as orderly as an inherently complex and disorderly process can be. It is simply that public and higher education policy leaders must take into account and respond to a wider range of factors in acquitting their organizational responsibilities than is identified in popularly held understandings of the policy process that fit with the conception of the rational organization. The range of relevant contingencies and organizational and political constraints bearing upon education policy leaders is very broad, extending from constitutional and statutory provisions of formal authority and role, to the dynamically changing configurations of informal organizational power both within and surrounding the organization in which the rank and file play a central role, to the very human considerations of personal liking or dislike, friendship, trust or distrust, commitment, and loyalty. The political strategies employed by education policy elites necessarily reflect the prevailing circumstances, and the judgment of leaders, in each of these related areas.

CONCLUSION

In the policy circles of government, and within the general public, there is an inadequate recognition of the importance of the close and politically ambivalent relationship between the public and higher education sectors. Even less have the political implications of this relationship for the education policy process within state government been fully explored and understood. This study has focused on the political relationships between state-level education policy elites because of the significant and comparatively recent institutional evolution in education governance structures nationwide that has changed the political context of education policymaking in the United States from what it has been historically. Currently, in the separate states relatively few individuals who represent complex organizational and social interests interact within the focused policy space of state government to make basic decisions on allocating, to both public and higher education, work to do and the public resources needed to get it done.

The political dilemmas analyzed in this book that recurrently confront state education policy leaders are rooted in two fundamental facts about state educational systems: first, the obvious functional interdependencies between public and higher education; and second, the intergroup dynamics inherent in complex organization, now focused in the coordinate status of each education sector within the policy structures of state government. The interdependencies between elementary and secondary education and higher education are often best addressed through cooperative strategies and behaviors; indeed, in this context competition between the two can be destructive of the public interest. But the organizational structure required for complex social endeavors in and of itself often engenders competition and even conflict, particularly between organizations that are closely related by function. These circumstances pose real—not merely apparent—dilemmas for state education policy leaders. They are abiding political dilemmas that cannot be resolved through the simple manipulation of organizational structure.

This study has identified characteristic organizational relationships and discussed several principles of organizational competition and cooperation that have been shown to apply to the state-level education policy process in the state of Utah. It remains to others to test their relevance, applicability, and usefulness in understanding and explaining the education policy process in other state jurisdictions. A beginning assumption of the study was that, while policy structures and political circumstances in the various states are as diverse as the states themselves, the dynamics of organizational competition and cooperation are universal. If this assumption is correct, these concepts and principles will have broad applicability and relevance. They are intended to support a more informed perspective of the education policy process in which the differences between education sectors, as well as their similarities and interdependencies, can be fully acknowledged and wisely acted upon.

Because of the deeply ingrained and institutionalized separation in the United States between public and higher education, our collective public thinking and discourse about education can easily degenerate into either short-sighted partisanship or blind insularity in which the public's interest in education, broadly conceived, is not served. We are faced with a circumstance in which our national well-being, as well as the individual welfare of our citizens, depends on the success of both education sectors. Because of the evolution of education policy structures, each sector is for the other the closest and most important competitor in state government for limited resources. At the same time, and more importantly, each education sector is for the other the chief and most abiding collaborator. The organizational exchange relationships between the two education sectors are intimate, continuing, and of fundamental importance. The central contributions of each sector are essential to the success of the other.

The political process will determine how public resources are allocated to public purposes, including education. The education policy process will inevitably be one in which policy elites in both sectors, in their efforts to support their own organizational interests, will intermittently employ political strategies of competition and cooperation as seems to suit them best.[9] If the purpose and problem of state-level education policy-making is not simply to effect thinking and rational choice, but to produce coordinated action in support of organization goals, then the political maneuvering associated with the organizational responsibilities of education policy elites within the arena of state government can be a functional aspect of the policy process.[10] However, if the public's interest in education is to be truly served, the politics of education within the states and the resulting education policy must be tempered and informed by widely held, dynamic understandings of the values, purposes, and continuing interdependencies of the two organizational complexes charged with education in our society.

APPENDIX

Each of the persons listed was interviewed one or more times on the issues dealt with in the study. The alphabetical listing states the relevant professional and/or political career positions held by the individual, followed in parentheses by the month and year in which the individual was interviewed. In total, sixty-three interviews were held with fifty-five individuals. The interviews averaged approximately fifty minutes in length. The great majority of the interviews were held between November 1989 and July 1990. Six of the interviews were held in November 1983 and focused exclusively on the cooperative budget strategy analyzed in this study.

The organizational listing groups the individuals by last name only according to their organizational placement within the education policy community in Utah. It should be noted that the names of several individuals appear in this list under more than one organizational heading. Interviews with these individuals were explicitly structured to take advantage of their broadened experience and perspectives.

ALPHABETICAL LISTING

Haven J. Barlow, senator, Utah State Legislature; chair, Public Education Joint Appropriations Subcommittee; formerly, president, Utah State Senate. (Interview: June 1990)

Elva M. Barnes, member, Utah State Board of Regents; member, State Board of Education/State Board of Regents Joint Liaison Committee. (Interview: April 1990)

173

L. Lowell Baum, executive director, Utah Education Association; member, Utah Commission on Educational Excellence. (Interview: March 1990)

Terrel H. Bell, U.S. secretary of education; commissioner of higher education, Utah System of Higher Education; U.S. commissioner of education; state superintendent of public instruction, Utah State Office of Education; superintendent, Granite and Weber (Utah) school districts. (Interview: June 1990)

John W. Bennion, superintendent, Salt Lake School District. (Interview: May 1990)

Richard J. Bradford, representative, Utah State Legislature; chair, Public Education Joint Appropriations Subcommittee. (Interview: June 1990)

W. Hughes Brockbank, member, Utah State Board of Regents; representative, Utah State Legislature. (Interview: March 1990)

Lee H. Burke, assistant to the president, Utah State University. (Interview: June 1990)

Dee S. Burningham, director of bargaining and political action; Uniserve director; Utah Education Association. (Interview: March 1990)

John Reed Call, superintendent, Granite School District; president, Utah Society of Superintendents. (Interview: May 1990)

Ted Capener, vice president for university relations, University of Utah; chair, Utah Commission on Educational Excellence. (Interview: February 1990)

Richard J. Carling, senator, Utah State Legislature; chair, Higher Education Joint Appropriations Subcommittee. (Interview: June 1990)

Don A. Carpenter, associate commissioner for planning and facilities, Utah System of Higher Education; president, Jordan School District Board of Education. (Interviews: July, November, and December 1989)

Stanford Cazier, president, Utah State University. (Interview: March 1990)

Keith T. Checketts,, member and chair, Utah State Board of Education; member and co-chair, State Board of Education/State Board of Regents Joint Liaison Committee. (Interview: March 1990)

Carol Clark, education advisor to Governor Norman Bangerter. (Interview: December 1989)

Diane Cole, education writer, *Salt Lake Tribune.* (Interview: November 1983)

Betty Condie, president; director of professional development, Utah Education Association. (Interview: March 1990)

John M. R. Covey, member, State Board of Education; member, State Board of Education/State Board of Regents Joint Liaison Committee. (Interview: April 1990)

Anna Marie Dunlap, education advisor to Governor Scott Matheson; member, Utah Education Reform Steering Committee; member, Utah Commission on Educational Excellence. (Interviews: November 1983; January 1990)

Harden R. Eyring, executive assistant to the commissioner, Utah System of Higher Education. (Interview: December 1989)

Emanuel A. Floor, chair, Utah Education Reform Steering Committee. (Interview: March 1990)

Robert Fox, assistant to the president, University of Utah. (Interview: November 1983)

Cecilia H. Foxley, associate commissioner for academic affairs, Utah System of Higher Education; co-chair, Statewide Library Study Steering Committee. (Interview: January 1990)

Ruth Hardy Funk, member and chair, Utah State Board of Education; member, State Board of Education/State Board of Regents Joint Liaison Committee; member, Utah Commission on Educational Excellence. (Interview: March 1990)

Bernarr S. Furse, state superintendent for public instruction, Utah State Office of Education; member, State Board of Education/State Board of Regents Joint Liaison Committee. (Interview: January 1990)

Brent H. Goodfellow, representative and member, Executive Appropriations Committee, Utah State Legislature; executive assistant to the president, Salt Lake Community College. (Interview: April 1990)

Kolene F. Granger, associate superintendent for development, Utah State Office of Education. (Interview: December 1989)

Bruce Griffin, associate superintendent for operations, Utah State Office of Education. (Interviews: July, November, and December 1989)

Darlene Gubler, president, Utah Parent-Teacher Association. (Interview: January 1990)

Donald B. Holbrook, member and chair, Utah State Board of Regents; member and co-chair, State Board of Education/State Board of Regents Joint Liaison Committee. (Interview: February 1990)

Richard E. Kendell, superintendent, Davis School District; associate superintendent for political affairs, Utah State Office of Education; member, Utah Commission on Educational Excellence. (Interviews: April and May 1990)

William Rolfe Kerr, commissioner of higher education, Utah System of Higher Education; member, State Board of Education/State Board of Regents Joint Liaison Committee. (Interview: January, 1990)

Clifford S. LeFevre, member, Utah State Board of Regents; member, State Board of Education/State Board of Regents Joint Liaison Committee; representative, Utah State Legislature. (Interview: April 1990)

Max S. Lowe, assistant commissioner for vocational education, Utah System of Higher Education; vice president for academic affairs, Salt Lake Community College; director, Salt Lake Skills Center. (Interview: January 1990)

Daryl McCarty, executive director, Utah Education Association; associate superintendent, Utah State Office of Education. (Interviews: November 1983; January 1990)

Oscar W. McConkie, chair, Utah State Board of Education; co-chair, State Board of Education/State Board of Regents Joint Liaison Committee; member, Utah Education Reform Steering Committee; formerly president, Utah State Senate. (Interview: January 1990)

Scott M. Matheson, former governor, State of Utah. (Interview: February 1990)

M. Richard Maxfield, member and chair, Utah State Board of Education; member and co-chair, State Board of Education/State Board of Regents Joint Liaison Committee. (Interview: March 1990)

Jay A. Monson, member and chair, Utah State Board of Education. (Interview: March 1990)

James R. Moss, state superintendent of public instruction, Utah State Office of Education; member, State Board of Education/State Board of Regents Liaison Committee; representative, Utah State Legislature. (Interview: May 1990)

C. Gail Norris, associate commissioner for finance, Utah System of Higher Education. (Interview: December 1989)

Chase N. Peterson, president, University of Utah. (Interview: July 1990)

Warren E. Pugh, senator, Utah State Legislature; chair, Executive Appropriations Committee; member, Public Education Standing Committee; formerly, president, Utah State Senate; member, Utah Education Reform Steering Committee. (Interview: January 1990)

Eileen Rencher, public information coordinator, Utah State Office of Education. (Interview: October 1990)

Peter Scarlet, education writer, *Salt Lake Tribune.* (Interview: January 1990)

Gerald R. Sherratt, president, Southern Utah University. (Interview: July 1990)

R. J. Snow, vice president for university relations, University of Utah. (Interview: November 1983)

Ron Stephens, superintendent, Murray School District; representative and member, Executive Appropriations Committee, Utah State Legislature; member, Utah Education Reform Steering Committee. (Interview: March 1990)

Donald W. Ulmer, deputy executive director, Utah Education Association. (Interviews: November 1983; February 1990)

Vickie Varela, assistant to the commissioner for government and media relations, Utah System of Higher Education; education writer, *Deseret News.* (Interview: January 1990)

Henry O. Whiteside, education advisor to Governor Matheson; staff assistant to the Utah Education Reform Steering Committee. (Interview: January 1990)

Raymond W. Whittenburg, superintendent, Jordan School District; president, Utah Society of Superintendents. (Interview: June 1990)

Sue Marie Young, member and chair, Utah State Board of Regents; member, State Board of Education/State Board of Regents Joint Liaison Comittee. (Interview: June 1990)

Dale O. Zabriskie, member, Utah State Board of Regents. (Interview: April 1990)

ORGANIZATIONAL LISTING

Public Education Sector

Utah State Board of Education	Utah State Office of Education	Local District Superintendents
Checketts	Bell	Bennion
Covey	Furse	Call
Funk	Granger	Kendell
Maxfield	Griffin	Stephens
McConkie	Kendell	Whittenburg
Monson	McCarty	
	Moss	
	Rencher	

Utah Education Association

Baum
Burningham
Condie
McCarty
Ulmer

Higher Education Sector

Utah State Board of Regents	Utah System of Higher Education	Institutions
Barnes	Bell	Burke
Brockbank	Carpenter	Capener
Holbrook	Eyring	Cazier
LeFevre	Foxley	Fox
Young	Kerr	Goodfellow
Zabriskie	Lowe	Peterson
	Norris	Sherratt
	Varela	Snow

State Government Representatives, Civic Leaders, and Journalists

Legislature	Executive and Advisors	Civic Leaders and Journalists
Barlow	Clark	Cole
Bradford	Dunlap	Gubler
Brockbank	Matheson	Floor
Carling	Whiteside	Scarlet
Goodfellow		Varela
LeFevre		
McConkie		
Moss		
Pugh		
Stephens		

NOTES

PREFACE

1. These classic studies are, of course, Robert A. Dahl's study of community power in New Haven, *Who Governs? Democracy and Power in an American City* (New Haven: Yale University Press, 1961), and Robert S. and Helen M. Lynd's study of evolving cultural conflicts in Muncie, Indiana, *Middletown in Transition: A Study in Cultural Conflicts* (New York: Harcourt, 1937).

2. The very significant role that minutes played in the interpretations made in the study invites a further brief explanation and justification. Formal meeting minutes are an important organizational artifact; they become progressively more important as organizations increase in complexity. This is particularly true if the purpose of the organization is that of formulating public policy. The minutes of policymaking bodies are a tool that leaders use to push their work along. They communicate expectations and desires, legitimize organization decisions and actions, and ratify common understandings and agreements in a permanent way that can be considered and reread by others at their leisure. (Minutes can also be ignored, of course.) Because of their policy importance, minutes are carefully prepared by those charged with producing them to assure that everything that "should appear" in them does appear, that nothing which "should not appear" in them is printed, and that the wording in sensitive and important areas is correct and matches the intent of the administrator. The importance of meeting minutes of policy bodies to the researcher lies in this fact: they are deliberate documents.

Minutes are highly instructive both for what they say, and for what they do not say. The fact that an organization's minutes do not reflect activity on an issue is as important to the researcher as the fact that they do. By comparing the activity reflected in the minutes with other sources in the wider environment, notably the personal experience of participants, the minutes of other relevant organizations, and events reported in the mass media, one can identify the point in time at which the organization, qua organization, begins to deal with an issue and judge how that

181

action relates to the actions of other organizations being studied. Used in this fashion, minutes were indispensable to this research in describing and interpreting the actions and reactions of each organization and its leaders in the issue area cases.

3. See Lewis Anthony Dexter, *Elite and Specialized Interviewing* (Evanston, Illinois: Northwestern University Press, 1970), and Robert K. Merton and others, *The Focused Interview: A Manual of Problems and Procedures* (New York: Free Press, 1956).

4. See the Appendix for a listing of persons interviewed for the study.

CHAPTER 1

1. For example, Schmidt and Kochan define conflictual behavior as, "Actions by one member which are inconsistent with the goals or objectives of some other member." They define "'member' (party to conflict) as any decision-making unit (individual or collective) acting interdependently with one or more other decision-making units." See Stuart M. Schmidt and Thomas A. Kochan, "Conflict: Toward Conceptual Clarity," *Administrative Science Quarterly* 17 (1972): 362. E. W. Kelley puts the matter even more explicitly. In his discussion of political coalitions, Kelley presents a commonly held assumption in analyzing coalition behavior when he writes, "An actor is a person or a group of people who interact with others. A group of people can be considered an actor only if one can observe behavior of the group. The interactions of individuals within the group are definitionally irrelevant." See E. W. Kelley, "Utility Theory and Political Coalitions: Problems of Operationalization," in *The Study of Coalition Behavior: Theoretical Perspectives and Cases From Four Continents,* eds. Sven Groennings, E. W. Kelley, and Michael Leiserson (New York: Holt, Rinehart and Winston, Inc., 1970), 467.

2. Max Weber, "Bureaucracy," in *From Max Weber: Essays in Sociology*, eds. H. H. Gerth and C. Wright Mills (New York: Oxford University Press, 1958), 196-244. In addition to hierarchical authority relationships, a system of impersonal rules, and permanency, bureaucracy operates on the principle of a division of labor and specialization in which tasks are assigned as official duties to those having special training and expertise.

3. Max Weber, "The Meaning of Discipline," in *From Max Weber: Essays in Sociology,* eds. H. H. Gerth and C. Wright Mills (New York: Oxford University Press, 1958), 253–55.

4. Talcott Parsons, "Some Ingredients of a General Theory of Formal Organization," in his *Structure and Process in Modern Societies* (Glencoe, Ill.: Free Press, 1960), 59–96. See also James D. Thompson, *Organizations in Action* (New York: McGraw-Hill, 1967).

5. Bacharach and Lawler, whose explicit focus is intraorganizational relations, propose a division of the organization analogous to that of Parsons's into three subgroups of workers, middle management, and upper management. They provide a thorough political interpretation of intraorganizational political dynamics that

takes into full account the political conflicts and tensions as well as the coalitions and interest subgroupings making up the larger organization. See Samuel B. Bacharach and Edward J. Lawler, *Power and Politics in Organizations* (San Francisco: Jossey-Bass, 1980), 47. Structural and functional differentiation is a source of conflict in the organization because to the degree that subunits develop autonomy and distinct functions they develop as well their own distinctive goals, values, norms, and role perceptions accentuating differences that will lead them to compete even while they must also cooperate. See Ronald G. Corwin, "Patterns of Organizational Conflict," *Administrative Science Quarterly* 14 (1969): 508.

6. William M. Evan, "An Organization-Set Model of Interorganizational Relations," in *Interorganizational Decision Making,* ed. Matthew Tuite, Roger Chisholm, and Michael Radnor (Chicago: Aldine, 1972), 188–90.

7. W. Richard Scott, *Organizations: Rational, Natural, and Open Systems,* 2d ed. (Englewood Cliffs, N.J.: Prentice-Hall, Inc., 1987), 9.

8. Defining the complementary concepts of competition and cooperation has occupied social scientists for years. Margaret Mead writes simply that competition is "the act of seeking or endeavoring to gain what another is endeavoring to gain at the same time." Conversely, cooperation is "the act of working together to one end." See Margaret Mead, *Co-operation and Competition Among Primitive Peoples* (New York: McGraw-Hill, 1937), 8. J. B. Mallor defines a competitive situation as "one which stimulates the individual to strive against other individuals in his group for a goal object of which he hopes to be the sole or principle possessor." A cooperative situation is "one which stimulates an individual to strive with the other members of his group for a goal object which is to be shared equally among all of them." See J. B. Maller, "Co-operation and Competition: An Experimental Study in Motivation," Teachers College, Contributions to Education No. 384, 1929. Regarding the closely related concepts of conflict and competition, there is some conceptual agreement on the substantive differences between the two. For Paul White competition entails an acceptance and observation by A and B of allocative criteria; conflict occurs under the same relationship of A and B to scarce resources, but "in the absence of agreement either on decision-making rules or on allocative criteria." See Paul E. White, "Intra- and Inter-Organizational Studies: Do They Require Separate Conceptualizations?" *Administration and Society* 6 (May 1974): 139. Clinton Fink develops a similar differentiation when he writes that competition "involves established rules or institutionalized norms which limit what the competitors can do to each other in the course of striving to reach their respective goals . . . but conflict is unregulated (i.e., involves the violation of the rules)." See Clinton F. Fink, "Some Conceptual Difficulties in the Theory of Social Conflict," *Journal of Conflict Resolution* 12 (1969): 443. Schmidt and Kochan present two apt metaphors for conflict and competition. Competition they liken to a race, in which there is "parallel striving"; conflict they liken to a fight, in which there is "mutual interference." The essential difference between the two relational states of competition and conflict thus lies in the interference or "blocking activities" engaged in by the parties. See Schmidt and Kochan, "Conflict," 361.

9. The literature in comparative politics on "consociational democracy" and

"neo-corporatism" provides a rich empirical and theoretical perspective on the universal relationships between elites and the rank and file as denoted here. For example, see Arend Lijphart, "Typologies of Democratic Systems," in Arend Lijphart (ed.), *Politics in Europe: Comparisons and Interpretations* (Englewood Cliffs, N.J.: Prentice Hall, 1969), 59–72; Hans Daalder, "The Consociational Democracy Theme," 26 (July 1974): 606–9; Gerhard Lehmbruch, "Liberal Corporatism and Party Government," *Comparative Political Studies* 10 (April 1977): 112; and Leo Panitch, "The Development of Corporatism in Liberal Democracies," *Comparative Political Studies* 10 (April 1977): 66.

10. David L. Rogers and Joseph Molnar, "Organizational Antecedents of Role Conflict and Ambiguity in Top-Level Administrators," *Administrative Science Quarterly* 21 (December 1976): 598–99, 601.

11. Robert Michels's analysis of European socialist parties is the classic description of the psychological dynamics upon which a differentiation and separation between leaders and rank and file is based. See Robert Michels, *Political Parties: A Sociological Study of the Oligarchical Tendencies of Modern Democracy,* trans. Eden and Cedar Paul (Glencoe, Ill.: Free Press, 1915).

12. The practice of deliberately isolating leaders from their rank and file so as to support decision making is demonstrated in an analysis of the European Economic Community in which the EEC Council of Ministers has attempted to decrease conflict, in part by "insulating itself from certain demands coming from within the community. The major step along these lines was the council's adoption of the rule to hold its meetings behind closed doors." See John E. Schwarz, "Maintaining Coalitions: An Analysis of the EEC With Supporting Evidence from the Austrian Grand Coalition and The CDU/CSU," in Groennings, Kelley, and Leiserson, *Coalition Behavior,* 241.

13. Henry Mintzberg, *Power In and Around Organizations* (Englewood Cliffs, N.J.: Prentice-Hall, 1983). The sources of organizational power include the control of a resource, a technical skill or a body of knowledge that is both essential to the mission of the organization and in short supply, the organization's formal authority structure, and even access to other individuals or groups that control sources of power.

14. Mintzberg sees the board of directors of the organization as being a separate category that actually lies at the interface between the Internal and External Coalitions, but he places them within the External Coalition because they are not full-time employees.

15. Mintzberg, *Power,* 28.

16. Ibid., 109.

17. When the external power is significant but roughly divided and balanced between a small number of individuals or groups with conflicting goals the result is a Divided EC. When the external influencers are numerous and dispersed with limited commitments to the organization, or when the organization itself through internal leadership, expertise, or "brute size" is able to overpower the external influencers, then a Passive EC emerges.

18. Scott, *Organizations,* 22.

19. Ralph Goldman, "Conflict, Co-operation and Choice: An Exploration of Conceptual Relationships," in *Decisions, Values, and Groups,* Proceedings of a Conference held at the University of New Mexico, ed. Norman F. Washburne (New York: Macmillan, 1962), 419.

20. Matthew Tuite, Roger Chisholm, and Michael Radnor, eds., *Interorganizational Decision Making* (Chicago: Aldine, 1972), vii–viii.

CHAPTER 2

1. Theodore Lowi sees all modern organizations, as varied as churches, insurance companies, universities, and agencies of government, as having "at least one common trait; they impose an administrative process on as much of their internal structures and on as much of their environments as they possibly can." See Theodore J. Lowi, *The End of Liberalism: Ideology, Policy, and the Crisis of Public Authority* (New York: Norton, 1969), 40.

2. Thomas R. Dye, *Politics, Economics, and the Public: Policy Outcomes in the American States* (Chicago: Rand McNally, 1966), 74. Education expenditures have grown as a proportion of the gross national product. Total expenditures of educational institutions in 1959 equaled 4.8 percent of the gross national product; in 1986, they equaled 6.8 percent. See Thomas D. Snyder, *Digest of Education Statistics,* 1988 (Washington, D.C.: U.S. Government Printing Office, 1988), 29.

3. Larry Sabato, and Ann Bowman and Richard Kearney describe and document the changing contours of American state governments that have supported a resurgence of the states within the federal system. They note an increased organizational capacity to deal not only with new responsibilities but also with policy areas that have traditionally been theirs, such as education. The comparatively recent evolution within the states of centralized education governance structures that have pulled education policy issues, particularly those of funding, into the state-level arena are specific manifestations of the generally increasing organizational capacity of state governments. A major factor in the growth of the states' role in education policy is the increased strength of state governments growing out of the government reform of the 1960s and 1970s, a period coinciding with reforms in public education finance and higher education governance which, taken together, have been most instrumental in moving the states to center stage in education policy matters. The centralization of state-level higher education governance is an extension of precisely the same organizational logic that prompted the severe reduction of independent agencies and commissions by bringing them within the line authority structure of a more rationalized executive. For succinct overviews of state government reform in this period see Larry Sabato, *Good-bye to Good-time Charlie: The American Governorship Transformed,* 2d ed. (Washington, D.C.: CQ Press, 1983), 57–95; and Ann O'M. Bowman and Richard C. Kearney, *The Resurgence of the States* (Englewood Cliffs, N.J.: Prentice-Hall, 1986), 3–29.

4. Both Robert Berdahl, and Michael Usdan and associates use the terms

"interlevel" or "educational levels" in describing relationships between elementary-secondary and higher education. For the purposes of the political analysis of this study the interlevel terminology, with its inevitable connotation of vertical relationships of sub- and superordination between the two, has been avoided. It has been thought to be more analytically useful and correct to use the phrases "education sectors" or, more broadly, "organizational complexes." The political problem addressed by this study is most usefully conceptualized as political interaction between two very different, yet co-equal, policy actors. See Robert O. Berdahl, "Secondary and Postsecondary Education: The Politics of Accommodation," in *The Changing Politics of Education: Prospects for the 1980s,* eds. Edith K. Mosher and Jennings L. Wagoner, Jr. (Berkeley, Calif.: McCutchan, 1978), 227–58; and Michael D. Usdan, David W. Minar, and Emanuel Hurwitz, Jr., *Education and State Politics: The Developing Relationship Between Elementary-Secondary and Higher Education* (New York: Teachers College Press, 1969).

5. There being no provision elsewhere in the Constitution for federally legislated and supported public education, the Tenth Amendment has been interpreted as reserving to the states the function of public education. (See Arthur E. Wise, *Rich Schools, Poor Schools: The Promise of Equal Educational Opportunity* (Chicago: University of Chicago Press, 1972), 93–94.) This relationship applies equally to higher education. Under the assumptions of dual federalism, in which specific governmental functions were to be dealt with, more or less exclusively by either the federal or the state government (whichever was more appropriate), early federal involvement was minimal.

6. Lerue W. Winget, Edgar Fuller, and Terrel H. Bell, "State Departments of Education Within State Governments," in *Education in the States: Nation-Wide Development Since 1900*, eds. Edgar Fuller and Jim B. Pearson (Washington, D.C.: National Education Association of the United States, 1967), 78.

7. There were both practical and theoretical reasons to support and justify this thoroughgoing decentralization of governmental power through local school districts. Local control and funding of schools had been a practice fully established during the colonial period, and in this respect, national constitutional provisions for education, or lack of same, simply mirrored practice. The major theoretical justification for what Paul Ylvisaker and others have referred to as the "areal distribution of power" as found, in this case, in the governmental structure of the local school district, is that it serves "to keep governmental power close to its origins, and government officials within reach of their masters." See Paul Ylvisaker, "Some Criteria for a 'Proper' Areal Division of Governmental Powers," in Area and Power: A Theory of Local Government, ed. Arthur Maass (Glencoe, Ill.: Free Press, 1959), 32.

8. Morton Grodzins and Daniel Elazar, "Centralization and Decentralization in the American Federal System," in *A Nation of States: Essays on the American Federal System*, 2d ed., ed. Robert A. Goldwin (Chicago: Rand McNally, 1974), 2-4.

9. See Thomas D. Snyder, *Digest of Education Statistics, 1987* (Washington, D.C.: U.S. Government Printing Office, 1987), 107.

10. Richard G. Salmon and S. Kern Alexander, *The Historical Reliance of Public Education upon the Property Tax: Current Problems and Future Role* (Cambridge: Lincoln Institute of Land Policy, 1983).

11. The intellectual bases of foundation formula strategies had been laid in the first quarter of the century by men like Elwood Cubberley, George Strayer, Robert Haig, and Paul Mort. See Robert H. Salisbury, "State Politics and Education," in *Politics in the American States: A Comparative Analysis*, eds. Herbert Jacob and Kenneth N. Vines (Boston: Little, Brown, 1965), 340–41.

12. The most well known of these cases was the California case of *Serrano v. Priest* (1971) in which the plaintiffs argued, among other points, that actual educational expenditures were a function of the taxable wealth within a school district, but that the equal protection provisions of the California constitution are based on the wealth of the state as a whole. On this claim, the California Supreme Court held that educational expenditures must be a function of the state's wealth in total. Court decisions comparable to *Serrano* were rendered shortly thereafter in a half-dozen other states. See Roald F. Campbell and others, *The Organization and Control of American Schools*, 5th ed. (Columbus, Ohio: Charles E. Merrill, 1985), 162. A federal district court decision that held that the Texas school finance law did not guarantee equal protection and was, therefore, unconstitutional, was appealed by the state of Texas to the U.S. Supreme Court. In *San Antonio Independent School District et al. v. Rodriguez et al.* (1973) the Supreme Court ruled significantly that the equalization demanded under the suit was a state, not a federal, problem. The Roderiguez decision shifted attention and responsibility back to the states where it has remained.

13. See Frederick M. Wirt and Michael W. Kirst, *The Politics of Education: Schools in Conflict* (Berkeley, Calif.: McCutchan, 1982), 236.

14. See Snyder, *Digest of Education Statistics, 1987*, 29.

15. Ibid., 107.

16. Ibid.

17. For data covering the years 1932 through 1962 See Winget, Fuller, and Bell, "State Departments," 78. For data for the years 1972 and 1977 see Deil S. Wright, *Understanding Intergovernmental Relations,* 2d ed. (Monterey, Calif.: Brooks/Cole, 1982), 10.

18. See Winget, Fuller, and Bell, "State Departments," 78.

19. R. L. Johns, "State Financing of Elementary and Secondary Education," in *Education in the States: Nation-Wide Development Since 1900*, eds. Edgar Fuller and Jim B. Pearson (Washington, D.C.: National Education Association of the United States, 1967), 207.

20. A relatively early, high-profile federal program, the National Defense Education Act (NDEA) of 1958, was intended to stimulate achievement in the study and teaching of "defense-related" subjects like science, mathematics, and foreign languages. Its passage by the Congress was prompted by the startling scientific achievement of the Soviet Union in launching the earth's first permanent artificial satellite. The direct impact of NDEA on public education has not been great.

21. Terry Sanford has written that "the national government came to the general support of education (mostly in the guise of national defense and help for disadvantaged children) because the states were not spending enough to reach the goals most Americans considered imperative." See Terry Sanford, *Storm Over the States* (New York: McGraw-Hill, 1967), 28. Probing Sanford's assertion, it is interesting to note that in 1964, before ESEA, the federal share of expenditures for public education was less than 5 percent. In 1980, fifteen years after ESEA's passage, the federal percentage was still less than 10 percent, a proportion that represents the high-water mark of federal spending on education, which has since declined. These modest federal percentages translate into large amounts of money and represent a considerable change in federal funding policy for education. For example, in 1982, Department of Education expenditures were $14 billion, whereas the Office of Education expenditures in 1964 had been only $673,005. See John Ellis, "Since 1965: The Impact of Federal Funds on Public Education," *Education and Urban Society* 15 (May 1983): 353. Nevertheless, it is still the states and the localities that provide more than 90 percent of the financial resources supporting the nation's public schools.

22. See Wright, *Understanding Intergovernmental Relations*, 20. Title I, the largest of the ESEA programs, provided funds that were to be administered through state offices of education for educationally disadvantaged children. Title V earmarked funds for the revitalization and strengthening of state-level education agencies.

23. Ellis, "Impact of Federal Funds," 358.

24. Wirt and Kirst, *Politics of Education*, 234.

25. In successive polls of the nation's governors taken in 1979 and 1981, 55 percent and 47.7 percent in each respective year perceived education as one of six major issues confronting a state governor on a perennial basis. See Thad L. Beyle, "Governors," in *Politics in the American States: A Comparative Analysis*, 4th ed., eds. Virginia Gray, Herbert Jacob, and Kenneth N. Vines (Boston: Little, Brown, 1983), 203–4.

26. Roald F. Campbell and others, *Organization and Control of American Schools,* 5th ed. (Columbus, Ohio: Charles E. Merrill, 1985), 58–60.

27. Susan Fuhrman, "State-Level Politics and School Financing," in *The Changing Politics of School Finance,* Third Annual Yearbook of the American Education Finance Association, eds. Nelda H. Cambron-McCabe and Allan Odden (Cambridge, Mass.: Ballinger, 1982), 53.

28. Bowman and Kearney, *The Resurgence of the States*, 205–6.

29. Berdahl, "Secondary and Postsecondary Education," 237–38.

30. See Richard Hofstadter and C. DeWitt Hardy, *The Development and Scope of Higher Education in the United States* (New York: Columbia University Press, 1952), 4–5.

31. John Marshall's written decision for the Court in the *Dartmouth College Case* (1819) established the legal inviolability of state charters to private colleges. Charters given to public institutions, in contrast to those given to private colleges, could be altered later by action of the state legislature. See John D. Millett,

Financing Higher Education in the United States (New York: Columbia University Press, 1952), 4.

32. See Hofstadter, *Development and Scope of Higher Education*, 28. The policy of the federal government to set aside a portion of the public domain for the support of education went back to the Articles of Confederation period and the Northwest Ordinance of 1787, when the Congress gave a land grant to the Ohio Company to support higher education. This policy reached its fullest expression in the Morrill Land Grant Act (1862) that ratified an established policy pattern in which by 1857, the year in which the Act was first introduced, Congress had granted four million acres to fifteen states for the endowment of state universities.

33. Specific manifestations of the "self-denying ordinance" as found commonly throughout the states include the following governmental practices with higher education institutions which differentiate them from other agencies of state government. In many states, constitutional recognition, in one form or another, is extended to higher education (as is the case as well for public education). Board members were either elected or appointed for longer terms than most other public offices, often with the provision that the selection be nonpolitical. Corporate powers have been conferred on the states' highest education boards that have the power to borrow funds, and to disburse them directly. Academic policy matters relating to programs and curriculum, graduation and degrees, and the administration of academic and professional personnel have come fully within the authority exercised by the institutions of higher education and their boards.

34. Lyman A. Glenny, *Autonomy of Public Colleges: The Challenge of Coordination* (New York: McGraw-Hill, 1959), 14.

35. Aims C. McGuinness Jr., "State Coordination and Governance of Higher Education: Implications for Governors," *State Government* 58 (Summer, 1985): 74. This number included all but three small states whose higher education institutions are so few in number as not to require a separate state-level board.

36. Glenny, *Autonomy*, 12.

37. Lyman A. Glenny, *State Coordination of Higher Education: The Modern Concept* (Denver: State Higher Education Executive Officers, 1985), 1, 4.

38. Data drawn from Thomas D. Snyder, *Digest of Education Statistics, 1988* (Washington, D.C.: U.S. Government Printing Office, 1988), 141.

39. John D. Millett, *Conflict in Higher Education: State Government Coordination Versus Institutional Independence* (San Francisco: Jossey-Bass, 1984), 6.

40. Snyder, *Digest of Education Statistics, 1988,* 143.

41. Ibid., 141.

42. Millett, *Conflict in Higher Education,* 6.

43. Snyder, *Digest of Education Statistics, 1988*, 141. While these figures are unadjusted for inflation, Millett calculates roughly that the adjusted increase between 1950 and 1980 was at least twelve times. See Millett, *Conflict in Higher Education*, 14.

44. Data drawn from Snyder, *Digest of Education Statistics, 1987*, 120. Dollar figures are not adjusted for inflation.

45. Lyman A. Glenny, "Higher Education and the Law," in *The University as*

an Organization, ed. James A. Perkins (New York: McGraw-Hill, 1973), 185. Most observers agree that the primary immediate reasons for the establishment of statewide coordinating and governance structures for higher education include several interrelated factors. See Glenny, *Autonomy,* 17–22; and *State Coordination,* 1–4, 20; Robert O. Berdahl, *Statewide Coordination of Higher Education* (Washington, D.C.: American Council on Education, 1971), 28–30; and Millett, *Conflict in Higher Education,* 26. The proliferation of academic programs, and particularly the actual or potential duplication of high-cost graduate and professional programs, has been an important source of both legislative and executive concern. In the face of increasing urbanization, it has often been the case that urban areas and institutions have sought the enriched programs offered by the rurally located research university. The highly visible conflicts between the aspirations of individuals representing separate institutions (often operated under separate governing boards) confronted legislators with difficult choices. Institutional lobbying, often self-serving and intense, was an irritant to legislators who had the unpleasant responsibility of distributing limited resources among too many institutions competing among themselves for students, programs, and dollars. See Aims C. McGuinness, Jr., "Status of State Coordination and Governance of Higher Education: 1985," in *State Postsecondary Education Structures Handbook, 1986* (Denver: Education Commission of the States, 1986), 2. It has often been the case that major reorganizations in higher education governance have come in the wake of less dramatic efforts at solving the problems that have failed. While critics of centralized state-level governance remain, Lyman Glenny renders the significant judgment that through coordination institutions of higher education enjoy a greater level of funding equity and security in their roles than would have been achieved through direct and unbridled competition among themselves.

46. See Millett, *Conflict in Higher Education,* 1. The report referred to, *Three Thousand Futures,* was published in 1980 by the Carnegie Council on Policy Studies in Higher Education.

47. Revised portions of this section were previously published by the author in the *Journal of Education Finance* 12 (Winter 1987) under the title "Political Competition and Cooperation Between Public and Higher Education Agencies of State Government." They are used here by permission of the publisher.

48. See James Q. Wilson, *Political Organizations* (New York: Basic Books, 1973), 261–80. Peter Blau makes the same point in this way: "Competition occurs only among like social units that have the same objective and not among unlike units with different objectives—among political parties and among business concerns but not between a party and a firm . . ." See P. M. Blau, "Social Exchange Among Collectivities," in *Interorganizational Relations,* ed. William M. Evan (Philadelphia: University of Pennsylvania Press, 1978), 63.

49. Aaron Wildavsky, *The Politics of the Budgetary Process,* 3rd ed. (Boston: Little, Brown 1979), 4.

50. Berdahl, "Secondary and Postsecondary Education," 234. See note 4 on "educational level" terminology used here.

51. Fuhrman, "State-Level Politics and School Financing," 59.

52. Thomas Dye writes that stable patterns of individual and group behavior may affect the content of public policy in that organizational structures may facilitate some policy outcomes and obstruct others. However, the relationship between structure and policy outcomes is not direct. See Thomas R. Dye, *Understanding Public Policy*, 5th ed. (Englewood Cliffs, N.J.: Prentice-Hall, 1984), 21–23.

53. See Stephen K. Bailey, "A Comparison of the University with a Government Bureau," in *University as an Organization*, 134. To expand on Bailey's insight, which he applied only to the university, we may say that public education as well as higher education are increasingly becoming a part of the political processes affecting all government agencies.

54. See Usdan, *Education and State Politics*, 227–30, 250. In this important work, Usdan and his colleagues focused their attention on the problem of the political relationships between public education and higher education within the context of state governments that were then clearly emerging as dominant influences in education policy. Their work identified several issues of particular relevance to both sectors of the education community, including state funding; community colleges (grades 13 and 14) and vocational-technical education, the education and certification of teachers for the elementary-secondary schools, and public school curriculum and academic standards. According to Usdan's analysis, these areas are of basic importance to both public and higher education, and within the context of state-level structures will bring them into increasing contact and require their interaction. Such interaction can take the form of either conflict or cooperation. Within the twelve states surveyed, Usdan found relationships ranging on a continuum from manifest conflict to latent conflict to quiescence, and finally, to cooperation. Manifest conflict and cooperation, the two extremes of the continuum, were usually found as responses to specific issues, and were most often temporary.

55. Twenty-two of these districts are countywide, thirteen are composed of a part of a county larger than a single municipality, and five districts correspond to the five cities in the state of the first and second class.

56. Roald F. Campbell, "Utah," in *Shaping Education Policy in the States,* eds. Susan Fuhrman and Alan Rosenthal (Washington, D.C.: The Institute for Educational Leadership, 1981), 103.

57. *Statistical Abstract of the United States,* 1988, xx.

58. In a 1983 study in Utah, legislators were asked to indicate which interest groups had been most influential during their tenure in the legislature. The Utah Education Association was ranked first in this category. Similar results were obtained in a 1966 study in which both legislators and lobbyists ranked education the most influential interest group in the state. For the results of the 1983 study and the comparison with the 1966 study by Zeigler and Baer see Ronald H. Hrebenar, Melanee Cherry, and Kathanne Greene, "Utah: Church and Corporate Power in the Nation's Most Conservative State," in *Interest Group Politics in the American West*, eds. Ronald J. Hrebenar and Clive S. Thomas (Salt Lake City: University of Utah Press), 119–20. Interestingly, a 1962 study of legislative politics in four other

states (not including Utah) found that education associations were among those interest groups regarded by legislators as least likely to be unselfish or public spirited, but most able to mobilize votes and affect the outcome of elections. John C. Wahlke and others, *The Legislative System: Explorations in Legislative Behavior* (New York: John Wiley and Sons, 1962), 336–37.

59. Campbell, "Utah," 106.

60. To avoid predisposing or leading the subjects' responses in one direction or another, as the interview was arranged and scheduled the topic was always described to the subject in the most general terms, such as "the politics of education in Utah." No mention was made at this stage of any interest in the competitive or cooperative interrelationships between the public education and higher education communities.

61. Campbell, "Utah," 107.

62. In fact, the 1992 legislature established a very formal nominating procedure for the State Board of Education that is intended to combine the benefits of the careful screening and review of qualifications associated with the gubernatorial appointment process with the democratic values of popular election. District nominating committees henceforth will present a list of up to five qualified individuals from which the governor will select two individuals to appear as candidates on the ballot. See *Utah Code Annotated* 53A-1-103.

63. Campbell, "Utah," 103.

64. McGuinness, "Status of State Coordination and Governance of Higher Education: 1985," 1.

65. Douglas L. Parker, "Senators Okay Single College Board," *Salt Lake Tribune*, 12 February 1969, A-1.

66. In language dating from 1911, Article Ten, Section 2 of the state constitution defined the composition of the public school system to include, "kindergarten schools; common schools, consisting of primary and grammar grades; high schools; an agricultural college; a university; and such other schools as the Legislature may establish" (Art. 10, Sec. 2).

67. Dave Jonsson, "State Supreme Court Backs Higher Education Board," *Salt Lake Tribune*, 1 February 1973, B-1.

68. See *State Board of Education v. State Board of Higher Education*, Utah 505 P. 2d 1193 (1973).

69. Dave Jonsson, "Board of Education Files Challenge on Control of Colleges," *Salt Lake Tribune*, 4 September 1971, 17.

70. Dave Jonsson, "Top Court Hears Views in School Board Issue," *Salt Lake Tribune,* 14 November 1972, 17.

71. John Cummins, "Handling of Education Suit Draws Challenge," *Salt Lake Tribune*, 1 September 1971, 19, 24.

72. Minutes of the SBE/SBR Liaison Committee, 9 May 1983.

73. In the course of an extended luncheon interview, one powerful state senator went to great lengths, including making a telephone call to the legal officer of the State Office of Education, to reaffirm to himself and to the author what the 1988 education amendment to the constitution had actually done.

74. See *Utah Code Annotated* Title 53A-1-501. Interestingly, the liaison committee is defined in Title 53A which covers the administration of public education at the state level, rather than Title 53B which deals with higher education.

75. In the context of the interview, it was equally clear to the author that legislators of highest importance to both public and higher education did know of the liaison committee.

CHAPTER 3

1. See, for example, Education Commission of the States, *State Postsecondary Education Structures Handbook, 1986* (Denver: Education Commission of the States, 1986); Council of Chief State School Officers, *Educational Governance in the States: A Status Report on State Boards of Education, Chief State School Officers, and State Education Agencies* (Washington, D.C.: U.S. Department of Education, 1983.); and Education Commission of the States, *State Governance of Education: 1983* (Denver: Education Commission of the States, 1983) for an informative presentation of both public and higher education governance structures nationwide.

2. Nils Brunsson writes that the primary purpose of the case study method should be "to generate theories formulated for and based on specific social situations, which have been studied empirically. These theories form 'languages' that provide means for understanding the situations studied. Such theories can then be used by people involved in similar situations, when they are trying to improve their understanding of their own reality. . . . In-depth case studies come to represent an important method and their presentation an important element in scientific reporting. . . . But the main purpose is to provide hypotheses, suggestions and options for readers trying to understand situations familiar to them." See Nils Brunsson, *The Irrational Organization: Irrationality as a Basis for Organizational Action and Change* (New York: John Wiley and Sons, 1985), 11.

3. Roald F. Campbell, "Utah," in *Shaping Education Policy in the States*, eds. Susan Fuhrman and Alan Rosenthal (Washington, D.C.: The Institute for Educational Leadership, 1981), 111.

4. U.S., Department of Commerce, Bureau of the Census, *Statistical Abstract of the United States, 1988*, 108th ed. (Washington, D.C.: Government Printing Office, 1989), xvii.

5. Ibid., xxiv.

6. Ronald J. Hrebenar, Melanee Cherry, and Kathanne Greene, "Utah: Church and Corporate Power in the Nation's Most Conservative State," in *Interest Group Politics In the American West*, eds. Ronald J. Hrebenar and Clive S. Thomas (Salt Lake City: University of Utah Press, 1987), 120.

7. See chapter 8 in Douglas M. Abrams, "Organizational Strategies of Political Competition and Cooperation: Public Education and Higher Education Interests in Utah, 1983-1989," Ph.D. diss., University of Utah, 1991.

8. James Q. Wilson, *Political Organizations* (New York: Basic Books), 13.

9. For the purposes of analysis, Bacharach and Lawler propose that "[i]nterest groups will form coalitions when the magnitude of outcomes expected as a part of a coalition multiplied by the probability of achieving these outcomes as a coalition exceed the magnitude of outcomes expected when operating as a single interest group multiplied by the probability of achieving these outcomes as a single interest group." See Samuel B. Bacharach and Edward J. Lawler, Power and Politics in Organizations (San Francisco: Jossey-Bass, 1980), 80–81.

10. Regarding the rationality of political and organizational decision making, Lewis Dexter describes the approach and orientation of students who have interviewed him as a person active in politics. He writes, "In most cases, it seems to me [interviewers] have tried to make the story I reported to them more coherent, more 'rational,' than in fact it was. . . . Some of the interviewers' imputations seem to have been that we acted in terms of power-oriented politics; other imputations were, I think, more oriented toward some kind of norm derived from administrative theory. But, in either case, the interviewers wanted answers reporting sharply motivated behavior, whereas in fact, so far as I could recollect, we acted in response to a complex and often inchoate set of desires and beliefs which could not be stated sharply." Dexter concludes that "the experienced person in any field knows that things happen in a subtle, confused, foggy, complex way, which cannot be stated or codified simply; the person without practical experience and without much contact wants to sharpen and simplify." See Lewis Anthony Dexter, *Elite and Specialized Interviewing* (Evanston, Ill.: Northwestern University Press, 1970), 19–20.

CHAPTER 4

1. Revised portions of this issue area case were previously published by the author in the *Journal of Education Finance* 12 (Winter 1987) under the title "Political Competition and Cooperation Between Public and Higher Education Agencies of State Government." They are used here by permission of the publisher.

2. Dwight Waldo, *The Enterprise of Public Administration: A Summary View* (Novato, Calif.: Chandler and Sharp, 1980), 185.

3. For the discussion that follows see chapter 13, "Competition and Coalitions," in James Q. Wilson, *Political Organizations* (New York: Basic Books, 1973), 261–80.

4. David B. Truman, *The Governmental Process* (New York: Alfred A. Knopf, 1953), 363–64.

5. For Wilson's discussion of political coalitions see Wilson, *Political Organizations,* 267; for his discussion of political alliances, see 278.

6. Ibid., 275.

7. In their empirical study of health organizations, Van de Ven and Walker present evidence that supports Wilson's hypothesis. They conclude that the greatest

amount of interorganizational coordination occurs in short-term, ad hoc, informal arrangements between pairs of organizations in which an entrepreneur within a single organization establishes ad hoc relationships to meet the needs of his organization. See Andrew H. Van de Ven and Gordon Walker, "The Dynamics of Interorganizational Coordination," *Administrative Science Quarterly* 12 (1984): 598.

8. Wilson, *Political Organizations,* 278.

9. Morton Deutsch uses the specialized terminology "promotively interdependent" to designate cooperative social goals, and "contriently interdependent" to designate competitive social goals. See his "Theory of Co-Operation and Competition," *Human Relations* 2 (1949): 132–33.

10. Diane Cole, "Regents Cut Plea for Funds Between Breaths," *Salt Lake Tribune* 12 October 1983, B-1.

11. Charles Seldin, "Higher Education Fund Erosion Perils Utah," *Salt Lake Tribune,* 21 October 1983, B-1.

12. Diane Cole, "Education Board Backs School Reform Package," *Salt Lake Tribune,* 19 November 1983, B-1.

13. In November of 1983 the author interviewed a vice president of university relations at the University of Utah on the joint funding strategy. Having concluded the interview, he cautioned the graduate student against "going around and stirring things up" because the alliance at that time was "like a house of cards."

14. See John W. Kingdon, *Agendas, Alternatives, and Public Policies* (Boston: Little, Brown, 1984). Kingdon suggests that for an issue to be placed on the public agenda and be acted upon requires "fertile soil" (a generalized concern over, or awareness of, a problem) in which new ideas can take root, coupled with what is often a fortuitous conjunction of specific circumstances, which creates a "policy window," a short period of time in which "something can be done."

15. Terrel Bell had been a district superintendent in the Weber School District, as well as in the state's largest district, the Granite School District. He has the unique distinction of having been the only individual to have served as the Utah state superintendent of public instruction (from 1963 to 1970), and the Utah commissioner of higher education (from 1976 to 1980).

16. National Commission on Excellence in Education, *A Nation at Risk: The Imperative for Educational Reform* (Washington, D.C.: Department of Education, April, 1983).

17. Kingdon, *Agendas,* 173.

18. Minutes of the State Board of Education meeting, 7 June 1983.

19. The commission membership included the president of the state PTA, a parent (who would later be elected to the State Board of Education), an official of the Utah Education Association, a teacher, a member of the school boards association, a vocational educator, a local district superintendent, a secondary school principal, and the state superintendent—all from the public education community. Three of the individuals appointed were board chairmen or presidents of major private business corporations; one was the executive director of the Chamber of Commerce. Representing higher education were the deans of the colleges of

education of the state's three universities, and the president of a junior college. The legislature was represented by a senator, and the Speaker of the House (who would later be elected governor).

20. The Utah Commission was divided into three subcommittees as follows: Subcommittee on Recruiting, Rewarding, and Retaining Good Teachers; Subcommittee on Restructuring the School Curriculum; and Subcommittee on How Time in School Can be Better Utilized for Purposes of Instruction. Each subcommittee prepared its own section of the commission's final report.

21. Utah Commission on Educational Excellence, Report of the Utah Commission on Educational Excellence (Salt Lake City, Utah: Utah State Board of Education, 7 October 1983).

22. Minutes of the State Board of Education meeting, 18 November 1983.

23. Minutes of the State Board of Regents meeting, 3 March 1983.

24. Minutes of the State Board of Regents meeting, 23 August 1983.

25. Minutes of the State Board of Regents meetings, 12–13 September 1983.

26. Minutes of the State Board of Education meeting, 30 September 1983.

27. The poll showed 71 percent of the population favoring a tax increase to finance public schools, with 46 percent "doubting" that higher education received enough money. See "Utahns Favor Tax Boost for Schools," *Salt Lake Tribune,* 16 August 1983, B-1. The results of the poll, very supportive of the committee's aims, were received and published at the crest of national debate on the quality of public schools. The Utah poll, commissioned by the *Salt Lake Tribune,* received results on a survey just before the legislature convened the following January in which public support for additional heavy spending in education had evaporated.

28. See Brent Steel and Taketsugu Tsurutani, "From Consensus to Dissensus: A Note on Postindustrial Political Parties," *Comparative Politics* (January 1986): 240.

29. Aaron Wildavsky, *The Politics of the Budgetary Process,* 3d ed. (Boston: Little, Brown, 1979), 16. For an enlightening treatment of a national culture in which the "fair-shares" principle conditions all political activity, as contrasted with the American political norm of "fair play, and the winner take all," see chapter 5, "Politics: Higher Interests and Fair Shares," in Ezra F. Vogel, *Japan as Number One: Lessons for America* (Cambridge: Harvard University Press, 1979), 97–130.

30. Minutes of the SBE/SBR Joint Liaison Committee meeting, 5 October 1983.

31. Minutes of the State Board of Regents meeting, 11 October 1983.

32. Ibid.

33. Ibid.

34. Utah Education Reform Steering Committee, *Education in Utah: A Call to Action* (Salt Lake City, November 1983).

35. Minutes of the State Board of Education meeting, 18 November 1983.

36. Utah Foundation, "1984-85 Funding for Education in Utah," Research Report No. 451, May 1984.

37. Mike Gorrell, "State Senator Raps Priority for Higher Education," *Salt Lake*

Tribune, 12 February 1984, B-1.

38. Minutes of the State Board of Regents meeting, 10–11 September 1984.

39. Ibid.

40. Ibid.

41. Minutes of the SBE/SBR Joint Liaison Committee meeting, 4 November 1984.

42. In the interview, the author had the impression that the phrase "lack of leadership" was intended as a subjective comment on the personal qualities of the individuals on the board, not as an objective observation that individuals formerly involved in the strategy had left the scene.

43. The standard term for the State Board of Education is four years, but McConkie's seat had been assigned a two-year term as the result of a redistricting plan implemented in 1982. McConkie's personal impact was so great that—in retrospect—even those working closely with him could hardly believe that he served as chairman for only two years. In an interview, former Governor Matheson expressed disappointment that McConkie had not run again: "He let me down."

44. Minutes of the SBE/SBR Joint Liaison Committee meeting, 3 November 1987.

45. James Moss resigned his position as state superintendent of public instruction in April 1990. He was the state's fourth state superintendent of public instruction in eight years.

46. Minutes of the SBE/SBR Joint Liaison Committee meeting, 8 March 1989.

47. Minutes of the SBE/SBR Joint Liaison Committee meeting, 11 September 1989.

48. Governor Matheson excluded the UEA from the steering committee as a principle of executive action that seeks the public, not special, interest. Interestingly, his education advisor in a 1990 interview felt in retrospect that the exclusion was a mistake, that the same result could have been achieved with the UEA having formal membership on the committee. Given the consistently adamant opposition of the UEA to the steering committee's program centered around merit pay, in the judgment of the author, this is unlikely.

49. Bacharach and Lawler, *Power and Politics,* 68.

50. Stanley Rothman, in a critique of the cross-cutting cleavages hypothesis of pluralist political theory argues that "it is not the rank and file which moderates demands, but rather a prudent leadership which seems to have a better conception of what political and social realities permit." In support of this assertion, Rothman cites the actions of English trade union leaders who have been more willing than the rank and file to accept wage restraints because of their awareness of objective economic problems. Had he chosen to continue his description of the reciprocal relationship between elites and rank and file he would also have noted the difficulty with which such union leaders maintain their office in the face of disapproval from their rank and file. (See Stanley Rothman, "Systematic Political Theory: Observations on the Group Approach," *American Political Science Review* 54 [March 1960]: 21–25.)

CHAPTER 5

1. Gary Dessler, *Organization and Management* (Reston, Va.: Reston Publishing Company, 1982), 435.

2. Stuart M. Schmidt and Thomas A. Kochan, "Conflict: Toward Conceptual Clarity," *Administrative Science Quarterly* 17 (1972): 365. See also Joseph J. Molnar and David L. Rogers, "A Comparative Model of Interorganizational Conflict," *Administrative Science Quarterly* 24 (September 1979): 406.

3. Vocational education includes prevocational and exploratory vocational education, industrial arts, home economics, career education, and an increasingly growing area of training in the use of high technology (automation).

4. There is a long-standing and continuing tension between the values underlying education and the life of the mind for its own sake (as espoused in academic or liberal education) and education as a means to a material end (as in vocational education). The contrast of the two goes back at least to Plato as he presents Socrates in the opening pages of *The Republic* making a metaphorical descent from Athens (the world of the mind—academic education) to the house of the merchant Cephalus at the Piraeus (the world of commerce and material gain—vocational education).

5. Utah Foundation, "Utah's Area Vocational Centers," *Research Report,* no. 506 (December 1988).

6. Vocational education has a legislative politics of its own outside both public and higher education channels. The author was invited to lunch by a leader of senate proponents of vocational education. Having concluded the interview with the author, the senator asked for the check and was informed that "the gentleman sitting in the corner" had already picked up the tab for the senator and his guest, and quietly left. Upon inquiry, it was determined that "the gentleman" was the director of the local Area Vocational Center.

7. Minutes of the SBE/SBR Joint Liaison Committee meeting, 24 September 1984.

8. In 1989, total state and federal funds, plus dedicated credits (tuition payments) expended in the AVCs alone equalled $14.3 million. See the Utah Foundation, "Utah's Area Vocational Centers."

9. A specific case in point of "legitimate" vocational education administered through higher education is a continuing education program servicing high-tech industries like the Thiokol Corporation in Box Elder County, Utah with noncredit/nondegree, high-skill instruction. The question raised here is of the partnership between the public and private sectors; the concept of economic development is now used to justify relationships that would have been questioned a decade ago.

10. Utah Foundation, "Utah's Area Vocational Centers," 162.

11. Minutes of the State Board of Education meeting, 16 October 1987. This discussion took place prior to the introduction of extensive short term intensive training in the community colleges.

12. See the discussion of this issue in chapter 2, pages 43–45.

13. Minutes of the State Board of Education meeting, 6–7 November 1986.

14. Peter Scarlet, "Vocational Education Needs Attention, Legislators Tell Regents," *Salt Lake Tribune,* 2 May 1988, S3.

15. Minutes of the State Board of Education meeting, 16 August 1988.

16. "State School Board OKs VoEd Changes, Stirs Squabble with Higher Education," *Salt Lake Tribune,* 20 August 1988, B6-3.

17. Minutes of the SBE/SBR Joint Liaison Committee meeting, 14 May 1984.

18. Minutes of the SBE/SBR Joint Liaison Committee meeting, 11 June 1984.

19. Minutes of the SBE/SBR Joint Liaison Committee meeting, 9 July 1984.

20. Minutes of the SBE/SBR Joint Liaison Committee meeting, 4 November 1984.

21. Mimeograph, SBE/SBR Salt Lake Skills Center Study Committee, *Summary Report,* 6 December 1985. The full text of the options given was as follows:

> 1. Support funding for the Salt Lake Skills Center as currently budgeted through the 1986 Utah Legislature, after which full funding and governance will be transferred to and assumed by the State Board of Regents, recognizing Skills Center functions as fully compatible with the role and mission of [the] Utah Technical College at Salt Lake.
>
> 2. Amend [the] Utah Code 53-16-5 pertaining to the State Board for Vocational Education, defining more clearly the role and mission of Area Vocational Centers and Skills Centers in harmony with the recently approved Utah Vocational Education Master Plan, and placing Skills Centers under control and management of the State Board for Vocational Education, with a stipulation that the Salt Lake Skills Center not become an Area Vocational Center.
>
> 3. Delay any movement to transfer funding or governance of the Salt Lake Skills Center until current higher education/legislative master planning committees can complete their findings and recommendations regarding the needs and demands of students and employers, and the most effective and efficient configuration of institutions and centers to serve those needs.

22. Minutes of the SBE/SBR Joint Liaison Committee meeting, 16 December 1985.

23. Ibid.

24. Ibid.

25. Minutes of the SBE/SBR Joint Liaison Committee meeting, 6 January 1986.

26. Ibid.

27. Minutes of the SBE/SBR Joint Liaison Committee meeting, 1 June 1987.

28. Minutes of the State Board of Education meeting, 9 April 1987.

29. Minutes of the SBE/SBR Joint Liaison Committee meeting, 13 April 1987.

30. Interestingly, during the next legislative session (the 1988 legislature) the house majority leader sponsored a bill that would do just this, move the AVCs under the Board of Regents. The state superintendent assured the State Board of Education that it would fail, which it did. See "Switch Reins of VoEd to Regents? House Bill Draws Stiff Opposition," *Salt Lake Tribune,* 12 February 1988, B1-6.

31. Minutes of the SBE/SBR Joint Liaison Committee meeting, 6 November 1987.

32. Utah State Board for Vocational Education, and the Utah State Board of Regents, *A Powerful Resource for Human and Economic Development Serving Students and Utah's Economy: Utah's 1988–93 Vocational-Technical Education Master Plan. DRAFT*, May 1988, 21.

33. Minutes of the State Board of Regents meeting, 11 November 1988.

34. Ibid.

35. Mimeo, SBR/SBE Liaison Committee, "Changes Made by the SBR/SBE Liaison Committee for Utah's 1988–93 Vocational-Technical Education Master Plan: A Powerful Resource for Human and Economic Development," 4 January 1989.

36. Minutes of the State Board of Education meeting, 6 January 1989.

37. Peter Scarlet, "Committee Says Liaison Can Solve Vo-Ed Feuds," *Salt Lake Tribune,* 29 January 1989, 10-B.

38. Ibid.

39. Ibid.

40. Minutes of the State Board of Education meeting, 7 February 1989.

41. In an interview, the commissioner said he felt the scenario had been realized in practice, citing the instance of a machinist course offered by the Ogden AVC using Weber State University facilities, with the joint use being planned and coordinated through the Regional Vocational Education Council.

42. The relationship of common goals to intergroup cooperation has been dramatically demonstrated by Sherif in what he called the "robbers cave" experiment involving initially hostile and conflictual groups of boys at camp. By planning activities such that desirable goals required the efforts of both groups they were, in effect, forced to cooperate to achieve the common, or "superordinate" goal. See Musafer Sherif, "Superordinate Goals in the Reduction of Intergroup Conflicts," *American Journal of Sociology* 63 (1958): 356.

CHAPTER 6

1. Thomas Hobbes, *Leviathan* (London: Oxford Press, 1909; reprinted from the Edition of 1651 with an essay by W. G. Pogson Smith). See part 2, chapters 24 and 29, pp. 193, 255.

2. See Susan B. Hansen, "Extraction: The Politics of State Taxation," in *Politics in the American States: A Comparative Analysis*, 4th ed., eds. Virginia Gray, Herbert Jacob, and Kenneth Vines (Boston: Little, Brown, 1983), 415–53.

3. Mary Frase Williams, "Earthquakes or Tremors? Tax and Expenditure Limitations and School Finance," in *The Changing Politics of School Finance*, Third Annual Yearbook of the American Education Finance Association 1982, eds. Nelda H. Cambron-McCabe and Allan Odden (Cambridge, Mass.: Ballinger, 1983), 140.

4. Ibid.

5. Hansen, "Extraction," 444.

6. Williams, "Earthquakes or Tremors?" 145.

7. Hansen, "Extraction," 442.

8. Williams, "Earthquakes or Tremors?" 164.

9. Ibid., 166.

10. Ibid., 150, 153.

11. Ibid., 169.

12. His specific suggestion on this point was to eliminate the twelfth grade year of high school.

13. Instead of suggesting the elimination of the twelfth grade year of high school, he suggested the elimination of the fifth day of the school week, clearly demonstrating a different perspective and set of priorities from those held by some legislators, and lending credence to an assertion voiced in the meeting by a board member that UEA proposals do not improve educational excellence, just teachers' salaries.

14. Minutes of the SBE/SBR Joint Liaison Committee meeting, 6 October 1986.

15. Utah Foundation, "Utah's 1988 Tax Limitation Initiatives," *Research Report*, no. 502 (August 1988).

16. Minutes of the State Board of Education meeting, 26 February 1987.

17. Minutes of the State Board of Regents meeting, 19 June 1987.

18. Minutes of the SBE/SBR Joint Liaison Committee meeting, 12 January 1987.

19. The Peoples Tax Act would roll back tax rates on income, sales, motor fuels, and cigarettes to the pre-1987 level. The Peoples Tax and Spending Limitation Amendments to the state constitution were modeled on Proposition 13 in California. They would first limit annual state appropriations to the previous year's total plus a specified percentage increase, and second, place a limit on ad valorem taxes on property. See Utah Foundation, "Tax Limitation Initiatives."

20. Peter Scarlet, "Utahns Unaware of Tax Limitation Consequences, Opponent Says," *Salt Lake Tribune*, 19 August 1988, G28-1.

21. Minutes of the State Board of Regents meeting, 6–7 August 1987.

22. A more demanding analysis made by the State Tax Commission later in the spring of 1988 projected a total loss of $346 million in tax revenues, an increase of 73 percent.

23. "Coalition: Tax Relief Headed for Ballot," *Salt Lake Tribune,* 24 March 1988, B2-4.

24. Paul Rolly, "3 Tax Initiatives to be Decided by Utah Voters," *Salt Lake Tribune*, 6 July 1988, B1-5.

25. One of these individuals sometime after the initiatives were defeated was named to the State Board of Regents by Governor Norman Bangerter. In 1992, this individual, Michael Leavitt, was elected governor of Utah succeeding Bangerter.

26. Dan Bates, "Campaign Gets Underway to Counter 3 Initiatives on Curbing Taxes," *Salt Lake Tribune,* 12 July 1988, B1-3.

27. Douglas L. Parker, "Tax Ax Hangs Over 10,000 Jobs, Warns Matheson,"

Salt Lake Tribune, 24 September 1988, B1.

28. Ibid.

29. "Initiatives Spell Disaster, Salt Lake Civic Leader Warns," *Salt Lake Tribune,* 13 April 1988, E8-1.

30. Paul Rolly, "Tax Rollback Will Devastate Colleges, Council Hears," *Salt Lake Tribune,* 25 June 1988, B1-3.

31. Dan Bates, "Campaign Gets Underway," *Salt Lake Tribune,* 25 June 1988, B1-3.

32. Dawn Tracy, "Tax Initiatives May Wipe Out U, Says Peterson," *Salt Lake Tribune,* 13 July 1988, B1-1.

33. "Cook Lambasts U Official in Tax Stand," *Salt Lake Tribune,* 19 July 1988, D8-3.

34. Mimeograph, "Draft Higher Education Plan: Informing Utahns of How Tax Initiatives Impact the State," Utah System of Higher Education, Summer, 1988.

35. Some higher education institutions worked to produce publications to communicate their value to the state in concrete, specific terms that would translate clearly into the daily lives of Utah voters. Perhaps the most ambitious such effort was a 132-page publication of the University of Utah. In a county-by-county review, the report listed the benefits accruing to local communities "from Tremonton to Ticaboo, Smithfield to St. George" through the University of Utah, even giving the names of local residents and organizations that had participated in and benefitted from University of Utah programs during the most recent year. Each county report listed prominently the county's resident student enrollment, both undergraduate and graduate. Even tiny Daggett County, with a total population of seven hundred, had one undergraduate enrolled at the university whose life would be changed if the initiatives passed. See University of Utah, Department of Public Relations, *The Impact of the University of Utah: A County-by-County Report* (Salt Lake City, Utah: University of Utah, August 1988).

36. The membership of the Education Coordinating Council as reflected in the minutes of the State Board of Education meeting of 27 February 1987 was as follows: the Utah School Boards Association; the Utah Society of School Superintendents; the Utah Association of Elementary School Principals; the Utah Association of Secondary School Principals; the Area Vocational Center Boards Association; the Vocational Directors Association; the Utah Education Association; the American Federation of Teachers/Utah Teachers United; the chairmen of the Education Committee and the Public Education Joint Appropriations Subcommittee of the Utah State Legislature; directors of Chambers of Commerce; representatives from the Colleges of Education of the University of Utah, Utah State University, and Brigham Young University; the Utah Parent-Teacher Association; the Utah Association of Private Schools; the Utah Home Schools Association; and representatives of the governor's office.

37. The fact of a seemingly rigid voting procedure within the HOPE committee is reflective of a diverse community that has established "folkways" for dealing with differing interests and conflicts. This approach contrasts markedly with the relatively free form, laissez-faire organizational approach used on the Taxpayers

for Utah steering committee.

38. Dawn Tracy, "40% of Teachers Back Tax Rollback Despite Threat to Jobs," *Salt Lake Tribune,* 18 August 1988, B1-1.

39. An official at the State Office of Education saw the turnaround in teachers' opinions on the initiatives to be indicative of the low trust level in the local districts in late summer as contracts are negotiated, with trust between the parties increasing (along with the proportion of teachers opposing the initiatives) as the school year progressed into the fall.

40. Peter Scarlet, "Don't Let Tax Protesters Bully You, Says PTA Leader," *Salt Lake Tribune,* 13 September 1988, A11-3.

41. Peter Scarlet, "Utahns Unaware of Tax Limitation Consequences, Opponent Says," *Salt Lake Tribune,* 19 August 1988, G28-1.

42. Minutes of the State Board of Regents meeting, 11 November 1988.

43. Minutes of the State Board of Education meeting, 11 November 1988.

CHAPTER 7

1. In Utah, sixty-nine cities and counties expended in excess of $22 million in 1988 to provide public library service (Utah State Library Division, Utah Public Library Service, 1988, 31). Counting only the publicly supported institutions of higher education, there are eleven academic libraries in the state which expended $12,482,000 for operations in 1988. In that same year, there were 644 public school libraries in Utah corresponding approximately to the number of public schools in the state. In the aggregate, public funds supporting all three types of libraries in the state are relatively substantial (Utah Foundation, "Public Library Service in Utah," *Research Report,* no. 520 [February 1990], 223).

2. The implicit policy connection between academic, public school, and public libraries in Utah is acknowledged in the fact that by state law representatives from the Utah State Office of Education and the Utah System of Higher Education sit on the Board of the State Library Division, the agency of state government that represents public libraries in state government. For a discussion of multitype library cooperation, see Douglas M. Abrams, *An Organizational Analysis of Multi-type Library Cooperation in Utah: A Consideration of Basic Issues for Laypersons and Librarians* (Salt Lake City: Utah Department of Community and Economic Development, State Library Division, 1987).

3. The first three of four elements to be addressed substantively in the study, as given in the legislative intent language authorizing the study, were as follows:

   1. Higher education library facilities and resources priority needs.
   2. An assessment of and recommendations relating to technological innovations and improved procedures which could alleviate the need for additional space or other traditional costly elements of college and university library service.
   3. Recommendations as to increased interlibrary loan capabilities, shared resources, and similar areas in which the public of the State of Utah could benefit from such

improvements in overall library services. This would include *higher education, public education,* and *community libraries* supported with tax resources. The emphasis would be on improved procedures, enhanced communications, and sharing of resources [emphasis added]. See Utah, Legislature, Executive Appropriations Committee, *Legislative Intent Language for the Statewide Library Study,* H.D. No. 327, 1988.

4. The quotation is taken from a five-page photocopied handout produced by the Utah State Office of Education in the summer of 1988. The consulting organization referred to is School Match of Westerville, Ohio.

5. Gillies Stransky Brems Architects and RMG Consultants, Inc., *Utah Statewide Library Study: Plans and Recommendations Regarding Facilities, Interlibrary Cooperation, and Technology from a Utah Statewide Library Study: Executive Summary,* January 1989, 1–9.

6. Utah, Legislature, House of Representatives, House Joint Resolution 21, 1989.

7. Significantly, the "crisis" (specifically deficiencies in collections and staffing) was attributable in large measure to the results of administratively established priorities within each sector, both at the local district level in public education, and at the institution level in higher education. The degeneration of school library media centers was attributable to the low priority set by local district administrators and boards, and condoned by the State Board of Education over an extended period. For their part, higher education administrators at each institution had presided over a local political process at each campus that had resulted in libraries being allocated what the outside study team found to be an inadequate percentage of the general and educational budget of each institution as compared to nationally established standards. Clearly, the heart of the problem in both sectors (with the significant exception of the academic library facilities needs themselves) would be solved in each sector by having administrators allocate a larger slice of the pie to library service. This was in fact the solution recommended explicitly for higher education, and implicitly for public education. However, the obvious solution to the problem was not palatable—for obvious reasons—to administrators. The common strategy followed by public education was to expand the pie.

8. Higher education system administrators consistently maintained an appropriately ecumenical name for the study (Statewide Library Study), rather than a more nearly descriptive name such as "Academic Library Facilities Study."

CHAPTER 8

1. In 1976, the number of regents was increased to the current sixteen.

2. In 1983, the number of seats on the State Board of Education was reduced from eleven to the current nine.

3. The model of rational organizational decision making has been fully discussed and critiqued in several works. See, for example, James G. March and

Herbert A. Simon, *Organizations* (New York: Wiley and Sons, 1958), 136–71; Charles E. Lindblom, "The Science of Muddling Through," *Public Administration Review* 14 (Spring 1959), 79–88; and Nils Brunsson, *The Irrational Organization* (New York: John Wiley and Sons, 1985), 15–34.

4. See Ronald G. Corwin, "Patterns of Organizational Conflict," *Administrative Science Quarterly* 14 (1969): 508. Because of these inherent organizational dynamics, this book should not be read as a tract either for or against any given arrangement of education governance structures in state government. The political relationships of competition and conflict between education sectors are based ultimately on the functional interdependencies between the two within a world of limited resources. These fundamental relationships cannot be changed by manipulating governance structures.

5. Lewis Anthony Dexter, *Elite and Specialized Interviewing* (Evanston, Ill.: Northwestern University Press, 1970), 19–20.

6. While it is the primary function of the public schools to transmit those basic skills, capacities, and understandings needed to live a useful and rewarding life, higher education focuses on transmitting higher-level cognitive skills and understandings, and on creating new knowledge through research. Attendance in the common schools by all children and youth up to a statutorily established age is mandated by the state, whereas attendance at institutions of higher education is optional, depending entirely upon the initiative of the individual adult and private individuals around him or her. Perhaps because of their primary function of socialization, which is supported by mandatory universal attendance, the public schools are largely congruent with the prevailing social values of the community, while institutions of higher education, for reasons that educators assert are directly associated with central purposes of the university, are typically in a state of tension with many of the social values of the broader community. A Carnegie Commission study confirms this point in its comparison of teaching staff in public and higher education: "While university faculty tend to be more liberal than the general community, public school faculty reflect more traditional middle-class, moderately conservative values." See Carnegie Commission on Higher Education, *Continuity and Discontinuity: Higher Education and the Schools* (New York: McGraw-Hill, 1973), 101–2. Robert Berdahl sees the autonomy and academic freedom of the professor in higher education as being a radically different pattern of accountability from that found in the public schools. See Robert O. Berdahl, "Secondary and Postsecondary Education: The Politics of Accommodation," in *The Changing Politics of Education: Prospects for the 1980s,* ed. Edith K. Mosher and Jennings L. Wagoner, Jr. (Berkeley, Calif.: McCutchan, 1978), 231–32. Teachers in the elementary and secondary schools experience a comparative restriction on what they teach, while academic freedom and teacher autonomy are hallmarks of higher education. There are basic differences in the economic relationships supporting each sector, as well. The widespread unionization of teachers supports the seniority system for determining teachers' salaries in the public schools, while the economics of the market—even in an environment becoming increasingly unionized—more nearly determine the salaries of professors in higher education. Historically, each sector

has drawn upon different sources for its funding. Traditionally, the public schools have been supported primarily through the local property tax, while higher education has relied on funds from the state and federal governments, student tuition payments, and private endowments.

7. Robert Frost, "Mending Wall," *Robert Frost's Poems* (New York: Washington Square Press, 1962), 94–95.

8. See Brunnson, *The Irrational Organization*, 89.

9. Neither competition nor cooperation is inherently good or bad for the organization. David Brown has worked creatively to deal with both the positive as well as the negative sides of conflict in a setting in which "organization interfaces" bring together organizations having both common and conflicting interests. The various mixes create the potential of too much, too little, or an appropriate level of conflict. Brown explains:

> Too much conflict produces interorganizational warfare that debilitates one or both parties. Too little conflict may lead to interorganizational collusion, in which important differences are suppressed in a kind of "unintentional merger" that preserves harmony at the expense of the organizations or the context. Or too little conflict may be associated with interorganizational isolation, in which important interdependencies are ignored for a "false independence" harmful to the interests of parties or context. Productive conflict, in contrast, brings organizations together for interorganizational bargaining, in which interaction over conflicting interests produces compromises based on recognition of underlying common concerns, or for interorganizational problem-solving, in which representatives explore differences as a prelude to discovering mutually beneficial solutions.

See L. David Brown, *Managing Conflict at Organizational Interfaces* (Reading, Mass.: Addison-Wesley, 1983), 258.

10. Nils Brunnson provides a persuasive defense of the functionality of irrational aspects of organizational activity. See Brunnson, *The Irrational Organization*, 15–34.

SELECTED BIBLIOGRAPHY

Abrams, Douglas M. "Organizational Strategies of Political Competition and Cooperation: Public Education and Higher Education Interests in Utah, 1983–1989." Ph.D. diss., University of Utah, 1991.

————. "Political Competition and Cooperation Between Public and Higher Education Agencies of State Government." *Journal of Education Finance* 12 (Winter 1987): 369–90.

Aldrich, Howard. "Organizational Boundaries and Inter-organizational Conflict." *Human Relations* 24 (1971): 279–93.

Assael, Henry. "Constructive Role of Interorganizational Conflict." *Administrative Science Quarterly* 14 (December 1969): 573–82.

Bacharach, Samuel B., and Edward J. Lawler. *Power and Politics in Organizations.* San Francisco: Jossey-Bass, 1980.

Bailey, Stephen K. "A Comparison of the University with a Government Bureau." In *The University as an Organization,* ed. James A. Perkins, 121–36. New York: McGraw-Hill, 1973.

Barnard, Chester. *The Functions of the Executive.* Cambridge: Harvard University Press, 1968.

Bentley, Arthur F. *The Process of Government.* Chicago: University of Chicago Press, 1908.

Berdahl, Robert O. "Secondary and Postsecondary Education: The Politics of Accommodation." In *The Changing Politics of Education: Prospects for the 1980s,* ed. Edith K. Mosher and Jennings L. Wagoner, Jr., 227–58. Berkeley, Calif.: McCutchan, 1978.

————. *Statewide Coordination of Higher Education.* Washington, D.C.: American Council on Education, 1971.

Beyle, Thad L. "Governors." In *Politics in the American States: A Comparative Analysis,* 4th ed., ed. Virginia Gray, Herbert Jacob, and Kenneth N. Vines, 180–221. Boston: Little, Brown, 1983.

Blau, Peter M. "Social Exchange Among Collectivities." In *Interorganizational Relations,* ed. William M. Evan, 55–68. Philadelphia: University of Pennsylvania Press, 1978.

Blau, Peter M., and Marshall W. Meyer. *Bureaucracy in Modern Society.* 3d ed. New York: Random House, 1987.

Bowman, Ann O'M., and Richard C. Kearney. *The Resurgence of the States.* Englewood Cliffs, N.J.: Prentice-Hall, 1986.

Brown, David L. *Managing Conflict at Organizational Interfaces.* Reading Mass.: Addison-Wesley, 1983.

Brunsson, Nils. *The Irrational Organization: Irrationality as a Basis for Organizational Action and Change.* New York: John Wiley and Sons, 1985.

Buntz, C. Gregory, and Beryl A. Radin. "Managing Intergovernmental Conflict: The Case of Human Services." *Public Administration Review* (September/October 1983): 403–10.

Campbell, Roald F., Luvern L. Cunningham, Raphael O. Nystrand, and Michael D. Usdan. *The Organization and Control of American Schools.* 5th ed. Columbus, Ohio: Charles E. Merrill, 1985.

Campbell, Roald F. "Utah." In *Shaping Education Policy in the States,* ed. Susan Fuhrman and Alan Rosenthal, 101–12. Washington, D.C.: Institute for Educational Leadership, 1981.

Carnegie Commission on Higher Education. *Continuity and Discontinuity: Higher Education and the Schools.* New York: McGraw-Hill, 1973.

Cambron-McCabe, Nelda H., and Allan Odden, eds. *The Changing Politics of School Finance.* Third Annual Yearbook of the American Education Finance Association. Cambridge, Mass.: Ballinger, 1982.

Corwin, Ronald G. "Patterns of Organizational Conflict." *Administrative Science Quarterly* 14 (1969): 507–20.

Coser, Lewis. *The Functions of Social Conflict.* Glencoe, Ill.: Free Press, 1956.

Daalder, Hans. "The Consociational Democracy Theme." *World Politics* 26 (July 1974): 604–21.

Dessler, Gary. *Organization and Management.* Reston, Va.: Reston Publishing Company, 1982.

Deutsch, Morton. "A Theory of Co-operation and Competition." *Human Relations* 2 (1949): 129–52.

Dexter, Lewis Anthony. *Elite and Specialized Interviewing.* Evanston, Ill.: Northwestern University Press, 1970.

Dye, Thomas R. *Politics, Economics, and the Public: Policy Outcomes in the American States.* Chicago: Rand McNally, 1966.

———. *Understanding Public Policy.* 5th ed. Englewood Cliffs, N.J.: Prentice-Hall, 1984.

Easton, David. *The Political System.* New York: Alfred A. Knopf, 1953.

Ellis, John. "Since 1965: The Impact of Federal Funds on Public Education." *Education and Urban Society* 15 (May 1983): 351–66.

Evan, William M. "An Organization-Set Model of Interorganizational Relations." In *Interorganizational Decision Making,* ed. Matthew Tuite, Roger Chisholdm, and Michael Radnor, 181–200. Chicago: Aldine, 1972.

Fink, Clinton F. "Some Conceptual Difficulties in the Theory of Social Conflict." *Journal of Conflict Resolution* 12 (1969): 412–60.

Fuhrman, Susan. "State-Level Politics and School Financing." In *The Changing Politics of School Finance,* ed. Nelda H. Cambron-McCabe and Allan Odden, 53–70. Cambridge, Mass.: Ballinger, 1982.

Fuller, Edgar, and Jim B. Pearson, eds. *Education in the States: Nation-Wide Development Since 1900.* Washington, D.C.: National Education Association of the United States, 1967.

Garms, Walter I., James W. Guthrie, and Lawrence C. Pierce. *School Finance: The Economics and Politics of Public Education.* Englewood Cliffs, N.J.: Prentice-Hall, 1978.

Garnett, James L. *Reorganizing State Government: The Executive Branch.* Boulder, Colo.: Westview Press, 1980.

Gerth, H. H., and C. Wright Mills, eds. *From Max Weber: Essays in Sociology.* New York: Oxford University Press, 1958.

Glenny, Lyman A. *Autonomy of Public Colleges: The Challenge of Coordination.* New York: McGraw-Hill, 1959.

———. *State Coordination of Higher Education: The Modern Concept.* Denver: State Higher Education Executive Officers, 1985.

Glenny, Lyman A., and Thomas K. Dalglish. "Higher Education and the Law." In *The University as an Organization,* ed. James A. Perkins, 173–202. New York: McGraw-Hill, 1973.

Goldman, Ralph. "Conflict, Co-operation and Choice: An Exploration of Conceptual Relationships." In *Decisions, Values, and Groups,* ed. Norman F. Washburne, 410–39. New York: Macmillan, 1962.

Gray, Virginia, Herbert Jacob, and Kenneth N. Vines, eds. *Politics in the*

American States: A Comparative Analysis. 4th ed. Boston: Little, Brown, 1983.

Grodzins, Morton, and Daniel Elazar. "Centralization and Decentralization in the American Federal System." In *A Nation of States: Essays on the American Federal System,* 2d ed., ed. Robert A. Goldwin, 1–24. Chicago: Rand McNally, 1974.

Groenings, Sven, E. W. Kelley, and Michael Leiserson, eds. *The Study of Coalition Behavior: Theoretical Perspectives and Cases from Four Continents.* New York: Holt, Rinehart and Winston, 1970.

Hansen, Susan B. "Extraction: The Politics of State Taxation." In *Politics in the American States: A Comparative Analysis,* 4th ed., ed. Virginia Gray, Herbert Jacob, and Kenneth Vines, 415–53. Boston: Little, Brown, 1983.

Hart, David K., and William G. Scott. *Organizational America.* Boston: Houghton Mifflin, 1979.

———. "The Organizational Imperative." *Administration and Society* 7 (November 1975): 259–84.

Hirschman, Albert O. *Exit, Voice, and Loyalty: Responses to Decline in Firms, Organizations, and States.* Cambridge: Harvard University Press, 1970.

Hofstadter, Richard, and C. DeWitt Hardy. *The Development and Scope of Higher Education in the United States.* New York: Columbia University Press, 1952.

Horowitz, Irving Louis. "Consensus, Conflict and Cooperation: A Sociological Inventory." *Social Forces* 41 (1962): 177–88.

Hrebenar, Ronald J., Melanee Cherry, and Kathanne Greene. "Utah: Church and Corporate Power in the Nation's Most Conservative State." In *Interest Group Politics in the American West,* ed. Ronald J. Hrebenar and Clive S. Thomas, 113–22. Salt Lake City: University of Utah Press, 1987.

Jacob, Herbert, and Kenneth N. Vines, eds. *Politics in the American States: A Comparative Analysis.* Boston: Little, Brown, 1965.

Johns, R. L. "State Financing of Elementary and Secondary Education." In vol. 2 of *Education in the States: Nation-Wide Development Since 1900,* ed. Edgar Fuller and Jim B. Pearson, 175–214. Washington, D.C.: National Education Association of the United States, 1967.

Johnson, David W., and Frank P. Johnson. *Joining Together: Group Theory and Group Skills.* 2d ed. Englewood Cliffs, N.J.: Prentice-Hall, 1982.

Kaplan, Morton A. *System and Process in International Politics.* New York: John Wiley and Sons, 1957.

Kelley, E. W. "Utility Theory and Political Coalitions: Problems of Operationalization." In *The Study of Coalition Behavior: Theoretical Perspectives and Cases From Four Continents,* ed. Sven Groennings, E. W. Kelley, and Michael Leiserson, 466–89. New York: Holt, Rinehart and Winston, 1970.

Kingdon, John W. *Agendas, Alternatives, and Public Policies.* Boston: Little, Brown, 1984.

Lehmbruch, Gerhard. "Liberal Corporatism and Party Government." *Comparative Political Studies* 10 (April 1977): 91–126.

Lijphart, Arend. *The Politics of Accommodation: Pluralism and Democracy in The Netherlands.* Berkeley: University of California Press, 1968.

———. "Typologies of Democratic Systems." In *Politics in Europe: Comparisons and Interpretations,* ed. Arend Lijphart, 46–80. Englewood Cliffs, N.J.: Prentice-Hall, 1969.

Lowi, Theodore J. *The End of Liberalism: Ideology, Policy, and the Crisis of Public Authority.* New York: Norton, 1969.

Lüschen, Günther. "Cooperation, Association, and Contest." *Journal of Conflict Resolution* 14 (March 1970): 21–34.

Maass, Arthur, ed. *Area and Power: A Theory of Local Government.* Glencoe, Ill.: Free Press, 1959.

McGuinness, Aims C., Jr. "State Coordination and Governance of Higher Education: Implications for Governors." *State Government* 58 (Summer 1985): 74–79.

———. "Status of State Coordination and Governance of Higher Education: 1985." In *State Postsecondary Education Structures Handbook, 1986,* 1–7. Denver: Education Commission of the States, 1986.

Maller, J. B. "Co-operation and Competition: An Experimental Study in Motivation." Contributions to Education No. 384. New York: Teachers College, 1929.

May, M. A., and L. W. Doob. "Co-operation and Competition." *Social Science Research Council Bulletin* 125 (1937): 15–31.

Mead, Margaret. *Co-operation and Competition Among Primitive Peoples.* New York: McGraw-Hill, 1937.

Merton, Robert K., Marjorie Fiske, and Patricia L. Kendall. *The Focused Interview: A Manual of Problems and Procedures.* New York: Free Press, 1956.

Michels, Robert. *Political Parties: A Sociological Study of the Oligarchical*

Tendencies of Modern Democracy. Translated by Eden and Cedar Paul. Glencoe, Ill.: Free Press, 1915.

Millett, John D. *Conflict in Higher Education: State Government Coordination Versus Institutional Independence.* San Francisco: Jossey-Bass, 1984.

———. *Financing Higher Education in the United States.* New York: Columbia University Press, 1952.

———. "State Governments." In *Higher Education in American Society,* ed. Philip Altbach and Robert O. Berdahl, 133–56. Buffalo, N.Y.: Prometheus Books, 1981.

Mintzberg, Henry. *Power In and Around Organizations.* Englewood Cliffs, N.J.: Prentice-Hall, 1983.

Molnar, Joseph J., David L. Rogers. "A Comparative Model of Inter-organizational Conflict." *Administrative Science Quarterly* 24 (September 1979): 405–24.

Mosher, Edith K., and Jennings L. Wagoner, Jr., eds. *The Changing Politics of Education: Prospects for the 1980s.* Berkeley, Calif.: McCutchan, 1978.

Myrdal, Gunnar. "A Methodological Note on Fact and Valuation in Social Science." In vol. 2 of his *An American Dilemma: The Negro Problem and Modern Democracy,* 1027–64. New York: Harper and Brothers, 1944.

Olson, Mancur. *The Logic of Collective Action: Public Goods and the Theory of Groups.* Cambridge: Harvard University Press, 1965.

Panitch, Leo. "The Development of Corporatism in Liberal Democracies." *Comparative Political Studies* 10 (April 1977): 61–90.

Parsons, Talcott. *Structure and Process in Modern Societies.* Glencoe, Ill.: Free Press of Glencoe, 1960.

Patchen, Martin. "Models of Cooperation and Conflict: A Critical Review." *Journal of Conflict Resolution* 14 (September 1970): 389–407.

Perkins, James A., ed. *The University as an Organization.* New York: McGraw-Hill, 1973.

Peterson, Paul E. *School Politics Chicago Style.* Chicago: University of Chicago Press, 1976.

Pondy, Louis R. "Organizational Conflict: Concepts and Models." *Administrative Science Quarterly* 2 (1967): 296–320.

———. "Varieties of Organizational Conflict." *Administrative Science Quarterly* 14 (December 1969): 499–505.

Rogers, David L., and Joseph Molnar. "Organizational Antecedents of Role

Conflict and Ambiguity in Top-Level Administrators." *Administrative Science Quarterly* 21 (December 1976): 598–610.

Rothman, Stanley. "Systematic Political Theory: Observations on the Group Approach." *American Political Science Review* 54 (March 1960): 15–33.

Sabato, Larry. *Good-bye to Good-time Charlie: The American Governorship Transformed.* 2d ed. Washington, D.C.: CQ Press, 1983.

Salisbury, Robert H. "State Politics and Education." In *Politics in the American States: A Comparative Analysis,* ed. Herbert Jacob and Kenneth N. Vines, 331–68. Boston: Little, Brown, 1965.

Salmon, Richard G., and S. Kern Alexander. *The Historical Reliance of Public Education Upon the Property Tax: Current Problems and Future Role.* Cambridge: Lincoln Institute of Land Policy. 1983.

Sanford, Terry. *Storm Over the States.* New York: McGraw-Hill, 1967.

Schmidt, Stuart M., and Thomas A. Kochan. "Conflict: Toward Conceptual Clarity." *Administrative Science Quarterly* 17 (1972): 359–70.

Schwarz, John E. "Maintaining Coalitions: An Analysis of the EEC With Supporting Evidence from the Austrian Grand Coalition and the CDU/CSU." In *The Study of Coalition Behavior: Theoretical Perspectives and Cases From Four Continents,* ed. Sven Groennings, E. W. Kelley, and Michael Leiserson, 235–49. New York: Holt, Rinehart and Winston, 1970.

Scott, Richard W. "Field Methods in the Study of Organizations." In *Handbook of Organizations,* ed. James G. March, 261–304. Chicago: Rand McNally, 1965.

———. *Organizations: Rational, Natural, and Open Systems.* 2d ed. Englewood Cliffs, N.J.: Prentice-Hall, 1987.

Sherif, Musafer. "Superordinate Goals in the Reduction of Intergroup Conflicts." *American Journal of Sociology* 63 (1958): 349–56.

Spiro, Herbert J. "An Evaluation of Systems Theory." In *Contemporary Political Analysis,* ed. James C. Charlesworth, 164–74. New York: The Free Press, 1967.

Steel, Brent, and Taketsugu Tsurutani. "From Consensus to Dissensus: A Note on Postindustrial Political Parties." *Comparative Politics* (January 1986): 235–47.

Thompson, James D. *Organizations in Action.* New York: McGraw-Hill, 1967.

Truman, David B. *The Governmental Process.* New York: Alfred A. Knopf, 1953.

Tuite, Matthew, Roger Chisholm, and Michael Radnor, eds. *Interorganizational Decision Making.* Chicago: Aldine, 1972.

Usdan, Michael D., David W. Minar, and Emanuel Hurwitz, Jr. *Education and State Politics: The Developing Relationship Between Elementary-Secondary and Higher Education.* New York: Teachers College Press, Teachers College, Columbia University, 1969.

Utah Foundation. *State and Local Government in Utah.* Salt Lake City: Utah Foundation, 1979.

Van de Ven, Andrew H., and Gordon Walker. "The Dynamics of Interorganizational Coordination." *Administrative Science Quarterly* 29 (1984): 598–621.

Vogel, Ezra F. *Japan as Number One: Lessons for America.* Cambridge: Harvard University Press, 1979.

Wahlke, John C., Heinz Eulau, William Buchanan, and LeRoy C. Ferguson. *The Legislative System: Explorations in Legislative Behavior.* New York: John Wiley and Sons, 1962.

Waldo, Dwight. *The Enterprise of Public Administration: A Summary View.* Novato, Calif.: Chandler and Sharp, 1980.

Weber, Max. "Bureaucracy." In *From Max Weber: Essays in Sociology,* ed. H. H. Gerth and C. Wright Mills, 196–244. New York: Oxford University Press, 1958.

———. "The Meaning of Discipline." In *From Max Weber: Essays in Sociology,* ed. H. H. Gerth and C. Wright Mills, 253–64. New York: Oxford University Press, 1958.

Weiner, Myron. "Political Interviewing." In *Studying Politics Abroad,* ed. Robert E. Ward, 103–33. Boston: Little, Brown, 1964.

White, Paul E. "Intra- and Inter-Organizational Studies: Do They Require Separate Conceptualizations?" *Administration and Society* 6 (May 1974): 107–52.

Wildavsky, Aaron. *The Politics of the Budgetary Process.* 3d ed. Boston: Little, Brown, 1979.

Williams, Mary Frase. "Earthquakes or Tremors? Tax and Expenditure Limitations and School Finance." In *The Changing Politics of School Finance,* ed. Nelda H. Cambron-McCabe and Allan Odden, 139–82. Cambridge, Mass.: Ballinger, 1983.

Wilson, James Q. *Political Organizations.* New York: Basic Books, 1973.

Winget, Lerue W., Edgar Fuller, and Terrel H. Bell. "State Departments of Education Within State Governments." In vol. 2 of *Education in the States,* ed. Edgar Fuller and Jim B. Pearson, 71–130. Washington, D.C.: National Education Association of the United States, 1967.

Wirt, Frederick M., and Michael W. Kirst. *The Politics of Education: Schools in Conflict.* Berkeley, Calif.: McCutchan, 1982.

Wise, Arthur E. *Rich Schools, Poor Schools: The Promise of Equal Educational Opportunity.* Chicago: University of Chicago Press, 1972.

Wright, Deil. *Understanding Intergovernmental Relations.* 2d ed. Monterey, Calif.: Brooks/Cole, 1982.

Ylvisaker, Paul. "Some Criteria for a 'Proper' Areal Division of Governmental Powers." In *Area and Power: A Theory of Local Government,* ed. Arthur Maass, 27–49. Glencoe, Ill.: Free Press, 1959.

INDEX

217

and reasons for failure of budget proposals, 92; on the 75:25 rule in vocational education, 97; cooperation with higher education on vocational education, 106; on the skills center issue, 115; response to tax limitation initiatives, 130; on the library study, 149; as a public education outsider, 114; perceptions as state superintendent, 136

Nation at Risk, A: impact across the United States, 67, 87; impact on Utah education policymakers, 52–53
National Commission on Excellence in Education, 67
National Defense Education Act (NDEA): impact on public education, 187 n.20
National Education Association (NEA): membership of Utah teachers, 32; involvement in opposing Utah tax limitation initiatives, 133
National government: support of public education by, 188 n.21
Neocorporatism: role of rank and file in, 183–84 n.9

Office of Planning and Budget (Utah), 39
Open systems: perspective of organization, 8; elements of, 157
Organization (formal): as a means of social control, 1, 11, 185 n.1; characteristics of (Weber), 182 n.2; theory of three-tiered, 2–3; functional definition of (in the model), 2, 54–56; political relationships within, 3, 159; open-systems perspective of, 8; as a structured pattern of behavior, 29, 154; roles within, 56, 157; autonomy of, 57, 61; sources of conflict within, 155, 159; systems of power (influence) within, 184 n.13; hierarchical model in policy process, 156; impact of personality on, 167–69; inherent competitive dynamics of, 170; conflict and cooperation in, 206 n.9;

Organizational decision making: study of, 8–9
Organizational ideology: defined, 164; in the open systems perspective, 157; impact on mediating organizational structures, 165
Organizational roles: in explaining leaders' actions, xvii, 9, 56, 157, 167, 169

Panitch, Leo, 183–84 n.9
Parent-Teacher Association (PTA): reputation of, 31; as a political power in Utah, 52; responses to tax limitation initiatives in Utah, 53, 126, 129, 132–34, 167
Parity principle, 57
Parkinson's Law, 123
Parsons, Talcott, 2, 182 n.4
Perkins, James A., 190 n.45
Personality: impact on political relationships between organizations, 167–69
Personalized Internal Coalition: and political strategies, 7; in tax limitation initiative case (Utah), 136. *See also* Internal Coalition
Peterson, Chase N. (university president): misquoted in the press, 64; on cooperative budget strategy, 78; opposition to tax limitation initiatives, 127–29
Political strategies: used to defend organizational interests, 154, 171
Power: distribution within the education sectors (Utah), 48–49
Presidents, council of (Utah), role of, 33; library facilities recommendations endorsed by, 144
Professoriate: as boundary personnel, 3; in the Internal Coalition, 5
Property tax: administration of, for public education, 13; and inequality of school funding, 14; used in funding public schools (Utah), 31
Public education: Internal Coalition in, 5; External Coalition in, 6; and local control of schools, 186 n.7; and finance reform as part of state

Utah State Board of Education. *See* State
Board of Education (Utah)
Utah State Board of Regents. *See* State
Board of Regents (Utah)
Utah Supreme Court, 43
Utah System of Higher Education:
institutional competition within, 43–
44; its budget request to conduct
library study, 139–40; and legislative
appropriation to plan library capital
facilities construction, 146; as source
of impetus for the Statewide Library
Study, 147
Utah Valley Community College, 98

Van Alstyne, Arvo (commissioner of
higher education): 63, 74, 78, 83
Van de Ven, Andrew H., 195 n.7
Vocational education: components of,
198 n.3; as a source of conflict
between education sectors, 46, 53,
93, 159, 163
Vocational education (Utah): governance
of, 30; control by State Office of
Education, 94; master plan, 47;
additional dollars for, in 1984 legislature, 80; legislative politics of, 198
n.6; drift away from in higher education system, 97; defining a principle
of division between education
sectors, 95–96; mutual perceptions
of commitment and performance
between education sectors, 96–98;

program review and approval of, 98–
99; as source of conflict between
education sectors, 101; regional
planning approach in, 106
Vocational-Technical Education Master
Plan (Utah), 106, 107

Walker, Gordon, 195 n.7
Weber, Max, 1, 2, 182 nn.2, 3
Weber State College, 97
White, Paul E., 183 n.8
Whiteside, Henry O., 69
Williams, Mary F., 120
Wildavsky, Aaron, 28
Wilson, James Q.: axiom on organiza-
tional competition, 27–28; on
organizational role of leaders, 57, 75;
on analysis of competition and
cooperation of groups, 61;
hypotheses on organizational
competition and cooperation, 87,
134–35
Winner-take-all, 57
Wirt, Frederick M., 187 n.13
Wise, Authur E., 185 n.5

Ylvisaker, Paul, 186 n.7
Young, Sue Marie, 114

Zero-sum game: and conflict, 163; in
vocational education case, 115